D0831693

*Number Fifteen: The Centennial Series of
The Association of Former Students of
Texas A&M University*

A Flying Tiger's Diary

A Flying Tiger's Diary

By CHARLES R. BOND, JR.
Major General USAF (Retd)

and TERRY ANDERSON

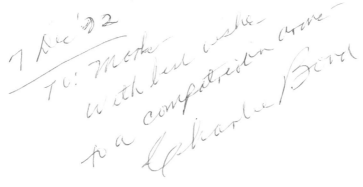

TEXAS A&M UNIVERSITY PRESS
College Station

Copyright © 1984 by Charles R. Bond, Jr., and Terry Anderson
All rights reserved

Library of Congress Cataloging in Publication Data

Bond, Charles R.
    A Flying Tiger's diary.

    (The Centennial series of the Association of Former
Students of Texas A&M University; no. 15)
    Bibliography: p.
    Includes index.
    1. World War, 1939–1945—Aerial operations, American.
2. Bond, Charles R.   3. World War, 1939–1945—Personal
narratives, American.   4. Air pilots, Military—United
States—Biography.   5. China. K'ung Chün. American
Volunteer Group—Biography.   I. Anderson, Terry H.,
1946–   II. Title.   III. Series: Centennial series of the
Association of Former Students, Texas A&M University;
no. 15.
D790.B59   1984   940.54'4973   83-40497
ISBN 0-89096-408-4 (pbk.)

Manufactured in the United States of America
Fourth Printing

To Mom and to Doris,
both of whom deserve all
my medals and more.
                    C . B .

Contents

MAPS

Preface

December, 1941, was a dark month for America. On the first Sunday the Japanese attacked Pearl Harbor. Just a few days later Adolph Hitler of Germany and Benito Mussolini of Italy declared war; the United States faced enemies off both shores. The first attacks close to home came later that month. German wolfpacks torpedoed American freighters in the heavy seas of the North Atlantic, and submarines were sighted off the coast of Florida. Just days before Christmas, a Japanese submarine surfaced and fired on California, slightly damaging a power station.

After these attacks Americans became nervous, even afraid. Officials on the West Coast ordered a blackout, resulting in chaos and numerous automobile accidents in San Francisco. In Seattle, citizens took action into their own hands when some businessmen forgot to turn out lights; factory windows were broken and light bulbs stolen. False reports flowed into government offices that a Japanese aircraft carrier had been spotted off California, and many people reported sighting Japanese Zeros. A thunderstorm in Los Angeles sent residents to their windows looking for enemy bombers, and rumors abounded that thousands of Japanese who had lived in the city were now back in their homeland preparing to return as a crack invasion force.

Similar concerns flared on the East Coast. Police reassured citizens that aircraft spotted off Long Island were not German bombers but patrol planes of the U.S. Navy. At Cape Hatteras, evening beachcombers envisioned and reported torpedo explosions in the Atlantic, and Georgians feared that Nazi subs were landing espionage agents on their beaches. Hotel owners in Charleston put sandbags on the roofs of their buildings, and city officials designated public schools and buildings as bomb shelters.

Even many midwesterners were worried. A civil defense pamphlet distributed in Illinois declared, "Chicago can be bombed," and contained an alarming map demonstrating that via the polar route the metropolis actually was closer to Germany than was New York City. Further north, the commander of the American Legion in Wisconsin proposed that the governor form an army of minutemen by enlisting the twenty-five thousand deer hunters residing in the state.[1]

Hysteria about possible invasion dissipated during 1942, but the military situation remained grave. While America mobilized and converted factories to war production, enemies made impressive gains. The German Afrika Korps swept eastward toward the Suez Canal, the lifeline of the British Empire, and the Wehrmacht advanced into the heartland of Soviet Russia. In the Pacific the Japanese attacked southward, invading and conquering the Philippines, advancing into the ricelands of Southeast Asia, and threatening India and Australia.

Indeed, for the first half year of America's involvement in the crusade against the Axis nations, news from the fronts was discouraging. There was one exception, however—the American Volunteer Group (AVG)—the Flying Tigers.

This is the story of that short-lived but famous organization based on the diary of one of its foremost fighter pilots, Charles R. Bond, Jr. At the end of each day in 1941 and 1942, Bond recorded events and thoughts in a small notebook, which he kept with his personal papers for the next thirty years. During the early 1970s he typed the diary, then he left it for another decade, until July, 1981, when he and I met.

As the oral historian for Texas A&M University, I was conducting a series of interviews with former students of the school who had military careers and eventually became generals. The interview with General Bond lasted eighteen hours, and during it he constantly referred to the diary, some three hundred pages of manuscript. Bond eventually informed me that he hoped to write a book using his diary—one also discussing his military career. I convinced him that he did have an interesting story and that I would be willing to help.

We initiated a joint project. I suggested the format—an introduction, diary chapters with introductions and conclusions, and an epilogue—and conducted research aimed at placing the story in military context and historical perspective. I also wrote first drafts of introduc-

[1] Richard R. Lingeman, *Don't You Know There's a War On? The American Home Front, 1941–1945* (New York, 1970), chap. 2. Also consult Richard Polenberg, *War and Society: The United States, 1941–1945* (Philadelphia, 1972), and John Morton Blum, *V Was for Victory: Politics and American Culture during World War II* (New York, 1976).

tions and conclusions and edited and annotated the diary. Meanwhile, General Bond rechecked his diary for accuracy and corroborated some events by contacting former colleagues and holding interviews. He wrote personal portions of the introduction and epilogue and approved the work I completed.

We hope the result of our effort is a book which reveals main events and personal experiences of the Flying Tigers—a representation of the daily life of the group, one which gives a different view from that recorded in the memoirs of AVG leader Lt. Gen. Claire L. Chennault. With the exception of his *Way of a Fighter*, other books about the group are either accounts by newsmen who visited China in 1941 and 1942 or later journalistic attempts to reach the mass market. These works usually have glamorized the pilots and in some cases even spread misconceptions. To date, no scholarly history has been written, nor has any pilot published his diary or a full account of the AVG.

This book is aimed to present an edited document, the diary, while at the same time providing sufficient background information that it can be considered a history of the Flying Tigers. Further, it is a personal history of a dedicated military officer who not only became an ace in the Flying Tigers but also returned to the United States Army Air Corps to complete a career as an Air Force major general.

In style the diary remains close to the original, but the reader has been spared needless punctuation, spelling has been corrected without comment, and insignificant entries have been deleted without the use of ellipses. Furthermore, for stylistic reasons the entire manuscript has been placed in the first person.

We are indebted to many for assistance. The Association of Former Students of Texas A&M University granted the funds to begin the oral history project, entitled "Aggies to Generals," which resulted in my meeting General Bond. To insure the accuracy of the manuscript, lengthy discussions were carried out between Bond and many of his former colleagues in the Flying Tigers, and sincere thanks are offered to Bob Neale, David "Tex" Hill, Charlie Older, Jim Howard, Bus Keeton, Pete Wright, Gregory "Pappy" Boyington, R. T. Smith, Skip Adair, and especially Dick Rossi for his detailed and constructive editorial comment on the entire manuscript. Special thanks are also expressed to Larry Pistole, nephew of Herbert Pistole, an AVG armorer, for sharing his knowledge, documents, and pictures of the AVG.

TERRY ANDERSON

A Flying Tiger's Diary

Introduction

American relations with China and Japan expanded during the last half of the nineteenth century. This was an age of imperialism, and while Britain, France, Germany, and Russia were interested in extending their influence, dominating trade, and establishing spheres of influence, the United States treated the Oriental giants differently. Instead of joining Europeans, officials in Washington espoused an "open-door" policy of free trade and territorial integrity for Japan and especially China.

Asians generally formed a favorable opinion of the "occidental friend," and American influence expanded in the Far East. Answering calls to help modernize the Orient, American experts supplied business skills, engineering advice, and capital. Educators traveled to Asia, and so did missionaries, who taught religion and English, the language of technology and development. By the turn of the century the people of China and Japan had initiated the enormous task of building modern schools and colleges and constructing factories and railroads, all in an attempt to change a society of peasants and landlords to one of businessmen and industrialists.

Change in China was slow, but not so in Japan, where the people were particularly astute at adopting western technology. In fact, they almost revolutionized their islands from feudalism to modernity in just five decades. By the early years of this century they were well on their way toward industrialization, and with their new economic muscle, their pride and nationalism expanded and were translated into a passion to become an empire.

To the Japanese, their manifest destiny lay in Asia. They attacked China in 1894 and scored an easy victory, forcing the sleeping giant to renounce all claims over Korea and to cede the islands of Formosa and the Pescadores. Japan also demanded the Liaotung Peninsula in Manchuria, but pressure from western powers forced the victor to with-

3

draw. Not to be daunted, Japan initiated plans for Korea and Man-churia, the same area which interested the Russians. The Japanese resolved the rivalry in 1904; without a declaration of war, they attacked the Russian fleet at Port Arthur. After a year of fighting, both sides were eager for peace. Russia agreed to give Japan the southern half of Sakhalin Island and to terminate the tsar's influence in southern Man-churia. Japan also received a new protectorate which it annexed in 1910: Korea.

During that era, the first decade of the twentieth century, America's relations changed significantly with the two giants of Asia. The Japanese were insulted by America's immigration policy of restricting Orientals. Californians openly discriminated against them, establish-ing separate schools for Asian children and refusing to allow Oriental adults to own property. In 1906, President Theodore Roosevelt signed the Gentleman's Agreement, by which the government of Japan agreed not to issue passports to their laborers seeking work in Amer-ica, and a generation later the process was complete when immigration acts excluded all Orientals. Moreover, Japan's resentment grew toward America because Roosevelt mediated the Portsmouth Treaty conclud-ing the Russo-Japanese War; they felt that they might have been able to gain more territory and influence if the referee had been someone more sympathetic to their aspirations in Asia. In Washington, officials became wary of Japanese plans and worried about the fate of China, emphasizing free trade and territorial integrity while voicing concerns about the aims of leaders in Tokyo.

Unfortunately, American apprehensions were substantiated by Japanese behavior during the First World War. While Euopeans were fighting for national survival in the West, Japan moved in the East. They seized areas formerly controlled by Germany, first regions of the Chinese coastal province of Shantung and then Pacific islands such as the Marianas, Carolines, and Marshalls. Japanese territory moved two thousand miles closer to California. More importantly, Japan made the Twenty-One Demands, a series of conditions designed to bring China under direct control of Tokyo. The United States protested, refusing to recognize these claims, and Japan, deciding not to test America's will, withdrew most of its demands and waited for a more opportune moment.

That time came in 1931 when the United States was immersed in the Great Depression. While America slid toward economic disaster, the Japanese Army occupied Manchuria. By 1933 Japan controlled the province of thirty million inhabitants and established a puppet state named Manchukuo. Again the United States protested. Secretary of State Harry Stimson declared a policy of nonrecognition, but that tactic had little impact on Japan. This time it would not withdraw.

Japan consolidated its gains for the next few years and then in 1937 returned to the offensive and attacked the remainder of China, the final act in its attempt to gain control of Asia. This conquest proved far more difficult than had been anticipated. The attack unified China. During the 1930s two rivals, Chiang Kai-shek and Mao Tse-tung, had been fighting between themselves, but after 1937 they formed an uneasy coalition and fought bitterly against the new aggressors. Although the Chinese armed forces were inferior in arms and training to those of the Japanese, China still had the advantage of the largest population in the world, some four hundred million, and it occupied one of the biggest land masses on earth. The inland campaign was long and costly. After four years of fighting, Japan was becoming more dependent on foreign supplies and still was years from victory.

The attack on China further strained relations between Japan and the United States. Americans were angered that Japan would assault China, and enraged when in December, 1937, Japanese fighter aircraft attacked an American gunboat, the USS *Panay*, anchored in the Yangtze River. Two sailors died, and the gunboat was sunk. Officials in Tokyo quickly proclaimed a mistake, apologized, and paid damages. Japan was not eager for war with the United States—at least not yet. Nevertheless, American opinion of Japan sank with the Panay and went still lower in 1940 when Japan signed a pact with Italy and Germany. By the next year only three percent of those Americans asked sided with the Japanese in the war against China, prompting more action from the administration of Franklin Roosevelt. By 1940 it was apparent that the policy of nonrecognition had failed, so FDR declared an embargo of strategic materials, such as scrap iron and steel, destined for Japan. The next year he began sending military supplies to China under the Lend-Lease Act. The Japanese complained, but continued their aggression on China and moved toward Southeast Asia. In July, 1941, after France had fallen to the Wehrmacht, officials in Tokyo announced a protectorate of former French colonies in Southeast Asia and began occupying Indochina. FDR responded promptly by issuing an executive order freezing Japanese assets in the United States, thus ending all trade with Japan, including exports of oil.

Both nations began preparing for war. Roosevelt established selective service, the first peacetime draft in American history, and troops in the Philippines began intensive training under the direction of Gen. Douglas MacArthur. In Tokyo, experts prepared plans for attacks against the Philippines and Pearl Harbor. There were negotiations during autumn, but neither side adopted a conciliatory position; the United States would not continue trade with Japan until the Japanese withdrew from China, and Tokyo would not withdraw, demanding that America recognize its new sphere of influence in Asia. It was a deadlock that was resolved on the Day of Infamy.

During the Sino-Japanese War the United States supported China, and nowhere was that support more apparent than in the actions of Claire Lee Chennault and the American Volunteer Group, later known as the Flying Tigers.

Claire Chennault was born in Texas, but his first memories were of northeastern Louisiana. Although he loved the outdoors more than his studies, he earned a teaching certificate from Louisiana State Normal School. He taught in a country school for a few years, but marriage and children brought demands for a higher salary, and he took jobs ranging from an English instructor at a business college in Mississippi to a factory worker in a tire plant in Ohio. At twenty-six, when he was the father of three, an international event changed his life—the United States entered the war against Austria-Hungary and Germany.[1]

Chennault was accepted for officer training and eventually became a pilot. Although he did not see combat during the war, he received a commission and began a distinguished military career. During the 1920s he was attached to a fighter group, and he became engrossed in aerial tactics. World War I had produced dogfighting, individual pi-

[1]The best source on Chennault's early life is his own memoir, *Way of a Fighter*, which was edited by Robert Hotz. See chaps. 1–3 of that work for his early life and career in the U.S. Army Air Corps. All books and articles about him rely on the memoir, for little is revealed about those years in his personal papers located at the Hoover Institution and on microfilm at the Library of Congress.

lots sparring for superiority in the air. Chennault labeled that superb sport but medieval warfare. Instead of individual combat he advanced the idea of formation tactics. Fighters should pursue in pairs or teams, using their combined firepower and maneuverability to destroy the enemy. He also supported the contemporary concept that airplanes could assist in ground warfare by dropping men behind lines as parachutists.

The young officer's ideas of tactics, however, faced stubborn resistance from the leaders of the U.S. Army Air Corps, especially the "bomber generals" who felt that heavily armed bombers would be the most potent planes in warfare. Convinced of the importance of fighters, Chennault challenged the generals by publishing his views in *The Role of Defensive Pursuit*. He advocated that if fighter pilots had radio intelligence, and especially an early warning system, they would be able to intercept and engage attacking bombers. In 1933 he proved his point; using his tactics, his fighters were the first to win war games exercises against bombers. But the victory was Pyrrhic, for instead of accepting the new tactics, the generals grumbled, and Chennault became involved even deeper in the controversy.

While the debate raged, Chennault became a fighter pilot instructor at the Air corps Tactical School. There he formed his famous group, "Three Men on a Flying Trapeze," with John H. "Luke" Williamson and Billy MacDonald. From 1934 to 1936 the trio staged air shows which included loops, spins, wingovers, chandelles, rolls, and Immelmann maneuvers. While pleasing spectators, Chennault was perfecting fighter tactics and again demonstrating the maneuverability of fighters.

By 1937 it seemed time to retire. The economic depression had resulted in severe cuts in training for fighter pilots, the outspoken lieutenant had been involved in bitter disputes, and he was ill; his hearing had been impaired during years of flying in open cockpits, and he suffered from low blood pressure and chronic bronchitis. Chennault was sent to the hospital, and while there he received a letter from China. The author was Roy Holbrook, who along with MacDonald and Williamson had left the United States and had become a flying instructor in China. The letter contained an offer of one thousand dollars plus expenses, a chauffered car, an interpreter, and the right to fly any plane if he would accept a three-month mission to survey the Chinese Air Force.

In April, Chennault resigned from the Army. In May he departed for the Orient.

Chennault arrived in Shanghai in June and met his former Air Corps colleagues and Madame Chiang Kai-shek. Soon he was back in the cockpit flying to the capital of Nationalist China, Nanking, where he met Generalissimo Chiang Kai-shek and began inspecting the Chinese Air Force.

Chiang's air force was in a shambles. Not until 1931, when Japan launched attacks against Shanghai, did the Chinese consider developing air power, for until then it seemed obvious that a naval blockade could isolate the ancient country from the rest of the world. The next year an unofficial American mission led by Col. Jack Jouett, with about twenty Air Corps officers, including Roy Holbrook, arrived and helped establish a flying school in Hangchow. Soon thereafter China had pilots but few planes and supplies. Officials in Washington were leery of more involvement, and thus the Chinese looked for help and accepted an offer from Italy. The Italian leader, Benito Mussolini, sent a general, forty pilots, and one hundred mechanics, who built a factory and began manufacturing planes. Thus, when Chennault arrived, the Italians controlled the Chinese Air Force. They produced planes and trained pilots but with unsatisfactory results. The "new" planes were so obsolete that the bombers could be used only as transports, and the flight school was a hoax. Every student who survived was given wings.

Chennault was investigating these problems on July 7, 1937, when the Japanese attacked the Marco Polo Bridge, igniting the final phase of the war for control of China. He wired the generalissimo and offered his services, believing that the event offered a chance to test his fighter theories and that Japan eventually would strike eastward and attack the United States.

Chiang agreed with Chennault and appointed him to serve under General Mow Pang-tsu at a flight combat training school at Hangchow. Problems at the school exemplified the situation throughout China. Pilots often killed themselves while flying simple training missions. One day China lost five pilots—not in combat, but while landing on a muddy runway. On the national scene, the navy consisted of a few gunboats, the army of recruits. Corruption was rampant. At one time officials sent the same plane to several cities pledging that it would be named in honor of each city if enough donations were collected; the money never reached the national treasury. Dishonesty often prevailed. Commissioners of the air force informed Chiang that some five hundred planes existed while the real number was less than one hundred. National unity was marred by warlords bickering for favors, along with the continual concern about the aims of the Communists. As Chennault put it, "China was a nightmare."

Chennault acted quickly that summer to prevent a Chinese disaster, implementing many of his theories and plans and scoring some early victories. In July he organized an air-raid warning net in the Shanghai-Hangchow-Nanking triangle, and with the aid of Billy Mac-Donald and Luke Williamson he selected the best Chinese pilots for special fighter tactics training. The results were impressive. When the Japanese attacked Nanking three times in five days, they lost forty-five planes. After Japan shifted to night bombing runs, they suffered 50 percent losses, and dive bombers sank the Japanese cruiser *Idzumo* at Shanghai. The Chinese Air Force even made the first bomb raid on Japan.

But by autumn the situation deteriorated: China could not cope with the massive war machine of Japan. The Japanese sent one hundred planes a day to bomb Nanking, devastating the city and its defending planes. By October only eight fighters remained in the Chinese Air Force. On the ground, Chiang's troops attempted unsuccessfully to drive the Japanese from Shanghai. Instead, the Japanese Army moved inland, and by the end of the year one could hear artillery in Nanking. Chennault wrote that defeat was just a question of time.

Then, during 1938 and 1939 the Japanese advance slowed, partly because of aid sent to China by the Soviet Union. After Japan invaded, China asked the international community to assist but received a response only from Moscow. Joseph Stalin had no love for Chiang Kai-Shek, since the latter had been fighting the Chinese Communists since 1927, but the Russian feared the aggressive tendencies of Japan more. Consequently, the Sino-Soviet relationship was a marriage of convenience aimed at weakening the Rising Sun in the Orient.

Considering the threat of Nazi Germany on its western border, Russia gave substantial aid to China. It supplied twenty million dollars in credit and became directly involved by sending an armored division and six regular squadrons from the Soviet Air Force. It built flying and artillery schools and opened a new overland supply route from Russian

Turkestan, a road that eventually carried more war material to China than the famed Burma Road. In 1938, China's benefactor was the USSR, but by the end of the next year aid decreased substantially, because Germany invaded Poland, sparking war in Europe.

China also received aid from an international squadron and some adventurous Americans. At first Chennault opposed the idea of recruiting foreign pilots, fearing a group composed of daredevils and undisciplined soldiers of fortune. Yet flyers were needed for newly acquried Vultee bombers, and the Chinese hired about a dozen pilots from France, Holland, Germany, and the United States. The group completed some successful bombing missions, but they were too susceptible to the bars and brothels of Hankow. Thus, the international squadron was disbanded late in 1938, about the same time Chennault recruited a dozen Americans to staff a flight training school at Yunnan. The latter group formerly were officers in the United States Army Air Corps such as Billy MacDonald, Johnny Preston, and C. B. "Skip" Adair, and they worked diligently to train pilots for the Chinese Air Force.

Nevertheless, foreign aid and advisers could not stop the Japanese. Their overwhelming power forced retreat, and by 1940 China had lost eleven provinces, all its major seaports, the centers of industry, and two main water arteries, the Pearl and the Yangtze. The best divisions of the army and the entire air force had been demolished, and waves of bombers dropped their loads daily on the wartime capital, Chungking.

The situation became desperate. In October, 1940, the generalissimo summoned Chennault to Chungking. He explained that the bombings must be stopped, wondered how long civilians could stand the horror, and stated that his government should buy fighters and hire pilots from the United States. He asked Chennault to accompany General Mow to Washington.

Chennault was pessimistic about securing aid from the United States. He knew that America was building as many planes as possible to expand their own air corps or that of the British. Any fighters left over probably would be obsolete, not able to cope with the new Japanese model, the Zero. Also, China had no cash, so the planes would have to be a loan or gift. But Chennault had been faced with obstacles all his life, and he carried out this mission with a typical amount of determination. During the early months of 1941 he met many influential people in Washington, including Chiang's brother-in-law and the representative of Nationalist China, T. V. Soong, a man who was a personal friend of Secretary of the Navy Frank Knox and Secretary of the Treasury Henry Morgenthau. Soong also introduced Chennault to two important reporters, Edgar Ansel Mowrer and Joseph Alsop, and Chennault pressed his case with two assistants of President Roosevelt, Thomas Corcoran and Dr. Lauchlin Currie, the latter a strong backer for increased aid to China.[2]

At the same time, Chennault searched for planes. After visiting many factories, he finally found hope at Curtiss-Wright. For years China had been a good customer of the company, and Chennault was friends with its vice president, Burdette Wright. The firm had one hundred P-40 Tomahawks destined for Britain, and Wright stated that if officials in London would waive their order, then the factory would send them a newer model more appropriate for the fight in Europe. Chennault went to work, and by January, 1941, Soong and Morgenthau had persuaded the British. In February the planes were resting on the docks of New York awaiting shipment to Rangoon.

Paying for and manning the planes were additional problems, especially since the Roosevelt administration had proclaimed neutrality in the China-Japan war. The United States could not aid a belligerent. That issue was resolved in March by passage of the Lend-Lease act, which allowed the president to lend, lease, or simply give any nation military supplies if he deemed it in the national interest. The administration then began aid to China's government, including twenty-five million dollars for the Tomahawks, and became more interested in supplying mechanics and pilots.[3] While generals and admirals squawked

[2] Chennault's relationship with Soong and important Americans such as Alsop, Corcoran, Knox, and Morgenthau is explained in two books by Michael Schaller, *The U.S. Crusade in China, 1938–1945*, chap. 4, and *The United States and China in the Twentieth Century*, chap. 3.

[3] American aid to China before Pearl Harbor consisted of a $45 million loan from the Export-Import Bank in 1939 which was restricted to civilian supplies; a $25 million loan after Japan occupied Indochina in September, 1940; and then Lend-Lease, which in 1941 only amounted to $27 million, or less than two percent of the total given to America's allies. An excellent book on the subject is by a former U.S. adviser to China, Arthur N. Young: *China and the Helping Hand, 1937–1945*, pp. 147–48, 402–403. Also see chap. 1 of Charles F. Romanus and Riley Sunderland, *Stilwell's Mission to China*

about losing trained men, the president intervened in April. He signed an executive order authorizing reserve officers and enlisted men to resign from the U.S. armed forces and join the American Volunteer Group destined for China.

The operation was secret, and the American government decided not to finance it directly but through the Central Aircraft Manufacturing Company (CAMCO), which was owned by William Pawley as a subsidiary of his Intercontinental Aviation Corporation. Pawley already had an airplane factory in South China at Loiwing and agreed to maintain and repair any planes damaged in combat. Also with American funds CAMCO would hire approximately 250 pilots and mechanics and pay their salaries and expenses.

American Volunteer Group fighter squadrons were called "advanced training units," and the fighters were labeled "advanced trainers." Chennault was the "supervisor." Eventually Chennault's passport listed him as a farmer, and while he commanded the AVG his title was "Adviser to the Central Bank of China."

During the summer of 1941 about 240 men signed contracts with CAMCO. Of those, about 85 then, and eventually 105, were pilots. I was one of them.

I was born in Dallas, Texas, on April 22, 1915, to Charles R. Bond, Sr., and Magnolia Turner Bond.[4] Both my parents were of Scotch-Irish and Welsh descent, and they came from similar backgrounds—large families, little schooling, and hard work. They married in Fort Worth early in the 1900s and started raising a family in Dallas. Hugh was born in 1910, and then two sisters, Jewel and Louise. I was the fourth, and afterwards came Perry and Jack.

Even in the Roaring Twenties before the Great Crash of 1929, it seemed that our family struggled with finances. Having learned to paint and hang wallpaper, my father established a small business. He worked long hours and did his best to provide an adequate income for the family. Life also was difficult for Mother, for she continually sacri-

---

(1953), which is the first book in their three-volume *The China-Burma-India Theater*, published by the Department of the Army, Washington, D.C.

[4] A complete oral biography is located at The Oral History Collection, University Archives, Texas A&M University.

ficed for us children. She was a remarkable woman, and her religious faith was the source of her strength and stamina.

Those years were not easy. Like my parents, my elder brother and two sisters left school to take jobs to help support the family. During summer all sons worked for Father to save for the family and to pay school expenses.

I worked hard in high school and became an honor student and a member of the National Honor Society. In addition, I participated in as many extracurricular activities as possible, the most enjoyable of which was Reserve Officers Training Corps. I advanced rapidly from a freshman private to the senior-class cadet colonel, the commander of the cadet corps at Forest Avenue High School. It was that experience which prompted me in my junior year to join the Texas National Guard.

At that time I began contemplating a military career and was interested in aviation and in earning a degree in aeronautical engineering. Though I wanted to attend Texas A&M, unfortunately the depression caused even tougher times for my family, and I could not afford college, so I investigated the possibility of obtaining an appointment to the U.S. Military Academy at West Point. I did not have the necessary political contacts but did learn of another possibility—selection to West Point through the enlisted ranks.

In 1935, I joined the army for one year with the understanding that I would be enrolled in the West Point preparatory school at Camp Bullis, Texas. A cram course, it aimed at preparing enlisted personnel for the academy entrance exam in March, 1936. About fifty young men reported to the school. It turned out to be an arduous and boring endeavor, and many dropped out and returned to complete their one year at Fort Sam Houston in San Antonio.

All of us were aware that through the preparatory schools there would be only twenty-six appointments to the academy and that Camp Bullis was just one of several such preparatory schools in the U.S. Army. The odds in my favor were poor, and although I earned a grade of 96 in the class, the score was too low to win an appointment. I was discouraged, and after finishing the one-year enlistment, I went home to work for my father in the painting business.

Nevertheless, I refused to give up, and I later discovered that a high school graduate could take a written examination in lieu of college for acceptance as a flying cadet in the U.S. Army Air Corps. I jumped at the opportunity and was directed to report for a full flight physical at Barksdale Field, Shreveport, Louisiana. Fourteen aspiring young men took the physical. I was the only one who passed, but I did have a problem—a deviated septum in one nasal passage, probably the result of boxing during high school ROTC summer encampments. It had to be removed, so I underwent surgery in Dallas. The written exam for the cadets was no problem, since I had studied similar topics at the Camp Bullis preparatory school.

In March, 1938, I reported to Randolph Field and entered Class 39-A of the flying cadets. It required nine months to complete the primary and basic phases of the training program. I soloed in a PT-13 in April after six hours of instruction, when my instructor climbed down from the rear seat and said, "Take it around the field, Bond, and land back here." He then walked off the field and sat down to watch. Full of confidence, I had no trouble.

After the nine months my class moved to advanced and specialized training at Kelly Field. By then I was set on pursuit—fighter—training rather than observation, attack, or bomber specializations. The acrobatics of flying were thrilling, as was the close-formation flying. I fantasized about fights in combat, and being in sole, complete control of an aircraft was the ultimate thrill.

When we moved to Kelly Field I checked out in the P-12, a tiny biplane that was highly maneuverable. I improved rapidly and before graduation in January, 1939, was honored by being assigned the number two position on the wing of the lead instructor for the final flyby formation. After the ceremonies we pinned on our gold second lieutenant bars and were sworn in as reserve officers in the U.S. Army Air Corps. We were proud.

The next day the assignments were posted, and we searched for our names. What a letdown; I was assigned to the Second Bomb Group, Langley Field, Virginia, a bomber outfit equipped with B-18s and four-engined B-17 Flying Fortresses. I charged over to my instructor and demanded to know why I had been condemned to bombers. He explained that there were insufficient graduates to meet the expanding needs of the bombardment units, and my name was skimmed off the top of the roster because it was in the first half of the alphabet.

In February, 1939, I went to Langley Field and reported to a B-17 crew as a copilot trainee with additional duty as assistant squadron operations officer. The squadron operations officer was a first lieutenant named Curtis E. LeMay. Cigar stuck in his mouth, LeMay was all business. He was not gregarious, nor did he smile very often, but he appreciated and enjoyed humor. When issuing orders he spoke softly, but his style of leadership was firm and forceful. A man of integrity, he would not compromise over a command decision in order to be political or polite. He was an expert concerning bombers, and anything that he told me to do I knew he could do better. He liked men who could accomplish a task, and I soon realized that this officer was destined for numerous command positions, perhaps even chief of staff.

With LeMay's guidance I studied the B-17 diligently, reading and re-reading the operations instructions and crawling all over the plane. After a few weeks I was copiloting for the squadron commander, Major Caleb Haynes. The first time he told me to take the controls while making an approach for a landing, I managed it to his satisfaction and thus became an exception to the proud rule of the veteran B-17 pilots: "You gotta be seven feet tall and a hunnert years old to be checked out in the B-17."

In 1939, with the behavior of Germany and Japan alarming officials in Washington, President Roosevelt became concerned about security in the Western Hemisphere. Of course his interest had been expanding earlier with his Good Neighbor Policy, and now it seemed appropriate to try to offset growing German influence in South America, especially Brazil. Thus, he decided to begin goodwill flights of the new four-engined Flying Fortresses to South America. It was a show of force, for Germany had nothing comparable to those bombers in the Luftwaffe.

At that time there were only fourteen B-17s in the entire Army Air Corps, and all of them were in the Second Bomb Group. We were ordered south of the border. LeMay was assigned as lead navigator for six bombers and planned the route with the aid of Pan American Air Lines, since at that time the Air Corps did not have logistical information about South America. Our itinerary consisted of Panama, Peru, Paraguay, and Brazil, with the return flight through Dutch Guiana

(Surinam), Venezuela, Puerto Rico, and Langley Field. During planning LeMay approached me and asked, "Charlie, do you have a mess jacket?"

I knew what he was driving at and replied, with a big grin, "No, but I can sure get one!" He then assigned me as the copilot for number six bomber, piloted by Lt. Don Olds.

Long-range, intercontinental, nonstop military flights were new in the 1930s, and we had a few problems. Ice tore off the radio antennas while we were flying at twenty-one thousand feet over the Andes enroute to Asunsión, Paraguay. Without our radio compass we strayed off course and had to land at Pôrto Alegre, Brazil. Another plane nosed over and bent all four propellers while taxiing on the soft ground at Asunsión, and on the return to Virginia my plane lost an engine and landed at Jacksonville, Florida.

After we returned, war erupted in Europe, and the president directed expansion of the armed forces. Our Second Bomb Group implemented plans to form cadres for another group and for a long-range reconnaissance squadron, which turned out to be a forerunner of the U.S. Air Force's strategic reconnaissance wings. In 1941 our Forty-third Bomb Squadron was ordered to MacDill Field, a new base that was still under construction at Tampa, Florida. The training there was more realistic, and we started practicing night bombing.

Shortly thereafter the United States began supplying bombers to Great Britain as part of Lend-Lease. The only available aircraft in the quantities England required was the Lockheed Hudson. Since RAF pilots were engaged defending their island, the president directed the Air Corps to ferry the bombers from the factory in Burbank, California, to Montreal, where Canadian pilots would continue the flight to England.

That effort eventually spawned the Air Transport Command of the Air Force and ultimately the Military Airlift Command. In March, 1941, I was assigned to the new U.S. Army Corps Ferrying Command in Long Beach, California. Because of my many hours flying bombers, I was made flight leader and settled down to a dull routine: ferrying bombers to Montreal, boarding airliners with my parachute and baggage, and riding back to Burbank. The job was monotonous except for one aspect which relieved the boredom. I usually made my first overnight stop at Hensley Field in Dallas, where I could spend time with my girl friend, Doris Walker. We had met in 1937 and over the years had written each other constantly. There was no doubt about our feelings, but we both realized that we were not ready for marriage.

I ferried aircraft for several months, and it seemed that bombers were my fate, when late one evening in June, 1941, I received a call from a friend who told me about an intriguing opportunity to get back into fighters—the American Volunteer Group.

1. *A Volunteer Sails for China*

During the spring and summer of 1941 Chennault began recruiting men for the American Volunteer Group. To help in the task he hired some assistants, Richard Aldworth, Skip Adair, Rutledge Irvine, Harry Claiborne, and Senton L. Brown, and one of them visited each of the seventeen air bases then in the United States. They carried letters authorizing freedom to talk with personnel, after which they offered one-year contracts to "manufacture, repair, and operate aircraft" for CAMCO. Monthly salaries ranged from $250 for mechanics to $600 for pilots and $750 for squadron commanders. In addition, traveling expenses and quarters would be furnished, and they would receive one month of paid leave. Although it was not stated in the contract, the recruiters hinted that pilots could earn a $500 bonus for each confirmed enemy plane shot down.

Over 300 men volunteered. Most of their surnames demonstrated either English or German ancestry, and they had been raised in forty-one states in the nation. Some had not graduated from high school, others had college degrees, and a few, a dentist and three physicians, had professional training. The group included many airplane mechanics along with cooks, orderlies, supply and finance clerks, radiomen, photographers, weathermen, and a chaplain. Eventually 110 pilots joined, the oldest being Louis Hoffman, forty-three, a Navy veteran who had as much flying time as Chennault, and the youngest, just out of flying school, being twenty-one-year-old Henry Gilbert.

Most of the pilots had been trained by the Navy, six were from the Marines, and fewer than half came from the Army. A Navy Catalina flying boat squadron contributed George "Pappy" Paxton, Ed Conant, Thomas Cole, Robert "Buster" Keeton, and Robert Layher. Robert Neale, Henry Geselbracht, Fritz Wolf, John Newkirk, and Frank Lawlor had been stationed aboard the USS Saratoga. Tom Haywood, Ken Jernstedt, and Charlie Older had learned to fly at the Pensacola Ma-

rine training base and had joined the group at Quantico. Fourteen U.S. Army Air Corps (USAAC) pilots volunteered from the First Pursuit Group, Selfridge Field, and Eighth Pursuit Group, Mitchell Field; they included Robert "Duke" Hedman, William McGarry, Arvid "Olie" Olson, and Robert Little. Finally, USAAC flight instructors Robert "Sandy" Sandell and Robert T. Smith signed up at Craig and Randolph fields.

Four women also volunteered for the AVG. Emma Jane "Red" Foster and Josephine Stewart, both nurses, joined in the United States. Olga Greenlaw, wife of Harvey Greenlaw, the executive officer of the AVG, and Doreen Davis already were in the Orient and performed office tasks in the headquarters at Kunming, China.[1]

The volunteers had various reasons for joining the AVG. Some disliked the military and saw the AVG as a way out. A few, like Marine 1st Lt. Gregory "Pappy" Boyington, needed money. Boyington was so deeply in debt that the corps ordered him to prepare a plan to repay his creditors. He signed on as flight leader at $675 a month. Others were more idealistic, hoping to boost democracy or Christianity in China; Paul Frillmann had been a Lutheran pastor at a mission in Hankow, China. One, interested in a good story, was the journalist Joseph Alsop. Nearly everyone desired action and adventure in China.[2]

I had my own reasons for volunteering. The late-night phone call in June, 1941, was from my old roommate, 1st Lt. Jacob J. "Jebbo" Brogger. Having spent many months together, we often talked of our future. Jebbo was aware of my intense desire to become a fighter pilot and to secure a regular commission for a career in the Air Corps. He asked if I might be interested in a wild scheme that he had just learned about from an old former Air Corps friend of his, Skip Adair. A retired pursuit pilot named Claire L. Chennault had obtained personal ap-

---

[1] Robert B. Hotz (with the assistance of George L. Paxton, Robert H. Neale, and Parker S. Dupouy), *With General Chennault: The Story of the Flying Tigers*, pp. 96–97. For a roster of the AVG, see Appendix B.

[2] Gregory Boyington, *Baa, Baa, Black Sheep*, pp. 14–26. For the stories of why Albert "Red" Probst, Loy "Sy" Seamster, Melvin H. Woodward, and Wayne Ricks joined the AVG, see Wanda Cornelius and Thayne Short, *Ding Hao: America's Air War in China, 1937–1945*, chap. 3. The voyage to Asia is described by Paul Frillmann and Graham Peck in *China: The Remembered Life*, chap. 3.

proval from the president to recruit pilots and mechanics from the U.S. armed forces for duty with an American volunteer group. These pilots would help China defend itself from the Japanese. He continued that Chennault had engaged some assistants to scour the military air bases throughout the nation to sign up volunteers for a one-year contract. If interested, I would be offered a contract by the Central Aircraft and Manufacturing Company for six hundred dollars a month. Traveling expenses and quarters would be furnished, and I would be granted one month of paid leave. Jebbo then hinted that AVG pilots might be paid a bonus of five hundred dollars for every confirmed enemy aircraft destroyed in combat. He gave me Skip's telephone number and hung up.

It was difficult to sleep that night, for I worried whether Skip would accept me because I had so much bomber time and no current fighter experience. The next morning I called Skip and told him about my conversation with Jebbo. After hearing my background and detecting my enthusiasm, he gave me the telephone number of a "Colonel Green" in Washington, D.C. Skip said, "If you want to join the AVG, just call that number and leave your name and duty station."

It did not take long for me to decide. The lure of adventure in a foreign country on the other side of the world was exciting. More important, however, was the unique and ideal manner in which this opportunity served to satisfy my dreams: a chance to get back into fighters, a chance for combat experience which might help me secure a regular commission, and a chance to earn fast money which would put me in a position to buy my parents a home.

The next day I called Colonel Green's office, giving name and duty station. In addition, I told the secretary the names of two of my closest friends, who also were ferry pilots—George Burgard and James D. Cross. Within twenty-four hours a wire arrived at our headquarters informing our commander that three of his pilots were resigning and were to be released immediately from active duty: Burgard, Cross, and me. Enraged, the commander called me abruptly, demanding a full explanation. I told him as much as I knew, and he relented, ordering us home, where we were to wait for word from CAMCO.

In early September I received a call and was told that an airline ticket was in the mail for a flight to San Francisco, where I should register at the Saint Francis Hotel, giving my occupation as "clerk." I was told to say nothing to anyone about the AVG. Arriving in San Fran-

cisco on September 21, 1941, I met about 25 other volunteers who com-
prised the last contingent of volunteers to leave the United States. The
first group, a small one, had left in June on a ship whose name had
been painted over. The second group, the largest, about 150, had sailed
on July 10 on the Dutch liner Jaegerfontein. *After that, small con-*
tingents followed on the Blumefontein, *the* Zandaam, *and my ship the*
Boschfontein. *In all cases the passenger manifests listed us as every-*
thing but pilots—acrobats, artists, musicians, salesmen, teachers, and
undertakers. There were other passengers on the ships, and we mixed
with them and wore civilian clothes.

*   *   *

September 24, 1941

We pulled away from the San Francisco pier at 1 P.M. sharp and soon were passing beneath the Golden Gate bridge—heading for Honolulu.

The SS *Boschfontein* is a Dutch motor ship, rather a small one compared to ocean liners, but our quarters are adequate. George Burgard, Jim Cross, and I are in the same stateroom. I lost in a throw of the dice and as a result got the only top bunk.

The ship's crew is Dutch and the stewards and waiters predominantly Javanese, very small people dressed in their native garb. They are courteous and efficient.

After a light lunch in the dining room and a brief afternoon nap, I went up on deck to watch the sunset on the Pacific, a beautiful sight. Had a few hands of gin rummy with Jim and George and then dinner.

Before retiring I talked with one of the missionaries who is returning to China. There are quite a few of them on board, and as a matter of fact the only females aboard are American missionaries going to China, some four or five. The other passengers are pilots and airmen and a few foreign businessmen.

I am turning in early and wondering if I am making a mistake in launching out on this adventure, probably because I am thinking deeply about Doris.

September 25, 1941

I woke in good spirits and immediately looked through the porthole to locate myself on the big ocean. Nothing but beautiful blue water under a brilliant sky.

We had our first fire drill this morning. George stayed in bed and said: "hell with it."

I spent most of the day reading and lounging on deck, but at noon I took over the duties of the officer of the day. We have established some semblance of military life. Also, we started immunization shots. I heard that the Dutch doc is actually a veterinarian, and I believe it after the way he gave me a tetanus in the back.

I began to sense a faint ache in my head and I'm wondering about sea sickness, even though the sea is as smooth as glass. It has dawned on me that I have not become accustomed to the continuing drum of the engines.

September 26, 1941

I ache all over from those shots. I seem lonely for some reason or other; guess it's dawning on me that I'm off on a trip for at least a year and I'll miss Doris. This thought dominated my entire day. How wonderful it would be if I could give Mom and Dad a trip like this.

September 29, 1941

First payday—$150, and I deposited it with the purser. The days pass slowly. I am watching flying fish, playing deck tennis, eating and drinking, and participating in the usual bull sessions with the guys.

September 30, 1941

I woke early this morning and there was Diamond Head. We docked and I still felt my wobbly legs after being on land for a few hours. In spite of a drizzle, we roamed about town to see the place, and it is full of the Army, Navy, and Orientals.

Jim, George, and I walked about the city and bought post cards and a few others items. I bought a loud sport shirt and then tried to contact some of my old Air Corps buddies but had no luck. Jim had better luck and met his friend Jim Cox, who drove us through some of the countryside. I saw my first pineapple fields. We also went to Hickam Field, the naval station, and Waikiki Beach, where we stopped to have a few drinks.

We lunched at the Alexander Young Hotel and wound up in the lounge. "Wound up" is an understatement! Pappy Boyington, Curtis

Smith, and the rest of us decided to remain there until sailing time. We had some drinks on the good old USA. As a result, we had to scamper to get aboard the ship by 3:45 P.M. Others were even later than us, resulting in a delay in our sailing. Finally we pulled out for the next stop: Surabaja, Java. Aloha, Hawaii. Hell, I'm already a world traveler!

October 1, 1941

The crew prepared a swimming pool in one of the holds, and it made our morning. Another cholera shot ruined the rest of my day—it hurt like hell!

I followed George's example and got a crew cut. I am now called Algonquin Indian.

October 2, 1941

Today was my turn in the crow's nest as lookout for enemy ships and submarines. After an hour I became bored while realizing I was looking for a possible attack. Just a few weeks ago in the U.S. there was little concern about war.

Several of us got in a good bull session with the chief engineer of the ship. He is a little pudgy Dutchman, old and experienced in the Orient. We drank several bottles of wine.

I started preparing for Father Neptune's Day celebration, which will occur when we cross the equator on our way to the bottom of the world, Australia. I am in charge of planning.

October 3, 1941

I had my second lesson in Chinese. My teacher is Mr. Woo Yaow Ta, one of the passengers returning to China.

October 6, 1941

No day! Last night we crossed the International Date Line, so today is really Tuesday, October 7, 1941. We skipped Monday.

October 9, 1941

I stood watch from 11:00 to 1:00 and got a thrill spotting land for the first time since Hawaii: the Solomon Islands. A look at the world map surprised me that we are going so far south on a course to Java.

October 10, 1941

Nine days out of Hawaii and I realized that I have begun noticing the dark Persian lady on board more than usual. We exchanged glances but not conversation. I wonder what that cute little photographer in Long Beach is doing these days. Cripes!

October 11, 1941

Neptune's Day was postponed today, even though we now are in the Coral Sea. We aren't ready yet.

I have been reading *Berlin Diary* by William Shirer and am becoming riled over the British and French activities vis-a-vis the Germans. It makes me itchy to get at the Japs in China.

October 12, 1941

A gorgeous day. I went to Sunday services and thought of Mom when we sang "Rock of Ages." What a dear saint she has been to me and the other kids. I just wish I had realized it more so when I was there, and then told her so. God grant me the power to make the lives of her and Dad as comfortable as I can the rest of their days.

October 13, 1941

Today was Neptune's celebration. What a day! By noon I was half stewed. Lewis Bishop was Father Neptune, and I was his queen. Dick Rossi was the barber, and Luke Gunvordahl and L. A. Hurst were policemen. Our faces were painted wildly with rouge and we dressed in shorts, for all of us expected to end up in the swimming pool. Dick had a large wooden straight razor and a pail of horrid-smelling goo that was shaving cream. It took several men to hold down the guy who got a shave, for the goo was made of flour, water, fruit juices, and fish soup which had been cooked days before and set out to spoil. A dishwashing mop was the shaving brush, and when the shaving cream was applied a load of it always got in the poor guy's mouth. That, together with the fact that he already was skunk drunk, meant that he usually ended up tossing his cookies.

All of us were thrown in the swimming pool, and I thought that I would drown; a couple of drunks held me under the water until I fought them off.

Those of us who were able to see through our glazed eyes spotted Australia. We now are skirting the east coast, inside the Great Barrier Reef.

24

October 16, 1941

I decided to back away from the table. We have been at sea fifteen days and I have put on twelve pounds.

We are in the Arafura Sea, and today we saw some gun emplacements on the northeast tip of Australia.

Same old routine: breakfast, reading, Chinese lesson, bull sessions, rolling dice for drinks, lunch, nap, shooting dice with Jim and George for a dime, deck tennis, sun bathing, shower, reading, evening formation, dinner, lounge, discussions, and watching the setting sun.

October 13, 1982

Everyone is becoming tense and irritable. Got into a hell of an argument with Jack Croft about something concerning the Neptune certificates. First time I was fighting mad on the trip, and I invited him on the deck. He wouldn't go. We're all drinking a lot.

October 18, 1941

George and Frank Adkins got into a scrap over something, and Smith got involved. George split Smith's lip. This stuff is bad business and will never help morale of the outfit.

October 19, 1941

We arrived at Surabaja, Java, a port city with about four hundred thousand people: a major Dutch Navy center. I watched the port activity as we picked up a pilot and eased into the pier. A swarm of Javanese waiters came on to replace ours. I changed some money, went into town, and stopped at the Oranje Hotel for a drink. Then I strolled over to an open-air lounge called the Hellendorn. We met some American flight instructors who were training Dutch pilots in Java. One instructor, Bill Eddy, and his wife, Nat, took us to their home for a visit, a lovely place. His pay must be good!

The city of Surabaja is typically Far East—hot, smelly, and colorful. Men wear flashy sarongs and everyone speaks Javanese or Dutch.

October 20, 1941

Up early to check out the possibility of a side trip to the island of Bali. Bought an elephant hat and some wood carvings, and then had lunch at the Shanghai Cafe.

Some of the guys decided to see what a Javanese "house of ill repute" looks like, so we went. I kidded the gals but had been fore-warned about Asian VD. No soap—left.

The little "dog carts" are interesting. They are small, two-wheeled buggies pulled by tiny ponies with jingling bells all over their harnesses.

Saw a naked Javanese youngster roaming the main street, and got my first experience haggling over purchases. He asks twice what he expects to get and we offer far less than we know we will have to pay. Eventually after much arguing—helped by many hand gestures—we strike a bargain and buy.

We met some of the CAMCO fellows. They are throwing in the towel and returning to the States. They painted a bad picture of the organization and raised doubts in my mind: what am I getting myself into? I'm still looking forward to getting into the cockpit of a P-40.

Many American-made PBYs and Ryan STs dot the sky of Surabaja. There seem to be preparations for war in the area. The Dutch are erecting harbor defenses.

October 21, 1941

The trip to Bali was arranged. A local Dutchman, Jack Dendien, owns a small Fiat and met George, Jim, myself, and two others, and we got away shortly after 9 A.M.

What a drive! It took only a few minutes to scare us out of our wits. Jack should have been a race-track driver—perhaps he was. With six of us crowded into that tiny Fiat, a trip of 180 miles was uncomfortable. Added to that was a demonic determination on Jack's part to keep the speedometer registering no less than 80 MPH at all times. At first we hinted tactfully about wiping out Javanese pedestrains from the sides of the narrow highways, but to no avail. In desperation George finally blurted: "Dammit, Jack! Slow down!" This helped for a few minutes, but soon we were whirling along again scattering the dogs, chickens, and children all over the countryside.

Today was the Mohammedan New Year, and the highways were seething with pony-pulled "dog carts," automobiles, bicycles, and an unbroken stream of people along the narrow shoulders of the roads. The small towns were even more congested. But we dashed through them, Jack relying on his horn. He never took his hand from the button until we cleared the city's outskirts.

To add to our discomfort, we were driving on the left side of the road. Our nerves were almost to the breaking point. When we met an oncoming vehicle, I leaned to my right to try in some way to get our car to the right side. It is incredible that we did not kill several people, but we certainly did get the day's bag of chickens, and we broke the legs of a small goat that did not get clear in time. We raced on, leaving it bleeding on the side of the road.

Our fear of this driving distracted us from enjoying the scenery of this exotic island. As we became more accustomed to Jack's wild antics, we did notice many rice fields with hazy mountains off in the distance. Hundreds of Javanese were planting the rice by hand, and all about were scarecrow structures to keep birds away. Each scarecrow is connected by heavy twine to a wire leading to a central straw hut. There sits a native who has the job of pulling the wire back and forth from time to time to activate the scarecrow arms. There is a job that does not exist in the States!

The jungles nearby are filled with banana and coconut trees. We drove across a low ridge just before entering the town of Banjoewangi. Suddenly the trees and bushes by the road were alive with hundreds of screaming, scampering monkeys. Jack said they were all over the island and that they would eat from your hand.

We had lunch in the village, and Jack refueled the Fiat while we amused ourselves by throwing pennies to inquisitive little Javanese boys.

At this town we boarded a ferry for crossing the strait to the island of Bali. We started across as the tide came in—about 8 P.M. Looking across the few miles to Bali and at the small sailboat that was our ferry, I wondered how we would ever do it. Our genial driver and friend, Jack, did not help matters; he explained that the tide is tortuous and that the water is infested with sharks.

We got the car on the boat with the help of several large timbers, a small ramp, and a lot of rope and chain wrapped about a small hand-operated winch. Our wisecracking and supervision were not only unheeded but also unappreciated. The natives merely grunted at us.

The boat was poled out into the deeper water and the sail was then put up. We had a rather sharp wind from our right rear, and soon we were skipping right along—at first in choppy water and then in rather deep swells. We helped balance the craft by standing on the windward edge of the siding. I didn't like the situation and the natives began yelling at one another. It was obvious that they, too, were a little nervous about the big load on their ferry. I divided my time watching the higher waves lapping at the boat and the lights on the far Balinese shore that were slowly getting closer and closer. Soon we were poled into our place at Gilimanuk, Bali.

We packed into our little Fiat again for the last wild ride to Denpasar, the capital of Bali, and then to our final destination. Kuta Beach. But this time it was night, and Jack was not the type of driver to be discouraged by darkness. We completely left the highway one time and ran off into an adjacent field. Several near repeat performances kept me from sleeping, although some of the others got used to the peril.

When we finally arrived in Denpasar, we were not able to arouse anyone to admit us into the Manx Hotel, so we drove on to Kuta Beach resort. There, a "number-one boy," or *djongas*, met us but was reluctant to awaken the manager since it was midnight. Jack finally prevailed in his Malayan tongue, and to our surprise we were received by a tall, blond American, who is the owner.

The hotel is much like a typical American resort. There is a large central clubhouse surrounded by many small cabana cabins, all made of bamboo and palm leaves. The cabins are furnished scantily with just a bed and lounge chair. A gas lantern burns brightly on the patio porch facing the beach, and a flickering kerosene lamp lights the interior of the cabana. There is a WC, the bathroom, and a small shower bath with clear, cool water.

We finally are turning in. What will tomorrow bring? Hopefully, a beautiful island and bare-breasted women in the Balinesian tradition!

October 22, 1941

I awoke this morning to the noice of Bob Koke, the American owner, beating the tong-tong and advising us to take a dip in the surf prior to breakfast. I got up and we spent a pleasant thirty minutes in the surf.

Breakfast was delicious: American-style pancakes and maple syrup. Bob suggested we take a bicycle ride to a nearby village to watch a Balinesian ritual—a "tooth filing" ceremony that is in effect a debut for a young lass who has just about reached puberty. He grinned when he suggested it and said, "I've seen one and I don't care to see another."

We pedaled out the drive and down the dusty little lane until we reached an intersection where we saw our first *kampong*. The word sounds a little like "compound" and that is an apt description of what the little village resembles. Several separate little thatched huts arranged in a square some two or three hundred feet on a side and a few storehouses and shacks among them. A high adobe and stone wall surrounds the settlement.

Balinesians were all about the place, and we finally saw the bare-breasted girls. Some are attractive; others are not. Their sole piece of clothing is a bright-colored sarong tightened at the waist. The older women are a bit more shy and tried to cover themselves with scarves or rice bags. I took several snapshots, for I knew the folks at home would find this hard to believe.

In the middle of the *kampong* there was a raised platform where an old man with white hair was sitting. Seems that he is the chief or mayor of the settlement. We were led past him and into a nearby hut. Tables and long benches were covered with food, money, and presents—all of which were brought for the family of the young girl who was to take her bow this day.

Our attention was diverted to another hut from which we heard strange music. It came from a chime box made of bamboo sections strapped together, and a native beat it rhythmically with a bone tied on the end of a wooden pole. There was no tune of any kind, just a tom-tom beat. In the middle of the floor was the young Balinesian girl, about fourteen or fifteen years old, kneeling on colorful pillows and making religious gestures toward an altar. She seemed to be in a trance. She had a flower in her right hand, and after a moment she placed it at the foot of the altar. Then she lay back across the pillows, flat on her back. A white sarong was laid across her body, and a bright yellow scarf was placed around the shoulders of a man, probably a religious authority in the *kampong*. He picked up a common metal file and dipped it in a can of water. Small wooden cubes were placed in her jaws between her teeth, and she clamped down on them, leaving her teeth separated about a half inch. She looked as though she had a huge smile. The music beat got louder an faster, and then he started filing her upper row of teeth. He paralled the gum line, filing down about halfway between the gum line and the ends of her teeth. Back and forth, stopping every now and then to wet the file in the water. She showed no signs of pain—not a grimace on her face, not even a word! There was no emotion in the crowd except for the girl's mother, who began to shed tears.

The file bit deeper and deeper into her teeth. My stomach warned me to get the hell out of there, and I did, as did the other guys. I just cannot comprehend the significance of such rituals, and I agreed with Bob: once is enough to see that.

On the way back to our beach hotel I spotted a young bare-breasted girl, about eighteen, standing with a group of other native boys and girls. She had a beautiful body, and her hair, bluish black, was tied in a knot and fell behind her head. Her eyes were dark brown and her skin was creamy white. She smiled, and there was no evidence of filed teeth. I stopped, hoping I could take a snapshot of her. I offered a coin to an old man next to her, gesturing that I would pay to get her picture with my camera. He thought I wanted to take his picture and posed boldly for me. I had to take his picture before I got things straightened out, and then I took several shots of the girl.

Bob told us that he had arranged for us to visit a temple and see the Balinesian Monkey Dance. When we arrived at the event we pushed our way through souvenir salesmen and took our seats in a small arena. The stage or performance area had a seven-foot pole in the middle. Five bowls of oil with bright flames were hanging from the top of the pole, and about a hundred half-naked young boys were squatting in a tight circle at the base. Suddenly they let out a loud howl and then buried their heads in their legs. The dance had begun, and the whole thing was performed in the squatting position. Constantly swinging their arms wildly, screaming and ranting, the boys imitated monkeys. There was a constant "sut-sut" coming from their lips, and in the background a single native chanted in a high shrill. Every so often one boy would jump to his feet and dance around the pole in wild, spasmodic convulsions. The dance lasted about thirty minutes and then it was suddenly over, when all the boys jumped to their feet and scrambled out of the temple.

October 23, 1941

I tried surfing this morning but was a miserable failure. After another luscious breakfast and goodbyes, we all stuffed ourselves back into the little Fiat for the dreaded drive back to Surabaja.

On the first part back to the ferry Jack drove rather slowly. I think George had bribed him to take it easy. The ferry ride was smoother, and soon we were back in Java and on our way back to our ship. This time we took a different route. The road was more mountainous, but it was a modern, well-paved highway. Then Jack revealed another one of his unique driving traits—as it grew dark he refused to turn on his lights! He nearly struck a native on the roadside, and then George roughly demanded that he use his lights. Jack did, but in an apparent retaliatory move he tried to intimidate us by racing madly with a Ford V-8 through the outskirts of Surabaja. He was going seventy-five MPH as he entered the city limits. We won the race, but came close to losing other things.

Arriving at the dock, we were aghast; the ship was not at the pier—gone! The customs officer informed us that we could catch it to-morrow at Semarang, some two hundred miles to the west. We re-signed ourselves to an overnight stay at the Sarkies Hotel and then a long train ride tomorrow. Now to bed—quite tired.

October 24, 1941

Arrived in Semarang and boarded the ship for Batavia.[3]

October 25, 1941

We pulled into the Batavia harbor and a tug berthed us between Australian and Panamanian ships. Close by was a Dutch motor ship, and we could not help but notice the three-inch gun at its prow. I won-der why we don't have one on our ship? Is war this close?

Soon we were in town and lounging at the Capitol Restaurant dis-cussing our Bali trip and the sights of the local city, which is the capi-tal of Java. About a hundred thousand people larger than Surabaja, I would think. A Dutch sailor and some Australian RAAF flyers joined us, and we were soon off on another drinking bout. The other patrons were quite amused at our loud antics, and we had the little combo play "God Bless America" for us as we joined in the chorus. A few hours of this was enough. We returned to the ship.

---

[3] Now Djakarta.

October 26, 1941

Another day, so we went off to the city again to meet the Dutch sailor and RAAF flyers. This time we went to a casino for swimming and dancing. We behaved ourselves today for some reason and soon were back on the ship.

Nothing to do but watch the unloading and loading, and that grew tiresome, so we made other plans. To break the monotony George, Jim, and I dressed in our formal military "monkey jacket" outfits, without all the Air Corps garbage, of course, and went back to town.

Passing by the Cozy Corner Night Club, I thrust my head into the door; not very impressed at first, but my eyes locked onto a very comely barmaid, and in we went. Eilene must have been about twenty-four, with black hair, lovely complexion, and dressed in a black evening gown that clung to a well-shaped body. She spoke good English. We could kill time here and have a dance or two. George taught the little combo "Maria Elena" and we danced.

We got into a heated discussion with a Dutch patron, who insisted that Americans in Arizona could not understand Americans from New York. Liquor made the argument much more heated, and we managed to dominate him, particularly when he claimed that I looked like a German officer. I suppose it is my crew cut. I resented the comparison, but we went back to the ship peacefully.

I learned tonight that the KLM Dutch shipping line is booked solid for the first two years after the European war is expected to end. The Dutch citizens in the Far East are uneasy about war in the Pacific.

October 27, 1941

I went to a movie and saw *Comrade X* with Clark Gable and Hedy Lamar. The local people like them as much as the Americans do. The news part of the movie was quite a show of the U.S. Navy's air force. I had to choke back a laugh when they showed pictures of the Air Corps's Randolph Field Training Center; it is obvious the U.S. has its propaganda wound up in the Far East. The local Dutch loved every minute of it.

October 29, 1941

We entered the port of Surabaja again this morning. During our visit to the city George and I ran into a Mr. Schmidt from Pennsylvania. He had been to China and is on his way home. He spent the evening telling us about China, and we ate it up—seems exotic.

October 30, 1941

A Dutch Ryan ST did a lot of buzzing above the ship this morning. It made me itch to get my hands on the controls of a P-40.

October 31, 1941

I watched the crew install three-inch guns on the bow of our ship. I guess these people are getting serious about the Japanese. It made me feel closer to war.

November 2, 1941

We were at sea when I was awakened this morning—on our way to Singapore. I was sitting in a chair putting on my socks when I heard a loud gunshot. Startled, I thought of an explosion and a sinking ship. Then I learned it was an officer testing the three-inch gun.

November 4, 1941

I spent the morning watching the small islands as we neared the port of Singapore. We stopped to pick up a pilot and then proceeded into the harbor and docked.

The cliffs and hillsides seem covered with pillbox fortifications— all camouflaged. Even the huge oil tanks are camouflaged. An airport must be nearby, for we have seen several British fighters in the sky.

We caught a bus and went to the Raffles Hotel. Enjoyed hearing the English language and had a few drinks. It seems that almost everyone is in uniform.

November 5, 1941

Jim and I went into the city this morning. First we bought some silk pajamas for the girls back home, then we hired a taxi and toured Singapore. There are some beautiful neighborhoods with huge, lovely homes with manicured lawns and colorful flowers. Practically every home has a private tennis court. This is the swanky part of town called Singapore Gardens. The downtown is much like an American metropolis with many large buildings and a lot of traffic. Trolley cars have overhead electric lines, no rails. The Chinese section is quite apart from the British area, definitely oriental and smelly. Thousands of shops and cluttered streets, and Chinese all seeming to be in a hurry, with the ever-pestering rickshaw puller tagging along asking us to take a ride.

Very prominent are the air-raid shelters in the business district. Concrete protective walls are built in front of doorways and large windows. War news and propaganda are posted everywhere. Servicemen are given a fifty percent reduction on theater tickets. Of course, all this war spirit is connected with England, which is now at war with Germany; the people here have the Japanese in mind. They expect war!

November 6, 1941

Read the local English paper with great interest. The British general Sir Archibald Wavell is visiting Singapore today. The Japanese have made seven demands on the United States; I read them in detail and think they are stupid. This article is dead serious.

Also, the Japanese notified the U.S. State Department and told them that American pilots flying for China and captured by the Japanese will be shot. I wonder how true this is. Some of the bunch are pretty pessimistic. I am still anxious to get into a P-40 at Toungoo, Burma.

Jim, George, and I went into town and got our Chinese visas.

November 7, 1941

About ten of us hired a taxi to see Johore, an independent state ruled by a sultan. We drove some forty kilometers to get there, and on the way went past many rubber plantations, a huge Ford plant, and several large British Army camps. When we arrived we were not permitted to enter the spacious grounds of the sultan's home; we had an Indian lieutenant for a guide, and he led us through the zoo, several mosques, a beautiful hospital, and a nine-hole golf course. The museum is impressive with millions of dollars in gold table settings and other ornaments. The sultan gives banquets for as many as 150 guests.

On the way back from Johore we stopped at a rubber plant to watch the production of crude rubber. The drying rooms were nauseating. The labor was Chinese, and they got about thirty cents a day, American.

Back in Singapore we visited the Tiger Balm House, where we examined one of the most valuable collections of jade in the world. All colors and all forms of jewelry and statuettes.

George ran into Harvey Greenlaw, the AVG executive officer, who flew from Rangoon to pick up some supplies for the AVG. He gave us a report on the setup in Toungoo, and it elevated our spirits. He made one comment that is puzzling; there are some awful flyers there in Toungoo flying for Chennault. I don't know if he is speaking of their character or their flying ability. I soon will find out.

I am eager to get going. I wonder what really is in store for us now with the great tension between the U.S. and Japan.

November 8, 1941

I ran into some of the AVG gang who are down with Greenlaw from Rangoon and discussed the setup at Toungoo. Robert Rogers, a crew chief and formerly an Army Air Corps enlisted man from New York, spoke highly of what we will find. I also spent some time with Andy Anderson, who told us about the Japanese bombing in China. He has been there since 1938.

The British antiaircraft troops practiced gunnery tonight, and the searchlights are all over the city. This place is bristling with defense activities.

November 9, 1941

We are on our way to Rangoon. I had another bull session with some of the gang, this time on the promenade deck, which is blacked out.

November 10, 1941

In the Bay of Bengal, and it is the same old routine at sea. Going to bed early tonight and thinking a lot of Doris.

November 11, 1941

Armistice Day—and here I am on my way to another war! We observed the day by a moment of silence all over the ship at 11:00 A.M.

I am a bit edgy today, and I think it is because of a lengthy bout of constipation. However, it makes me feel better to know that I am not among the group who already have picked up venereal disease.

I spent a lot of time talking with an NBC newsman about the war situation. He did not conceal his apparent contempt for our AVG gang. I wonder how we will do in our mission.

Practically everyone had champagne tonight since this is the last night of our long cruise to the Far East.

November 12, 1941

I awoke this morning as we were easing up the Irrawaddy River prior to docking at Rangoon. Off in the distance is a tall, golden spire, one of the many pagodas I will be seeing during the next weeks in Burma.

2. Training in Toungoo

After our arrival in Burma we traveled some 170 miles north to Toungoo, and 7 miles outside the town we occupied RAF barracks at Keydaw Aerodrome. The training base was in a valley surrounded by dark, damp jungle. Heavy rains alternated with torrid heat, producing the atmosphere of a Turkish bath. The teakwood barracks had thatched roofs and woven rattan walls. Also, they had no screens, so they housed not only the men, but also numerous insects. The food was "American" but poorly prepared, and eating proved to be something of a challenge; the insects fought us for dinner and sometimes won.

We were unaware of the knotty negotiations between the Chinese and the British concerning the use of the RAF base, for that had preceded our arrival by several months. The British were hesitant to become embroiled in anything that appeared supportive of China, fearing the aggressive mood of Japan. After discussions, Chennault finally prevailed with the help of the generalissimo; the British agreed to let us train at Toungoo with the understanding that as soon as we could fly the P-40s we would move north to China. Little did they realize that within weeks they would be clamoring for the AVG to remain in Burma.

Chennault was eager to begin training but had to wait for the Tomahawks. The planes had arrived in Rangoon, but still were in crates and had to be assembled, fitted with radios, and armed for combat. In early August a few AVG pilots had begun ferrying the P-40s to Keydaw. By the end of the month twenty-two planes had been assembled, but all ninety-nine were not at Keydaw until the end of November.

The "Old Man" or "Colonel," as we called him then, also had problems with many of the volunteers. After two months at sea, eating four or five meals a day, the men were soft and overweight. Chennault cut transportation around the base to a minimum, forcing most of us to buy bicycles, and began regular schedules of calisthenics, baseball, and volleyball. Some men had poor attitudes, and after arriving at Toungoo, five immediately returned to the United States. As Chennault put it, most volunteers "considered themselves extremely hot pilots. After their long voyage bragging to fellow passengers about their prowess as fighter pilots, many of them were convinced they were ready to walk down the gangplank at Rangoon and begin decimating the Japanese Air Force."[1] Some of the fresh graduates from flying school thought they could not learn anything from Chennault—"a beat up old Army captain who had been buried in China." Although he had desired to recruit pilots of ages twenty-three to twenty-eight with three years' experience, he was able to find only a dozen volunteers who met those standards. In fact, just half had flown a fighter, and only a few had ever sat in a P-40.

To minimize these problems, Chennault instituted what he called a kindergarten for the AVG. The course consisted of seventy-two hours on the ground and sixty in the air. We spent most mornings in the classrooms and afternoons getting familiar with the P-40s. Chennault taught everything he knew about fighting the Japanese. He emphasized that their pilots fought by the book, then he handed out Japanese flying and tactics manuals that had been captured and translated into English. He said that enemy pilots were brave fighters with plenty of guts, but that they lacked initiative and judgment. They went into battle with a set plan and followed it no matter what happened. Bombers always held their formations, and fighters always tried the same tricks, regardless of the combat situation.

Chennault compared the P-40 to the Japanese Zero. Designed in 1939, produced by Mitsubishi, the Zero was a formidable fighter. It was armed with two 7.7-mm machine guns and later with two 20-mm cannons. It was light and maneuverable. With a 925-horsepower radial engine it had a top cruising speed of about 330 MPH and could climb quickly to thirty-four thousand feet. To get such maneuverability, however, the designers skimped on armor plating and sacrificed protection for fuel tanks and pilots. The P-40 was much heavier, with a larger engine—a 1,150-horsepower Allison that was liquid-cooled, meaning that a hit in the radiator could cause overheating and disaster. It had a

[1]Chennault described training and tactics in *Way of a Fighter*, pp. 109–15.

slower cruising speed, about 300 MPH, and a ceiling of thirty-two thousand feet. When loaded for combat, the plane could not climb and turn well above twenty-two thousand feet. Yet the P-40 was heavily armed with two .50-caliber and four .30-caliber machine guns, and it had armor protection for the pilot.

The Old Man stressed these comparisons so that in combat we would make best use of the strengths of our plane against the weaknesses of the Zero. The P-40 had the advantage in a dive and superior firepower, whereas the Zero could climb faster, turn sharper, and cruise higher. Chennault trained us to attain higher speeds by descending on the enemy, closing in, firing, and peeling off. Our greatest defensive strength in combat was the power dive. He also warned us always to fly in pairs—stick together. If we found ourselves alone after engaging the enemy, we should search the sky and join another P-40. We should always enter combat with the altitude advantage and trade altitude for speed—dive, hit, and run—press the attack, fire in short bursts, and only break off at the last instant. If the enemy got on our tail, then we should go into a split-S power dive with full throttle, pull away, and then regain altitude to make a vertical attack. Never were we to try horizontal combat with a Zero.

We practiced these tactics for weeks over the skies of Burma, and of course this daily activity increased the possibility of accidents. Some pilots misjudged the fast landing speed of the heavy P-40. The first time Pappy Boyington tried to land, he bounced along the runway and had to use full throttle to avoid crashing, making it in on the second try. Others had similar problems. One afternoon six pilots overran the runway, causing considerable damage to their planes. A seventh plane was damaged that same day when a mechanic accidentally ran into it on the service ramp of the runway. Eventually a dozen P40s were destroyed during training.

There were also more serious accidents. Jack Armstrong of Kansas died in a collision with another plane while practicing aerial combat. The other pilot parachuted to safety. Maax Hammer of Illinois crashed while attempting to land during a monsoon storm, and Peter Atkinson of West Virginia was killed when he was unable to pull his plane out of a power dive.

These accidents naturally produced doubts in the minds of some pilots about the P-40. They complained that the liquid-cooled en-

gine was too vulnerable and that the plane was too difficult to fly for combat. Some even carped that the United States had given the good planes, such as the Brewster Buffalo, to the British as part of Lend-Lease. Chennault realized the problem and so on November 20 arranged a mock dogfight between Erikson Shilling in his P-40 and an RAF pilot flying a Buffalo. Shilling clobbered his opponent and demonstrated that if flown properly, the P-40 could be a formidable fighter.

Because of unexpected problems, training took much longer than planned. Although we first engaged the enemy in December, 1941, we still had eighteen pilots not prepared for combat as late as March, 1942.

*   *   *

November 12, 1941

When we docked at Rangoon, Bill Pawley, the CAMCO owner, came aboard to welcome us. We were paid immediately in rupees, my first pay except for expense money, from CAMCO.

Jim, George, and I took a rickshaw ride around the central part of the city before catching the train north to our training base and final destination—Toungoo. We have been traveling for some fifty days since San Francisco.

When we pulled into the Toungoo station, we were greeted by some members of the AVG—Skip Adair, Eriksen Shilling, and George McMillan. We drove to our training base, the RAF field, and had coffee and doughnuts before walking over to the barracks. George, Jim, and I are in the same outfit, the First Pursuit Squadron.

I am happy about everything so far, and content as I douse the light and lie down in my bunk in Burma—halfway around the world from home, folks, and Doris.

November 13, 1941

Reveille was supposed to have been 5:30 A.M., but we were allowed to sleep in this first morning. I had a good breakfast, roamed around the housing area and hanger briefly, signed some paperwork, and went into the little town of Toungoo to buy a bicycle. From what we are told, a bike is essential here. I paid 107 rupees for it, about thirty-two dollars.

I pedaled back to the base, took a short nap, and then began thinking over this deal. What is the situation here? Why did I come? How will it turn out?

The setup is not as bad as some of us were led to believe by rumors from disgruntled ones. The American Volunteer Group is headed by Colonel Claire Chennault with a very small administrative staff of selected men from volunteers from the Navy, Army Air Corps, and Marines. We have about one hundred pilots and about two hundred maintenance and support personnel. No military titles. Everything is run like a civilian business, somewhat like an American airline company. However, there is an underlying, subconscious aura of military relations between the officers, pilots and staff, and the enlisted men, maintenance and support people. Discipline is more a matter of each individual's own behavior and his personal regard for the other man.

Each individual is a volunteer and was hired for a particular job in the organization—staff materiel officer, finance clerk, squadron leader, armorer, vice squadron leader, crew chief, flight leader, radio operator, wingman, propeller specialist, and so on. The pay is in American dollars, as much of it deposited in U.S. banks as each man wants. It varies from as much as $750 to some $250. Practically everything is furnished—food, lodging, official transportation and expenses. But we do provide our own clothing, and it varies considerably. For most, the British-style bush jacket and shorts are the most popular. Most of the flying clothing seems to be that which the other pilots have brought from the Navy, Army, and Marines.

I was hired as a wingman to start at six hundred dollars a month, with verbal promises of rapid advancement because of my longer service back home. Many others have just graduated from flying school, and a few pilots have only three or four hours of night flying.

The RAF base here at Toungoo has one macadamized runway about four thousand feet long with no overruns. One fair-sized hanger accommodates several P-40s, and several other maintenance and supply buildings complete the hangar layout. We have shoot-in butts across the field, and another shorter runway is being built.

The field is in a wide valley with some fairly lofty mountain ranges to our east separating Burma from Thailand. To the west are the flat fields where the natives raise rice.

We have an improvised control tower which consists of a small open-sided hut about eight feet square resting on four heavy poles about five feet above the ground. The controller is one of the pilots assigned to duty for the day. Air-to-ground communications is one channel, a very unreliable system. Our transmitters and receivers in the planes are cheap commercial sets.

The barracks and living area are separated from the hangar by about a mile, but by cutting across the end of the runway we can shorten the distance by a third. The barracks and administrative buildings are made of teak wood frames covered with woven bamboo. Several of the support buildings on the hangar line are of the same construction. Roofs are metal sheets of corrugated tin, very popular in the U.S.

Besides our bicycles we have a few Studebaker station wagons and a couple of small buses.

Our dining hall also serves as the club and bar, and we eat at 6 A.M., 1 and 7 P.M. Food is prepared American-style and it is adequate.

We have no hospital, only a small infirmary. Doc Lewis "Rich" Richards and Doc Sam Prevo impress me, and all of us love our two nurses, Red Foster and Jo Stewart. As a matter of fact, Red and Joe are the only women in the outfit right now.

Each day we take a vitamin D and a salt pill. Softball games and bicycle riding are the main forms of exercise, and we have movies which are imported from the States. Latrines are dry outhouses in the rear of our barracks, as are the bath shacks and washstands. Burmese natives take care of the menial jobs and food preparation. An elderly one had turned out to be our barber. Thank the Lord we don't have to worry too much about our looks, for the haircuts would be our ruination.

At this time Chennault is known as "the Colonel" and is the boss, leader, chargé d'affaires, commander, and any other title that is indicative of the fact that he runs the AVG. Skip Adair is what we call the G-4, or materiel staff officer. The three squadrons are initially organized on the basis of eighteen assigned P-40s. Chennault also has a twin-engined Beechcraft light transport for traveling back and forth to China and frequent supply runs to other parts of Southeast Asia.

Pedaling our bikes into Toungoo over the seven-mile stretch when the station wagon is not available is getting our legs in good shape.

I have already learned the terrific importance of mail from home—
a great morale booster. Read a letter from Doris tonight several times
before turning in.

November 14, 1941

Hit the floor at 5:30 this morning to the clanging sound of Joseph's
gong. He is our number-one Burmese barracks boy. He walks up and
down the open-bay barracks every morning that is a workday and beats
the hell out of that gong.

We new arrivals reported to the line this morning for our first day
of work. There were about thirty-five of us, and we swelled the
strength of the group to about 70 percent of its ultimate manpower of
volunteer Americans. Our instructors and teachers are composed of
the previous contingent which arrived here a few months earlier.

Our first lecture was on the P-40 and its operation and the local
flight rules and regulations. Edgar Goyette, an ex-Navy man, did the
talking, and I was impressed. He was assisted by Noel Bacon, another
ex-Navy pilot. We had our pictures made and were issued our para-
chutes. Goyette gave me a cockpit check, and I studied the G-file thoroughly the rest of the morning.

In the afternoon we had our first ball game. Each squadron has a
team, and I played shortstop on the First Squadron team. My defensive play was far superior to my hitting. I fanned out time after time.
As usual, I was trying to hit the home run as I use to do in grade-school
softball. I got a lot of razzing about it.

November 15, 1941

More studying of the G-file and cockpit familiarization today. I
checked my parachute for a good fit. The Chinese writing on it means
"umbrella insurance."

I discussed the P-40 flying characteristics with "Mortimer Snerd"
Shilling. I also made out a will and filed it with headquarters.

About ten of us went into town tonight in the station wagon to the
local Baptist mission to have dinner with Mr. Walker and Mr. Johnson,
who are very fine people and want to know us better. While discussing
the world situation over coffee after dinner, I noticed a magazine section of a British newspaper on the table. I was attracted by the picture
of an Australian P-40 on the front page that was exactly like ours, but
with one exception—the lower nose section around the oil scoop inlets

was brightly painted red, white, and green in the shape of a snarling tiger shark mouth wide open with teeth exposed.

Gee! I'm going to paint my P-40 that way! I discussed it with the others and they thought it was a good idea. Fortunately, Chennault likes the idea as well.[2]

November 16, 1941

I was quite sore this morning. I suppose it is from pedaling into town for the paint to jazz up the planes. A good game of softball got rid of it.

November 17, 1941

I arose excited today, for I anticipated my first flight in the P-40. But because of my recent experience flying the B-17s, they wanted me to break in on a BT-14 first. I went along with it, but they couldn't get it in commission.

Jim and George, meanwhile, checked out okay on the P-40. Both did well, and Jim even did better when he had his first forced landing. His engine threw a rod and caught on fire, and he had to make a belly landing in a nearby rice paddy, wheels up. I heard, and was worried about his condition until he walked into the dining hall—just in time for lunch—with a smirk on his face!

I took a nap this afternoon. We have to use the mosquito bar. Bugs and ants are all over the place.

November 18, 1941

This was the day! I made my first flight in the P-40. I was confident of my ability to handle the plane and was relaxed and at ease only a few minutes after being airborne. Having been trained as a pursuit pilot in P-12s and BT-8s (the forerunner of the P-35) at Kelly Field in 1939, I was eager to try acrobatics during my first flight. Slow rolls,

---

[2] During the next weeks we painted the noses of our planes with teeth of a snarling tiger shark. CAMCO representatives also asked Walt Disney to develop an insignia, and his illustrators created a winged tiger leaping forward from the base of the letter V, which represented victory over Japan. Thus, the teeth under the nose cowling and the leaping tiger became the symbols of the AVG, which became famous as the Flying Tigers. That name was popularized by the American press after Chinese newspapers in March, 1942, began referring to the pilots as *fei-hu*, or "flying tigers." Malcolm Rosholt, *Days of the Ching Pao: A Photographic Record of the Flying Tigers—14th Air Force in China in World War II*, p. 8.

loops, and Immelmans were smooth after a few tries. The one characteristic of the plane which is new to me is the sharp increase of rudder-pedal pressure required to offset an extreme yaw to the left, particularly in high-speed dives. At 400 MPH in a vertical dive it is almost impossible to hold enough left rudder to correct for the drastic yaw without maximum rudder trim. My first landing approach drew a few gasps from some of the old hands, but the touchdown was good—wheels first with tail up. I had been warned of the ground looping tendency of the aircraft. In all, I was very happy with my first flight.

Freeman Ricketts came in on a subsequent landing attempt with his wheels only half down. He damaged the aircraft badly but was unhurt. The whole group now is temporarily grounded for the rest of the day.

All of us were scheduled for our "short arm" physical today. Seems like too many of the guys were suspected of having VD. Doc Tom Gentry is from Dallas, so we hit it off right away.

November 19, 1941

Apparently the Old Man was still teed off about Ricketts's landing yesterday, for no flying was scheduled today. We just cannot afford aircraft losses from accidents, since we do not have all the P-40s on hand yet. I was disappointed, but I stayed busy by helping Ed Rector paint the tiger shark on the nose of his plane.

Our Burmese number-one boy gave me a haircut today, and the dry shave about the ears made my skin crawl. I will have to get used to it, or take time to teach him to use soap and water.

Went to the movies tonight and watched Paulette Goddard in *Ghost Breakers*. During an undressing scene the moans and howls from all of us could be heard all over the base.

November 20, 1941

I was assigned to the First Pursuit Squadron today as assistant operations officer under Frank Schiel. He seems like a very fine person.

No flying today for me. I was control tower officer for most of the day.

An RAF pilot in a Brewster Buffalo flew up from Rangoon. He and Shilling put on quite a dogfight show for all of us right over the base. Shilling whipped him soundly. We could not say much for the RAF pilot. He did not strike us as a "tiger."

November 21, 1941

Chennault gave us a talk this morning on the organization once we move up to Kunming, China. We will be under the directives of Generalissimo Chiang Kai-shek, which in effect puts us in the Chinese Air Force. Some 996 Chinese will be assigned to support us. Ultimately, we might get some P-43 aircraft, a high-performance fighter with a turbosupercharger. That will provide us with a much higher altitude capability than we have now with the P-40.

The Old Man still has a military air about him. With his tan RAF bush jacket and sun helmet, he impresses us as a commander rather than a director or manager.

He extolled the virtues and advantages of the P-40 over the Japanese Zero. Particularly, he stressed our superior diving capabilities as compared to the Zero's. He emphasized that over and over, and told us never, never try to dogfight with a Zero, particularly in turning combat. Hit and run! Hit and run, dive, and then come back to altitude. Of course, always try to stay in groups of at least two. As soon as you find yourself alone, search the skies to rejoin someone.

I like the Old Man. His voice is not too high, although he is hard of hearing. His face is heavily pocked, and that jutting lower jaw is the outstanding feature. It is easy to understand why he often has been called "old leather face." He has a good sense of humor and likes to be around us when permitted by his administrative duties.

I had three flights today totaling a little over two hours. One was a formation flight led by Bob Little. What a flight! We did everything in the book. I was a mass of sweat after the hour-and-twenty-minute rat race. My landings are much better now.

Went to bed rather early tonight, but awakened around midnight scratching my head. Finally it dawned on me that something was crawling all over my head. I flipped on my flashlight and found the problem: hundreds of little ants all over my pillow. My head was alive with them. It was probably the cheap Burmese hair oil I was using. Dousing my head under the water tap in the rear of the barracks seemed to solve my problem. Tomorrow I'll find some cans, fill them with water, and place the legs of my bed in them.

November 22, 1941

No flying today, Saturday. I went to the infirmary to have Doc check my eyes—conjunctivitis. He gave me some salve. I hung around and talked to Red and Jo, the nurses. Great gals!

I assumed duties at noon as officer of the day (who the hell says we are not a military outfit?). I actually got dressed up a little with clean starched slacks, flight cap, shiny belt buckle, and a black tie. I realized how slovenly I have gotten, as have all of us. The tie was uncomfortable, and I dragged it through my soup at lunch. Hell's bells!

It was a bad day to have the job of OD. Perhaps because it is Saturday. It seems that everyone decided to get a snoot full. My patience was taxed to the utmost by six airmen when I tried to close the canteen at 11:30 P.M. They finally gave in. Jim and George got loaded, and I loaned George forty rupees for a crap game. Jim and Donald Knapp decided to go into town with me to make rounds of the restaurants, bars, and so on to make sure that the AVG boys were not getting out of hand. The railway refreshment room was a popular place known as the China Hotel, which really is a cat house. What a filthy joint. None of our men were there, and I was glad to get out of the place.

As I turned into the barracks area, I heard a pistol shot. In my eagerness to get to the scene, I ran over a bicycle—ruined it. I'm not about to accept the responsibility for that. Getting out of the car, I found Ed Conant really "out," and he was shooting his pistol into the sky. Robert H. "Snuffy" Smith, equally maggoty, was with him and not helping the situation. I tried to get Ed to give me the gun so I could hold it for him overnight, but he refused. He said he was on his way to the China Hotel. I was at the point of bashing him one, but gave up, telling Snuffy that he was responsible. Snuffy was now half sober, for he had fallen into the ditch several times. He agreed to take care of Ed.

I got two letters from Doris today. I am sure she loves me as much as I know I love her.

November 23, 1941

I was up at 6:45 this morning, having breakfast in the dining hall. Had to do this as part of my OD duties. Everyone else slept in.

November 24, 1941

I had my first six-plane formation today. Enjoyed it. I continued operations discussion with Frank Schiel, and he seems to appreciate my interest in his problems as operations officer.

Later, I attended a lecture on P-40 armament. The plane has six forward-firing fixed machine guns—two .50 calibers firing through the propellers and four .30-caliber guns, two in each wing root. We have them harmonized for some 250 yards out front. Those .50 calibers sound awesome when fired compared to the .30s.

November 25, 1941

I had my first ground gunnery exercise today. Lots of fun, but I need to improve a lot.

November 27, 1941

Thanksgiving Day! I flew a six-plane formation flight this morning and ended up in a twelve-ship dogfight when we met up with another flight towards the end of the mission. I figure our side won.

We had the day off after 11 A.M. Our dinner was the same as usual. I really miss the old traditional Thanksgiving turkey with all the trimmings.

Saw *Typhoon* with Dorothy Lamour at the movie tonight.

November 28, 1941

More strafing practice today. One of my .50 calibers ran away after I pulled off the target. All six guns were firing perfectly, and five of them stopped as I released the trigger on the stick. One, however, kept right on firing. I reached up and charged it, and then locked it. It stopped. I don't know what was the problem.

I packed up a trunk to send ahead to China in preparation for our move north.

November 29, 1941

Our squadron decided to have a picnic, and we took a truck into the mountains east of the city. I was the only one that did not drink beer. Had I drunk it, I am sure that I would have had a merrier time. Everyone got tighter than a tick.

We stopped at a little stream where the jungle seemed impenetrable. The stream looked inviting and we took a long swim. Giant oak trees stood over a hundred feet, and beneath them were banana trees, ferns, bamboo, and all kinds of exotic jungle growth.

On the way back to the base we stopped in Toungoo. Some of the guys had lost their shoes and had to buy another pair. It was something else watching the haggling between an enterprising Burmese merchant and a smashed American pilot. Pappy Boyington sighted a stray cow in the street and for some reason decided to wrestle it to the ground. What a sight! In the meantime, Bob Prescott and John J. "Five-Star" Hennessy took it upon themselves to kibitz Pappy's antics to the great delight and entertainment of the gathering crowd of natives. While waiting for the action to subside, I bought a pair of British-made calf-length boots for flying.

In a bull session tonight I learned that we are leaving for Kunming the day after tomorrow. Also, I heard that the Japanese bombed Kunming yesterday. I guess we are going to see some action real soon.

November 30, 1941

Today is Sunday, but all of us were up early getting the ships ready and peaked up for the flight to Kunming. My ship is No. 5. I have one bad tire, and the engine is missing. A lot of work has to go into preparations. My crew chief, Walt Dolan, and I labored long. I have my doubts about the outfit being ready for action, but we are preparing for it.

Had another gunnery mission today, and I still did not do well enough. I'm beginning to wonder if score means anything. I suppose that time and combat will tell.

Got all my personal things packed and ready to ship north.

December 1, 1941

Payday! I drew 321 rupees, about a hundred dollars. I have decided that I would be able to make it each month on a hundred bucks and put the other five hundred dollars in the National Bank of Fort Sam Houston in San Antonio. Was shocked to learn that the CAMCO company had not paid my insurance premiums, and I must take care of that immediately.

Lots of talk about the Japs. Heard they took Bangkok yesterday, and that is getting close. We are now keeping our ships dispersed as much as possible. We are even discussing the possibility of a night flight to Kunming. It would minimize the chances of the Japs intercepting us, but I doubt if all of us would get there with our few navigation aids.

I am not sure what is beginning to affect the morale of the guys, but it is certainly getting bad. Seems that some believe the Old Man has misrepresented the facts to us. We are outnumbered terrifically by the Japanese Air Force. However, there are rumors that the RAF will be sending in three squadrons of Brewster Buffaloes and a squadron of bombers. I wonder how long we will last?

December 2, 1941

Spent the early morning getting my plane peaked. Took off on a high-altitude indoctrination flight and leveled off at twenty-three thousand feet. The P-40 is just about at its maximum ceiling that high, and the Zero is supposed to be much better. I did slow rolls, loops, the whole gamut. It was relaxing.

Shortly after landing, I was scheduled to go right back up to ten thousand feet, where Pappy Boyington and I practiced individual combat. He won the first one, but I decisively won the second. Pappy is an ex-Marine and a fine fighter pilot. He is built like an ox and we have about the same number of hours in the P-40. He tried to turn too violently in our second set-to and snaprolled the damn thing. Of course that made it easier for me to get on his tail. I loved it.

December 3, 1941

Another ground gunnery mission, but this time it was a different story. Strictly a matter of anticipation, smooth flying, and good judgment with that iron sight on the P-40. Some previous discussion with Bob Little must have helped. I feel a hell of a lot better now.

I had a long talk with Skip Adair. He told me I was number one for advancement in the outfit. He thinks we will get about fifty-five Lockheed Hudsons to form a bomber outfit. I am anxious to get a position of more responsibility.

December 4, 1941

Another terrific formation flight and a grand windup, a rat race involving twenty-four aircraft. What a riot!

Went on a spending spree and bought a jade and white sapphire ring for Mom and an opal stone for Dad. Total: thirty-three dollars.

December 5, 1941

I had a long personal session with Chennault. I let my hair down about some improvements. I guess I am too much military to watch the lax attitude and the freedom from rules and regulations. Poor discipline! I believe that is what is happening to the morale, and I told him so. He is one hell of a fine guy. Chennault told me that he had heard

Left: My official U.S. Army Air Corps picture taken in April, 1938, while I was in pilot training at Randolph Airfield, San Antonio, Texas. In the background is the cockpit of the PT-13 trainer. *Right:* With Doris in front of a B-18 bomber I flew from Florida to Dallas in early 1941. At that time I had never heard of Chennault, and I was courting Doris.

The highly maneuverable PT-12B trainer, the model I learned to fly at Kelly Field in late 1938. (*Courtesy, U.S. Air Force*)

BT-9 trainers on the flight line at Randolph Field, San Antonio, in the late 1930's. (*Courtesy, U.S. Air Force*)

Aboard the Dutch ship *Boschfontein* in the Pacific en route to Burma in September, 1941. I am on the left. Standing behind me is Lewis Bishop, while Bob Prescott is in the middle and then Dick Rossi. In back of Dick is Ralph Gunvordahl.

We joined together: George Burgard, Jim Cross, and me aboard the *Bosch-fontein* in September, 1941.

Left: My official AVG picture taken at Toungoo in November, 1941. The Burmese barber charged two cents for the haircut, which is what it was worth. *Right*: A more candid shot at Toungoo, the same month. The mustache lasted only a few weeks.

Burmese crew at Toungoo refueling my No. 5 after a flight over Burma in November, 1941. (*Courtesy, Larry M. Pistole*)

AVG pilot barracks at Toungoo, Burma. Note the mosquito bars, the crowded bunks, and the woven rattan walls at the end of the barracks. (*Courtesy, J.J. Harrington*)

One of the British Royal Air Force's Brewster Buffaloes used in the defense of Burma from December, 1941, to March, 1942, on the field at Rangoon. (*Courtesy, J. J. Harrington*)

A Hurricane fighter of the early type used by the British in the Far East in late 1941 and early 1942. (*Courtesy, U.S. Air Force*)

Jim Cross by his P-40 with two versions of the First Squadron Adam and Eve insignia. The one on his left is a duplicate of my original design. (*Courtesy, Jim Cross*)

Japan's Mitsubishi Type 97 bomber was in common use in the Burma and China areas. (*Courtesy, U.S. Air Force*)

A British Blenheim bomber similar to the ones used against Japanese forces in Burma. (*Courtesy, U.S. Air Force*)

The Westland Lysander, though developed as a utility aircraft, was used as a bomber in Burma. This one, at Rangoon, is ready for a mission. (*Courtesy, Jim Cross*)

The Japanese Type 97 fighter was often encountered and shot down by the Flying Tigers over Burma and China. (*Courtesy, U.S. Air Force*)

The famous Japanese Model Zero (this one a captured specimen) was a more formidable fighter than either the Type 96 or Type 97. (*Courtesy, U.S. Air Force*)

good things about me and talked long to build my ego. At least that was my impression.

Before leaving, the Colonel told me that the insignia I had designed for our First Pursuit Squadron just would not do.

"Why? I think it is good," I said.

Chennault said, "The red apple looks too much like the Japanese Rising Sun, Charlie. It won't do."

I now had a problem. Since we were the First Pursuit Squadron, I had designed an insignia which represented the first pursuit, Eve chasing Adam.[3] It is a big red apple with a black snake coiled around the middle of it with a white female chasing a male across the face of the apple. I thought about it for a while and decided that the Old Man is right. But there are green apples as well as red ones, and that was the answer. Everyone laughed, but agreed, as did the Old Man. Now we have the "Adam and Eve" First Pursuit Squadron of the American Volunteer Group.

December 6, 1941

I finished the painting on No. 5, and the insignia looks great. The Second Squadron has become the "Panda Bears" and the Third the "Hell's Angels."

Got my insurance payments straightened out finally. The way things look here, that is one thing to have current—just in case. What a thought!

Rumors are that Japan is about to quit China, but that I will wait to see. Frank Schiel came in with the news that England has declared war on Finland, Hungary, and Rumania. The thing is spreading fast.

December 7, 1941

Saw my first monsoon rain today. Hard and blowing, practically rains horizontally. The roofs do not leak, to my surprise.

Got in a discussion with Joe, the barracks boy. Learned that he is not Burmese, but Indian. He hates Hitler and loves Gandhi.

December 8, 1941

Today will go down in history! Last night the Japs hit Pearl Har-

---

[3] Dick Rossi and Bob Prescott also claim authorship of Adam chasing Eve as the "first pursuit," and probably we all were in the same conversation. The design of the insignia, however, was my idea.

bor, also Manila. The reports are unbelievable; we are stunned. By the time we had our first alert flight lined up, and every guy was on the line, we realized that we are right in the middle of one hell of a big war!

We kept our engines warm. With no radar warning we have little time to get off. Many of us scan the eastern skies continuously—as if we would have a chance to scramble if we caught sight of an incoming Jap raid. We expect to be hit, but I presume they are working on Singapore right now. Who knows?

We may stay right here now instead of moving north to Kunming. Tonight is blacked out—and from now on.

Poor Mom and Dad. I'll bet they are worried to death about me. And Doris. How I'd love to have her here with me tonight.

We may be bombed before daylight.

December 9, 1941

Was up at 4:30 for a full-day alert program. We expect the Japs at any time. All of us have sidearms on. I have borrowed Einar "Mickey" Mickelson's .25-caliber automatic pistol. It is a good four inches long and is not much larger than a .22. Everybody gets a big kick out of seeing me sporting it at my side.

Those of us on morning alert lounge around in the shack near our planes. We are ready to rush to the cockpits at the sound of the siren. We have been told that the RAF has radar in the hills to the east, but I'm not convinced.

As the morning wore on, Bob Little, Bob Neale, Snuffy Smith, Jim Cross, George Burgard, and I took off for a patrol along the Burma Road southwards toward Rangoon. We leveled off at eighteen thousand feet. I must admit that I was a bit tense. I was ready for anything: but nothing. We returned to base, and I noticed that I had barely more than fifteen gallons of gas left in my ship.

At about 4:00 P.M. we had a scare. Saw a shiny object reflecting in the sky almost over our base heading southeast. Bob, Jim, and I took off, but we didn't have a chance of getting to that altitude and catching it—whatever it may have been.

The news is disheartening about Pearl Harbor and Manila. I wonder when we'll get a chance at them. We are very tense and prepared to do our best, but we have no replacements.

December 10, 1941

At about 3:30 this morning we were startled out of our bunks by the wailing siren. Air raid! Within ten minutes most of us were on the line. My crew chief had not showed up yet, and I forgot to pull the prop a few times before starting up. It caught anyway and settled down to a sweet roar: I was ready to go.

The six night-alert pilots already were in the air, circling the base. We expected Japs any minute, but none came over.

About 5:00 A.M. we began to call in the night alert for landing. Hell, we hadn't been practicing any night missions, and we had no night landing aids of any kind. We lined the runway with lanterns and hoped for the best.

David "Tex" Hill came in first. He overshot the runway and rolled into a heap at the end of the strip. Fortunately, he wasn't scratched.

We decided to light the runway approach by using the headlights of the station wagon and Studebaker sedan. It helped, and the other five pilots felt their way onto the narrow strip. All got in okay.

As dawn broke we continued our tense alert. A flock of birds in the southwest scared the hell out of us.

Bob Little, Ed Leibolt, Jim Cross, and I took off to escort Lacy Mangleburg back from a photo mission over Thailand. We had heard that the Japs had moved into Chiang Mai, Thailand, east of us, and we are jumpy about it. But we didn't see any Japs, nor did we pick up Mangleburg on his return leg. We all returned to the base.

Reports are prevalent about our departure for Kunming, but it seems that the RAF wants us to remain in Burma. I have a hunch that we might go down to Rangoon.

After a day like this I am ready to hit the hay.

December 11, 1941

Up early again this morning for routine alert in anticipation of mixing it up with incoming Japanese bombers. But nothing. We lay around, played poker, and talked about the war.

We drew our steel helmets and gas masks. Barbed-wire barriers are going up everywhere, and others are digging bomb shelters and foxholes.

Went up with Bob Little for about an hour of combat training. He beat me handily, and I thought of Phil Cochrane and Johnny Alison back at Langley Field, Virginia, in the Eighth Pursuit Group where they trained Bob to fly fighters. Bob has some 375 hours in fighters and is damn good—one of the best in the outfit. I am learning a lot from him, and hopefully his lessons will make me a better fighter pilot.

December 12, 1941

Five-Star Hennessy woke me early this morning with his eerie moaning. No telling what his nightmare was, but it took me a while to get back to sleep.

George Burgard had a narrow escape. In a dogfight mission with Matt Kuykendall he got in an inverted spin and then went into an uncontrollable dive we call a "flop." I have never experienced this maneuver, but those who have say the aircraft acts like a pendulum with the nose down swinging wildly back and forth. George got control of the ship just in time. He was really shook up.

December 13, 1941

Up and at 'em again—if we could ever find them! Our spirits seem to be improving, and I'm not exactly sure why.

Bob Little and I were given a mission over northern Thailand, basically a visual reconnaissance of Chiang Mai airfield. We leveled off at twenty thousand and cruised some two hundred miles to the airport. No activity, so Bob went down for a closer look while I circled overhead. He rejoined me and we headed back to Toungoo. Bob Neale, with a flight of four, rendezvoused with us at midpoint of our return leg and escorted us back to base, just in case.

We had another air raid, but it proved false before we got off the ground.

An unidentified civilian aircraft flew nearby and we took off after him and made him land. He was a businessman going north to Lashio.

Tired tonight. Thirteen and a half hours a day is long enough, especially under the strain of alerts. Saturday night means nothing.

December 14, 1941

Same old day, except for an unusual incident. The air-raid siren went off, and I was right in the middle of a nature call, on the can near the alert shack. Never in my life have I cut anything so short!

I took off on a patrol mission, climbing slowly to twenty thousand feet. My engine overheated quickly. Back to base, where I found that some mechanic had left a rag in my oil cooler duct.

We hear that the Japs are on their way to Burma. It is rumored that we will depart for Kunming tomorrow, so I packed everything.

I am tired tonight, but Allied news of bitter fighting heartens me. I keep wondering when we will see our first action.

December 15, 1941

A dull day. Felt a little ill before noon but was okay after lunch. Wonder if it is my nerves? Played a little ball and read some to pass the time. No air raids today. The barbed wire is still going up everywhere. Hell, I got so bored I decided to shave off my mustache.

December 16, 1941

Heard that Chennault was meeting General Brett in Rangoon tomorrow. The RAF sent up a Blenheim bomber to pick up the Old Man. Wonder if plans are being laid to induct us into the U.S. Army Air Corps?[4]

A Chinese National Airways Corporation (CNAC) DC-3 picked up quite a few of our maintenance personnel to ferry them to Kunming. This has being going on for several days; maybe we'll move now.

---

[4]A few days later, on December 21, Chennault and Lt. Gen. George Howard Brett, the U.S. air commander for Southeast Asia, met Field Marshal Sir Archibald Wavell and Chiang Kai-shek in Chungking for the first Allied Conference. The aim was to coordinate efforts against the Japanese, but a War Department memorandum concluded that the conference achieved "very little, in a way of concrete results." Charles F. Romanus and Riley Sunderland, *Stilwell's Mission to China*, p. 57. Neither Chennault nor Stilwell cared for the British "superior race complex" in Asia. Joseph W. Stilwell, *The Stilwell Papers*, ed. Theodore H. White, p. 61; Chennault, *Way of a Fighter*, pp. 141–42.

3. *The First Taste of Battle*

During the first months of war the Japanese advanced rapidly in the Pacific and Southeast Asia. While attacking Pearl Harbor, they also struck Hong Kong, Malaya, and the Philippines. On December 10, Thailand capitulated. Officials in Bangkok and Tokyo signed an alliance aimed against the British and the United States. During the next week the Japanese occupied Guam and Wake Island, and on Christmas, British forces surrendered in Hong Kong.

The advance continued during the new year. On January 2 the Japanese occupied Manila, and nine days later they began their conquest of the Dutch East Indies. By the end of the month they had captured Celebes, Rabaul, New Ireland, Amboina, and the Solomon Islands. In February the British surrendered Singapore.

Attempting to stop the onslaught, Britain and China devised a strategy for Southeast Asia. The first aim was to defend the Burma Road, the famous supply route that meandered over seven hundred miles through the mountains connecting Kunming, China with the northern Burmese city of Lashio. From Lashio a railroad continued south to the port of Rangoon. With the Japanese in control of the Chinese coast, the route from Kunming to Rangoon remained the only cross-country way of supplying China.

The Burma Road was China's jugular vein, and it had to be saved, but China and Britain disagreed on strategy to defend the nation. Chiang Kai-shek felt that troops must confront and block the Japanese advance, and he offered to send six divisions. The British, however, were leery of Chinese intentions in Southeast Asia and refused the offer, instead asking the generalissimo if he would allow the AVG to operate under the command of the Royal Air Force. Chennault vehemently opposed this idea, and eventually a compromise was arranged: one squadron of the AVG would assist the RAF in defending Rangoon. We would work with the British but remain under the command of Chen-

nault. The other two squadrons would be stationed at Kunming to defend southern China and the Burma Road.

In mid-December the AVG left Toungoo and redeployed into combat positions. Led by Olie Olson, the Third Squadron "Hell's Angels" flew to Mingaladon aerodrome on the eastern edge of Rangoon on December 12 and joined the RAF. Meanwhile, airmen loaded supplies and equipment in Toungoo and started the long drive north to China.[1] Chennault and his staff boarded transports on December 18, and along with the pilots and planes of the First and Second squadrons, flew to Kunming.

The city sat high on a cool, dry plateau in Yunnan, an old province situated on the unmarked borders of Indochina, Burma, India, and Tibet. In ancient times the area was on the trading routes linking east and west and had been traversed by numerous traders, including Marco Polo. During the thirteenth century the kings of Burma had fought the hordes of Kublai Khan. The province was famous for spices, copper, tin, and its principal export—opium.

Chennault knew the area well, for he had visited in 1938. By 1941 the Chinese had constructed a new base and airstrip at Kunming. There were an aerodrome and two modern hostels, one at the field and another at an old university dormitory in the city. The facilities included a library, a small hospital, and, most important, hot showers. For the long idle hours we could play tennis or baseball or use the pistol range.

After landing, we taxied to our operations area and parked our planes in an alert posture. We had thirty-four P-40s operational, and more qualified pilots. We were eager and excited to meet the enemy, and we did not have to wait long. The next morning the Japanese attacked. It was my first taste of battle.

*   *   *

December 18, 1941
I went to breakfast and when I returned to the barracks all the

<hr>

[1] For an interesting account of evacuating southern Burma and driving up the Burma Road to Kunming, see Frillmann and Peck, *China: The Remembered Life*, chap. 6.

pilots were packing up to head north—a 670-mile flight over some awful-looking terrain and impossible in case of a forced landing.

Decided to send holiday greetings to the family and Doris because of the uncertainty of communications out of China.

Just before taking off we got word that Kunming had been bombed this morning by ten Jap bombers. When we started taking off, George Burgard was ahead of me. I watched him start his roll, and his engine cut out about halfway down the runway and he went off into the boondocks and tore off his landing gear. I rolled on and took off. As I cleared the pavement and started my wheels up, I dropped one wing slightly to check George's ship as I flew over it. George was on the wing and waved. He was okay.

We had eighteen ships in the formation, and our flight level was twenty-one thousand feet. I and one other were "weavers" above the formation by a thousand feet. Our job was to criss-cross the formation, always flying at an angle to the flight path, to get a better view of the rear and flanks in case of Japanese interception. Weaving, I had to use a higher manifold pressure, which meant more fuel, and I was sweating it a little. No Japs, but we were ready. En route John Dean's oxygen tube came loose, and he passed out and started down out of the formation. As he got to a lower altitude he regained his senses and managed to figure out what the problem was, fixed it, and rejoined the formation.

We caught sight of the field just northwest of a huge lake and southeast of the city of Kunming. The elevation of the field is six thousand feet. An uncompleted runway stretches the entire length of the field practically down the middle. The field is large and has been battered by many Jap bombings. Bomb shelters are everywhere, and there are thousands of Chinese soldiers swarming all over the area.

George landed later in another P-40 and told us about his escapade. He also said that Freeman Ricketts taxied into Chennault's car at Toungoo and chewed it up with his propeller. The other squadron didn't make it; for some reason they had to turn back. The Third Squadron was deployed in Rangoon.

We went to our hostel, which was about a mile from the airfield. Immaculate rooms for each pilot with a comfortable bunk, chair, table, chest of drawers, and small desk. In the middle of the room is a small charcoal heater; it is cold here. The service is good, and my number-one boy's name is Ma. He grins all the time. The food is American and much better than in Toungoo, and so is the atmosphere. Another thing: Hot water! Yeowee!! I thought I would never get out of the shower, and shaving is no problem anymore. Even our bar is more cozy and inviting. They have prepared for us.

Mickey Mickelson told us about touring the bombed part of the city this evening. Bodies scattered all over the place, literally blown to bits. It is so easy after listening to such description of misery and woes to react violently and hate the guts of the Japs.

As I finish these notes tonight I am reflecting about the sights of the countryside over which we flew—wild and beautiful mountains with few rivers and fewer roads. I am sentimental and thinking of the family and Doris. The first thing I did in my room was to put up her picture.

December 19, 1941

Up at 4:30 and having a terrific breakfast of real bacon and eggs. Wow! But it's cold as hell here. Ice all over the ground: six thousand feet elevation makes a lot of difference, as does some 650 miles further north.

Rode down to the alert line to warm up my ship, but as I approached I was sharply challenged by a Chinese guard. He caught me by surprise; we had no such security in Burma. "American! Friend! OK!" I yelled. Anything to let him know I was on his side. These soldiers are really on the ball.

Got my ship preflighted and then wandered over towards the alert shack. It is made of adobe brick and plaster and is surrounded by dirt revetments with an opening for us to scamper through to get to the planes for a scramble. Machine gun emplacements are everywhere, and trenches connect them in an elaborate network.

Soldiers and coolies swarm over the area. I watched the coolies, thousands of them, trotting back and forth with their baskets of crushed stone and pots of slimy mud to complete a hard-surface runway down the middle of the field. How pitiful. They stared at me as much as I stared at them. In a discussion with an interpreter I learned that Kunming has a population of about three hundred thousand.

The field is on the edge of a huge lake. High mountains surround the area, and there always seem to be threatening clouds. At one end of the field is a bombed-out hanger, and across to the southeast is a dive-bombing range.

We keep our ships prepared for takeoff at all times. We are in much better shape here than in Burma, since we have a hundred miles of early warning. The Chinese observer corps works very well. Individuals sit on the mountainsides with binoculars and by various means of communications can warn us of incoming enemy planes.

We were issued some winter flying gear, U.S. Navy stuff, and it was welcome.

Sandy Sandell, our squadron commander, called me in about noon and said he and the Old Man wanted me to do a job for them. They wanted me to go on a reconnaissance mission to Mengtzu, China, about 125 miles southeast of Kunming towards Hanoi, to look over that airfield to see if it was operational. I was to ride in the rear seat of a BT-9 as the observer, and a Chinese pilot would fly the mission. We took off and flew just below the mountaintops and dodged the low-hanging clouds. We picked up the railroad running southeast and followed it through the valleys and gorges of the mountainous countryside. The mountains run up to about ten thousand feet in some cases, and the railroads and dirt roads find their way through the valleys between the peaks. Must have seen two dozen tunnels on the flight. The airfield was unusable. Deep furrows were dug across the entire area. It would be suicide to try to land on the field. We returned and reported this to the Old Man.

Jim and I got in a bull session about the price of things in China. A U.S. dollar brings 38 Chinese National dollars, and I saw one pilot with 5,000 CN in his pocket, over $130. A fifth of scotch costs 450 CN, or a hefty $12.

December 20, 1941

Took off at 6 A.M. for patrol duty in case of an early dawn attack by the Japanese. It was my first night takeoff in a P-40. Exhaust flames trailed back from the Allison engine on both sides of the fuselage as the throttle was opened. They were bright blue way back to my cockpit. I now can understand the story told during my flight training back in 1938 about a young trainee on his first night flight who took off and quickly returned to the field screaming that he was on fire.

Nothing happened on the patrol flight. Returned to the field and went on alert duty. About 10:00 we scrambled on another air-raid warning.

This time it was the real thing! We leveled off at twenty thousand feet in an area southeast of Kunming, where we sighted Japanese raiders—ten bombers in tight formation. They saw us and immediately aborted their objective of bombing Kunming and began scurrying back to Hanoi. I was in Frank Schiel's plane, since he had the day off and my plane was being repaired. We were practically full throttle at twenty-thousand, indicating 225 MPH, and it still took us a good eight to ten minutes to overtake them and get into attacking position. Bob Little was my flight leader. He dove down into the lower clouds to come up from below and the right quarter, while I climbed and veered off to the right to attack from above and off their right beam. I charged all my guns and turned on my gun sight and gun switch. The Japs were in a tight formation. As we closed in, they lowered their "dustbin" rear-fighting guns to defend against us. As a result they slowed down.

I was tense but more excited. I was about to taste combat. I thought in terms of shooting down airplanes and gave no thought to the fact that there were men in those ships.

I fingered my oxygen mask to secure it tightly and set the regulator control for twenty-one thousand feet. The plane needed a little left rudder trim for a diving speed that would be much higher than what it was indicating while I positioned for my attack. I wanted the bubble centered when I squeezed the trigger. I was about a thousand feet higher than their formation and a couple of thousand feet off to the left. I rolled and started down. As the nearest bomber eased within the gunsight ring, I squeezed the trigger on the stick. Damn it, nothing happened!

I took a quick look at my gun switch. In my excitement, I had checked it so many times that I had turned it off! I was closing in fast on the outside bomber and not firing. I broke off violently—down and away and then back up to my original position for another attack.

I went in for a second attack, and all guns were blazing this time. I saw my tracers enter the fuselage of the bomber. At the last second I broke off, and then I felt a quiver in my control stick but thought nothing of it. I attacked again and again. Two bombers began to lag behind, trailing smoke. Many of the other guys were after those two ships, so I concentrated on the main formation. I could see only seven. Three evidently had gone down, but I could not yet claim that I shot one down. Some of our guys followed the bombers down and watched them explode against the mountains.

We were hitting them from all directions—right, left, above, below. Sandy Sandell even tried a front quarter pass while attacking. On one pass I barely missed colliding with Bill Bartling. I was too keyed up to give it much thought. After another pass I pulled away and up into clouds and immediately had to go on instruments before I came out above the layer.

I had to give the Japanese pilots credit. They kept a tight formation throughout repeated attacks of our fighters. Their "dustbin" gunners—the ones who had not been killed in their turret positions—kept up their fire. They were twin-engined bombers with a single tail and a light green color with that prominent red sun on the fuselage and wings. There was a large black cross on the rear fuselage of one of the ships which I saw when closing within one hundred yards on one pass.

Sandy began calling us off and wagging his wings for join-up. By this time we were some two hundred miles from our Kunming base, and our fuel was low. Fourteen of us had taken off, and we couldn't afford to lose any aircraft after such a fight. We were lost at first but soon located ourselves. All of us were not back in formation, and I was concerned about lost aircraft. We found the base and landed. The stragglers followed in one by one.

When on the ground in the parking area I found to my amazement that I had bullet holes in my right aileron, right stabilizer, and rudder. That was the quiver in my controls.

Fifteen minutes after landing, we had to scramble again. This time I was in No. 5. We patrolled above the field at twenty thousand for about forty-five minutes, but nothing developed. Back to the field we dove and pulled up in slow rolls as we crossed the field in a loose right echelon string.

We critiqued the fighting in detail and concluded that we had gotten four of the bombers for sure and several more as probables. I felt fairly convinced of having contributed to the loss of that left wingman. We were in high spirits. Chennault was elated. It was our first taste of combat and our first test. We had not lost a man. It is the first time Japanese bombers have been turned back from bombing Kunming.

Gen. C. C. Wong, a friend of Chennault's and the Chinese officer in charge of the area, treated us to a banquet tonight to express the gratitude of the Chinese people.

My eyes are giving me fits, conjunctivitis again, and Doc Rich gave me something for relief. Tired, I was heading for my bunk when Pappy Boyington came in and wanted to discuss reorganizing the outfit. An undercurrent of dissatisfaction seems to be growing in our squadron. Neither the pilots nor airmen seem to like Sandell, our squadron commander. It's Sandy's personality. He is a small fellow with a mustache and a very cold manner. Boyington, Burgard, Kuykendall, and I drove over to the field and talked with Frank Schiel. We asked him what should be done, if anything. We expressed a lot of dissatisfaction about organization and leadership. Many suggestions were offered, and if they are adopted, I believe the situation will improve considerably.

December 21, 1941

Quite a lot of talk is still going on about our fight with the Japanese bombers. A Chinese intelligence colonel extended the personal thanks of Generalissimo Chiang Kai-shek.

Frank Schiel prepared a memorandum for the Old Man after our meeting last night. It was quite harsh. Pappy Boyington approved it, and so did I. Tonight Pappy, Frank, and I got together with Sandy Sandell about the morale situation. He flew off the handle; he did not like our attitude. At first he would not talk to me, but he condescended and we talked at length—I did most of the talking. We finally decided that we would have a meeting tomorrow with all the pilots of the squadron.

December 22, 1941

A day off, but dammit, I have been so used to getting up at 4:30 that I could not sleep.

I worked most of the day on a speech about who should be responsible for what in the squadron, and then Bob Little, Bob Neale, Jim Cross, and I went into town. Kunming is filthy. The streets are narrow and barely paved with large stones. The stores are jammed together and have never seen any paint. The city bank, however, is a very modern building. The streets are literally jammed with humanity—men, women, children, ponies dragging carts, rickshaws, a few old cars, motorcycles and go-carts, and myriads of soldiers in faded khaki uniforms. There is a hustle and bustle in the air. The food carts are everywhere, although I would not dare eat anything from them. The dress of the average Chinese is a drab blue jacket and trousers—most are dirty and ragged. It is really pitiful. I have never seen so many people afflicted with eye diseases. Doc Richards says it is VD.

We were strolling along one of the main streets when all of a sudden the people began to run in all directions as though in panic. We stopped spellbound, wondering what could transform this crowd into such a seething riot. Bob Little answered the question—he pointed at the orange ball at the top of a pole at the end of the street. *Jim bao!* Air raid! One orange ball at the top of the pole means the enemy bombers are on their way. This is usually one hour's warning in Kunming. When the second ball goes up to join the first one, they have about twenty minutes' warning. When the balls are brought down, everybody stays put wherever he might be. If anyone tries to change his position, he stands a good chance of being shot on the spot. The falling bombs usually tear the shops and homes to bits and pieces—they are nothing but straw and mud. Great holes are left in the streets, and bits of human bodies are found all over the place. The bombs killed over four hundred people in the raid before we came. We returned to base, but nothing happened there.

Tonight we had a squadron meeting to discuss introducing more militarism into the outfit. It seemed that everyone was in favor of it. I gave the talk and discussed the advantages. They agreed, and I am now the adjutant and personnel officer. I have a free hand to enforce more disciplinary measures. I feel good about it.

I heard that Sandy "busted" Frank from being operations officer for being late with his dawn patrol flight. I think it was planned, and I shall never forgive Sandy for it.

December 23, 1941

Had another alert today and took off to the west and climbed to twenty thousand feet. Nothing happened. Was called back in and we buzzed the field before landing. I was hitting about 400 MPH when I passed over the field at just grasstop level. Pulled up in a slow roll and turned onto base to get in the landing pattern.

About 5:00 P.M. we fourteen pilots who were in the fight the other day were lined up to be decorated. The governor of Yunnan Province was the honored guest. A large contingent of Chinese soldiers was present, and a Chinese band murdered the "Star Spangled Banner." When the governor finished his speech, fourteen Chinese officials came forward with bright red silk sashes and draped them about our shoulders and waists. The red meant "joyful." In the background thousands of firecrackers were set off. Next came fourteen Chinese girls—really attractive young belles—and they gave each of us a bouquet of flowers. Following this there were gifts of hams and fruits.

Right in the middle of this gala occasion we got another air-raid alarm, but by the time the Second Squadron pilots got to their planes, it was called off. We are getting real touchy.

Tonight we had a meeting with the airmen of the squadron concerning the idea of putting some more militarism in the outfit. This took a little bit of persuasion on my part. I learned that the big problem was Sandy Sandell—the men just did not like him. George, Jim, and Frank spoke to the men. We have a problem on our hands. I am not sure how it will turn out.

December 24, 1941

Another alert this morning. We took off about 10:00 expecting to intercept twenty-three Jap bombers. Patrolled at twenty-two thousand feet, but no sign of anything.

It's a funny feeling to sit there in my cockpit at twenty thousand feet, straining my eyes to pick out the intruding enemy bomber formation. I am in winter flying boots and jackets and trousers. My head is squeezed into my helmet with earphones, goggles, and oxygen mask hanging on all sides. I have winter mittens on. My hand is not relaxed on the stick, nor on the throttle. It is cold, but the engine purrs smoothly, particularly when I ease the mixture control over to "automatic lean." I see the squadron commander ahead with his three wingmen in right echelon, but I am back here in my flight as a wingman, flying number three below the number two man. We fly a loose pattern, several miles over the field and to the southeast of the city, constantly craning our necks to pick up the enemy formation.

The thoughts that come and go so quickly, one after another, are technical matters and tactical data: move the throttle a bit forward on the outside of a turn; watch my rearview mirror; look to the left, right,

65

and below at my wingman, glance at the fuel gauge, oil and fuel pressure okay; there is a slight fluctuation of the fuel pressure indicator; hydraulic fluid temperature is okay; oil temperature okay; look around again, to the right, the left, up into the sun particularly; sneak a glimpse of the squadron commander's ship; look across the gunsight and practice aiming at something; adjust my seat for the hundredth time; adjust my oxygen mask; cut back on the throttle on the inside of the turn; check my oxygen regulator; and a thousand other things— one after another. I do this over and over, as all of us do, almost unconsciously on every flight.

We got word today that the Third Squadron, which was deployed to Rangoon, had a mixup with fifty-four Japanese bombers accompanied by fighter escort. They got nine bombers and a Model Zero. But I hated to hear about the losses: Henry Gilbert was shot down in flames, and Neil Martin is missing.

December 25, 1941

Christmas Day! As I returned to my room from breakfast, I found a Chinese saber on my bunk. A Christmas gift from Jim Cross. God bless his heart. What a guy!

Heard this morning that Eriksen Shilling, Lacy Mangleburg, and Ken Merritt got lost flying CW-21's from Lashio to Kunming and crash-landed. The CW-21 is a lightweight Curtiss Wright fighter plane. China bought a few of them, and the guys were trying to get them up to Kunming so we might use them in our outfit. Shilling is okay, but the other two are bad off. Mangleburg burned to death upon landing, and the other is hurt badly. What a mess. Doc Richards went out to pick them up, about fifty miles from here.

Chinese intelligence has recovered some of the parts of the bombers we shot down. The flexible defensive machine guns are 7.7 mm. Chungking confirmed that we destroyed six of the bombers. That means three thousand dollars divided fourteen ways, and it gives credence to my belief that I shot one down. I feel good about it.

Bob Little and I went into town today to take some pictures. I bought a pair of sunglasses and a Chinese officer's cap. I tried my meager Chinese in bargaining and thought Bob would crack up. We ran across a Chinese student who could speak some English, and he took us to a place where we had "chops" made of our signatures. A chop is a piece of ivory about one inch square, on one end of which our name is translated into Chinese and etched in the ivory. The little stamp is encased in a larger ivory box with one end containing a stamping ink. When I have to sign my name, I simply ink the end of the chop and stamp my signature on the paper. I also bought one each for Jim and George.

We were issued the Chinese "blood chit" emblems to sew on the back of our jackets today. It is about six by ten inches and has the Chinese flag on it. Also Chinese writing that directs the people to assist us in any way possible—that we are their friends.

Not much of a Christmas Day, but I'm glad I'm alive and healthy. I hope my people aren't worrying too much about me.

December 26, 1941

Spent some time with the so-called first sergeant today about problems of the airmen and also had a long talk with Sandy Sandell. I just do not understand his problem.

Olie Olsen's Third Squadron in Rangoon is doing great. They shot down nineteen Japs yesterday and got twelve the day before. Cripes, I wish I was there!

December 27, 1941

Chennault has me working on some AVG regulations. I heard that a San Francisco radio station says that we are the hardest-fighting outfit of our size in the world.

Unfortunately, Neil Martin was found dead yesterday after the fight in Rangoon.

December 28, 1941

Still working on AVG regulations. I wonder if Chennault really intends to use these?

Saw Shilling today. He looks okay but a little scratched up. He doesn't want to talk about the fiasco much—feels bad about it.

Heard that the Japs are moving in on the Philippines and are within two hundred miles of taking Singapore.

Went to the movie tonight at the first hostel. The movie was so old I couldn't remember it, *Here Is My Heart* with Bing Crosby. The projector was so noisy we couldn't hear the sound, so I gave up and went back to my room.

December 29, 1941

Still working on AVG regulations: twenty-one pages and about two-thirds finished.

Had an air-raid alert and patrolled about forty minutes. Nothing. I actually believe it was a false alert as a result of the Second Squadron leaving for Toungoo and Rangoon to replace the Third. That probably alerted the Chinese ground observation corps (GOC) net.

The local Chinese authorities gave us a Christmas dinner tonight. I tried to use chopsticks, and what a mess. When I stood up to participate in the *gombay* toasts with that rice wine, I actually thought I would get sick right at the table. I noticed several of the fellows sneaking away with green faces. When I found chicken feet in one of the dishes we were served, that was the end.

After the dinner we went upstairs to the entertainment. A Chinese officer, General Huang, was the MC, and we sang songs and Christmas carols. General Huang presented Colonel Chennault with a gold and silver saber, a beautiful thing. Chennault made a moving speech, promising victory if it meant his death. It was good.

December 30, 1941

God! What a head this morning! Must have been that rice wine last night.

I heard that San Francisco radio devoted a good ten minutes last night to telling the world what the AVG has been doing for the American cause. Made me feel proud, and I hope Doris and the folks heard it.

Finally finished my versions of what I thought were proper AVG regulations and turned them over to Harvey Greenlaw. He acted grateful and even went so far as to admit a morale and leadership problem in our squadron. I talked freely with him. I feel sorry for Sandy, but doubt if the little guy will ever change.[2]

---

[2] Other pilots in the squadron had similar feelings. George T. Burgard wrote in his diary on December 22: "There is a reorganization coming within the Squadron—Bond is to be the new adjutant, with Little in Operations. Sandell has practically a mutiny on his hands. It seems to me that we need a more stable C.O.," and on December 30: "Bond found out today that a change is brewing in our squadron—it can't come too soon for the good of the organization. I like Sandell fine, as far as I am personally concerned, but he is a terribly inefficient Squadron head. Boyington would be the man for the job. Bond would also be a dandy if he only had the pursuit experience."

December 31, 1941

Was on the dawn patrol this morning. The weather has been bad every morning. I am not sure whether this is better for us or for the Japs. They can't find Kunming in weather like this, but we are not an all-weather fighter squadron, either. At any rate, a lot of pilots have bad colds or sinus problems—many are in bed.

On a reconnaissance mission John Dean and Albert "Red" Probst got lost and had forced landings. We had a report of Dean circling, which is our signal to the Chinese GOC of being lost and asking for help. That was about thirty miles from here. I took off to get him and lead him in, but he had already tried to land in a valley before I got to him. He is okay but washed out his landing gear.

I went to bed early to sleep in the New Year.

January 1, 1942

Thought we had an alert this noon, but it proved to be the Third Squadron returning from Rangoon after being replaced by the Second Squadron. We had hours of discussion with those pilots about their combat experiences at Rangoon with the Japs—tactics, tricks, habits and peculiarities of the Japanese pilots.

Colonel Chennault published an order involving rules and regulations today, and I was quite surprised and frustrated when I saw that very few of my recommendations were accepted. It made me wonder what he thought of me now! I felt quite bad about the whole thing.

One of the squadron crew chiefs, Charles Kenner, came to my room today to get a lot off his chest about the morale of the squadron. He talked to me about an hour. I just listened, and I suppose that this has turned out to be one of my jobs.

I rearranged my room and am going to bed, depressed as hell. I hope the Japs come over tomorrow. I don't feel like I'm doing my part.

January 2, 1942

Heard a rumor today that Lt. Gen. George Brett, chief of the U.S. Army Air Corps in the Southwest Pacific, has made arrangements to incorporate the AVG into the AAC. This has started lengthy discussions throughout the outfit. The general consensus is to stay the way we are, but I doubt if we will. I am willing to go back into the Air Corps right now if they will give me a regular commission.

I was promoted to flight leader today along with three others; some progress anyhow.

Red Probst and John Dean approached me this evening with the idea of handing in their resignations in order to get things moving to change our command setup in the squadron. I persuaded them not to do it. For some reason Padre Paul Frillmann, our chaplain, and Doc Richards came by tonight. We had a good old bull session until the wee hours of the morning about everything in general. I went to bed wondering if I were now becoming another "chaplain" along with the Padre.

January 3, 1942

The squadron bickering continues, and the dissatisfaction is quite evident. Just a lot of petty gripes. I am wondering what is at the core of all the malcontent. There is no doubt about everyone's natural dislike of Sandy, and his cold, aloof manner is apparent to everyone. On the other hand our squadron has not come up for our rotational turn at Rangoon, where most of the combat is going on. The Second and Third squadrons have had the lion's shares, although our squadron was the major one in the recent combat near Kunming. Maybe it's a matter of not doing anything. I'm sitting on alert and not getting any combat. Also there is the uncertainty of our status, since the U.S. is now in the war against Japan. That has not helped the temperament of the men throughout the AVG, not just our squadron. This is definitely unhealthy.

Pappy Boyington and I decided to call on Chennault, but he was down with the flu, so we talked at length with Harvey Greenlaw, who might be considered second in command. No results there, so I went over to see Skip Adair, who might be considered the chief of staff. One thing was cleared up to my relief. Skip told me that neither I nor Pappy was considered to be behind all the turmoil. That made me feel much better. The guys talk to me or Pappy because of our greater experience in the military. It is just natural that they come to us.

I led a flight today and got quite a morale boost out of it. Also George McMillan brought my star sapphire ring from Toungoo—looks good.

January 4, 1942

Got reports of the Second Squadron getting seven more Jap planes at Rangoon and losing none. That makes the score seventy-five to two!

It appears true that the Army Air Corps is seriously dickering with the local "powers" to induct us as a unit into the U.S. military. We had to turn in a written report of our military background to the Old Man today. I am wondering what will come out of all this.

January 5, 1942

Got into a bull session with Bob Little and got a good argument going as to whose plane was the best. He refers to my ship as a bucket of bolts. He's quite a guy, well liked in the squadron and one of the better flight leaders.

Accompanied Sandy to the clubhouse tonight to talk to the men in an attempt to develop a closer feeling between them. Sandy has changed some, and the morale seems to be a bit better.

Wrote a masterpiece to Doris. Wonder how much of it the censors will permit to go through?

January 6, 1942

Got reports of some more Second Squadron action at Rangoon, but this time it was a little different. They were hit with a Japanese fighter sweep of about forty planes. Pappy Paxton, John Bright, and Allen Christman were shot down. Fortunately, they are okay. They bailed out near the base. Three Jap planes were shot down.

Was paid today in Indian rupees. I remain a bit worried about my insurance. Jim and I got George to agree that we should wire his dad to check into it for all three of us. We are asking him to pay it for another year.

January 7, 1942

Had quite a bull session tonight in my room: George, Jim, Doc Rich, Bob Little, Ed Leibolt, and Charlie Sawyer. As usual the topic was our future destiny, just speculation. We learned that Chennault is now a brigadier general in the U.S. Army Air Corps and is in Chungking in conference with the generalissimo. We are reasonably sure the discussion concerns our status, but we don't know what the outcome will be. The word around here is that CAMCO is through with us. I am glad, for I have lost faith in their administrative capability.

January 8, 1942

Did something different for a change. Several of us went to the

Nan Ping Theater in town and saw *Dr. Cyclops*. Really a first-class movie theater. Completely forgot about being in China for a while.

January 9, 1942

A day off! Slept until about 9:00 A.M. and had a good, leisurely breakfast. Then went on a country drive with our hunting rifles, which took us about halfway round the big lake.

The countryside is really beautiful, especially the cliff on the south side of the lake. The mountain there must be at least two thousand feet above the lake. On the western end of the cliff is a huge Chinese temple, and at the bottom of the cliff are huge piles of fallen rock, where a city of Chinese laborers hammers and chisels the rocks into smaller pieces and carries them away in shoulder baskets for runway construction at the base.

We were traveling in a jeep and attempted to drive up a dirt road over the crest of a sharp ridge in an endeavor to go completely around the lake. Through sign language a Chinese ox-cart driver warned us that we would never make it. Believe it or not, there are many swanky homes in that area. This is the area where the rich Chinese of Kunming have chosen to live in order to evade the Japanese bombing. The biggest surprise is the large number of Buicks and Cadillacs. These Chinese must be connected with the trucking business, since Kunming is the terminus of the Burma Road.

Further down the face of the cliff are many cave homes dug into it. The atmosphere and appearance there are the complete reverse of the affluent area. These are poor coolies living in the caves. They are barely clothed and look filthy. Apparently this is where the coolies live when they are not crushing up the rock at the base of the cliff.

Many small factories are built in the hillsides and cleverly camouflaged smokestacks rise out of the ground in the most inconspicuous places.

Got word today that Ken Merritt was killed in Rangoon. I never did get the full story, but it seems that one of our pilots was coming into Mingaladon, our airfield, on a night approach and hit him with his landing gear. Also heard Charles Mott was lost in action. That makes four of our pilots lost in action so far.

January 10, 1942

Jo and Red, the two nurses, came over to our First Squadron dining hall tonight for dinner. They have quarters across town in another larger hostel that houses the other squadrons and the group staff, also the Old Man. They helped cheer us up a little.

January 11, 1942

Made a test flight in old No. 5 plane this morning and buzzed all the fishermen on the lake. She runs like a sewing machine.

Napped a little in the early afternoon. Still feel depressed and have a cold like may of the men.

Several of us decided to go into town just to be doing something. Went into a filthy tea room with the idea of listening to the music. That was a dud. Just rhythmic beats on some bamboo instruments. A Chinese gal pinched Charlie Sawyer on the butt and walked out the door. Just for fun we started tracking her but soon lost her in the back alleys.

January 12, 1942

Same old routine! I wonder where in hell the Japs are? The guys in Rangoon have started going on strafing missions in Thailand. Do I envy them. This sitting on my fanny is getting me down. I wish we had some action. Perhaps this is what caused all the morale problems lately, and it is now getting to me.

Eight of our guys were selected to go to Rangoon today to take some of the heat off the Second Squadron. I had a chance but a poor one. Four names were put in a hat for the eighth guy, and my name was one of the four. I was not the lucky one.

What the hell! I am now acting as squadron vice commander, operations officer, adjutant, and personnel officer. Maybe I will be busy enough to keep from getting bored.

Jim and George told me this afternoon that some of the guys did not take kindly to our promotions to flight leader. Mickey Mickelson told me the whole deal was just a matter of jealousy, but some of the pilots were riled at me because I lost in trying to get the squadron reorganized. I told him I had dropped the idea because most of the pilots are too reactionary. I am afraid that some of them may get into trouble. Others have asked for transfers to the other squadrons. My ability as a fighter pilot and as a squadron leader, I learned, is highly respected by all of the men.

Got a cable from my oldest sister, Jewel, that upset me the rest of the day: "Daddy sick in hospital. Jack has measles. Need money." It was a knife in my heart. For some reason or other I had been sensing trouble at home for the past few weeks. I still do not know about Dad's trouble. I am sure Jack will pull through. I wonder how poor Mom is holding up under all the strain. I sent a cable and four hundred dollars to help them. Went to bed feeling awfully low.

January 13, 1942

General Chennault tells us that now there are no firm plans to incorporate us into the Army Air Corps. He says we are getting some new versions of the P-40, a better plane with six .50-caliber guns in the wing roots. Also we will get some P-43s. He even says we are getting more pilots and mechanics, which really surprised me. Perhaps we will continue as the AVG.

An order was published today giving anyone a chance to resign and return to the States. We have until 20 January to decide, no later. I am staying here.

Some of the pilots have elected to leave. Seven are going home tomorrow, two or three out of our First Squadron. They must arrange for their own transportation. That was one of the catches in the order that gave them a choice to go or stay. It'll cost them at least two hundred dollars just for boat fare from India to the U.S. Many reasons are dreamed up for leaving, but the main one, I think, is a yearning just to be back in the good old U.S. Some of them admit that they will reenter their respective services upon returning to the States. Otherwise, they will be drafted.

Chennault is classifying each resignation and discharge as dishonorable. He feels that anyone leaving now while we are at war and in actual contact with the enemy waxes of dishonor! It makes sense, and perhaps he is right. But will such a discharge from the AVG mean that much back home? I don't know.

A few of the guys ran across a Chinese prostitute in town last night and they are daring any of us to go look at her. Puss and scabs in her navel and all over her belly. Left breast wrapped in a swath of bandages. Cripes, what's happening to us?

January 14, 1942

A Russian-built Chinese bomber came into our field yesterday. It is a light bomber with two in-line engines and external wing racks under each wing. Rumors are that there will be a squadron of them here.

What I would give to have a squadron of some kind of U.S. bombers here in our AVG.

Jim and George came into my room tonight, and I could tell immediately that they had some serious things on their minds. They had obviously been doing some serious talking about the decision to go home or stay.

One thing that is a big factor in their thinking is that the Old Man disapproved of their promotions to flight leader. We talked for some time. I went over all the background of our coming to China, our being together throughout the whole deal, the squadron morale problems, their lack of experience in fighters. Both of them have a feeling that we three are not as close as we have been in the past. I tried to explain that cliques are bad for any outfit without saying that our clique of three has really been resented by the other men. I suppose the core of the matter is that I got my promotion and they did not. One thing is sure: we are still fast friends.

January 15, 1942

My promotion to flight leader was effective January 2, meaning an increase of seventy-five dollars a month gold.

For some reason the sunrise got to me this morning, so I wrote Doris a masterpiece. How I love that little gal.

Went into town with Ed Leibolt to see his Canadian girl friend who had come over on the boat with us. Her assistant is a well-educated Chinese girl. We discussed the war at length and the future.

On the way back to the barracks I bought a Chinese propaganda leaflet. It shows some crude pictures of the horrors of war, mostly death scenes of bombing raids and rape cases.

January 16, 1942

The generalissimo's photographer came this morning to get snapshots of us, still and moving. For what I am not sure.

Had a short flight this morning involving some "combat." I got in an awful spin, my first one in a P-40 unintentionally. Got out of it about a thousand feet above the surface of the lake. Shook me up.

Four of the guys quit today and got ready to go home. Also, Mickelson and John Farrell said, "No more P-40 flying." They decided they did not like fighters and have agreed to fly the Beechcraft light transport.

There are many "red asses" and "independents" in this outfit. It is pathetic! I get quite frustrated and enraged. Even Jim, George, and I are getting at cross words now. Some of the guys seem to be off their rockers. I wonder?

Tonight I broke out in a rash in my bunk and started scratching like mad. Doc Richards said it was the hives. He gave me some capsules and I finally fell asleep.

January 17, 1942

My hives are still with me. The Doc has given me a dose of salts in hopes of getting rid of the problem.

Later in the morning we had an alarm, and I took off with John Dean and Joe Rosbert on my wing. Sandy told me to circle the field until I got radio instructions. In the meantime the Third Squadron pilots got off and went down to Mengtzu, some 125 miles southeast of Kunming. They met a Jap bombing force and got three planes.

I was disgusted. Why in hell were we not sent down? I later found out my antenna was busted and no one could talk to me. Rosbert's radio was bad, and Dean had no earphones. What an outfit!

We got into the movie business this evening. We flew formation attacks against the Beechcraft while they took movies of us. The photographer in the Beechcraft was really shook up. We broke off the attacks at the very last second.

January 18, 1942

Off today because of my hives. Sat around most of the day and scratched!

Doc Richards really shot me full of stuff tonight. George brought Bob Prescott over, and we opened a bottle and had a good bull session. That helped my hives to some extent.

January 19, 1942

Wow! Those pills Doc gave me. I was up all night. I am sure that he is convinced that if he can get everything out of my guts he has the problem whipped. Perhaps he is right. I am sick. On top of that he gave me a dose of Epsom salts this morning. Cripes! My guts will shine like a mirror soon.

January 20, 1942

Slept late and felt much better.

Pappy Boyington returned from a trip to Rangoon today and told me of watching the Japs come over Rangoon at night on their bombing raids with their running lights on! Unfortunately, it looks like the Japs will have no problem in taking Singapore and Rangoon.

Tonight the Doc shot me in the vein with something. I had some temporary relief, but about 10:00 P.M. I was in misery. My face swelled like a balloon. He gave me a codeine tablet and I fell asleep.

January 22, 1942

Feeling better. I borrowed Jim's blouse and am having a Chinese tailor copy it for me. It is an old U.S. Army Air Corps officer of the day blouse, only it is made of a beautiful soft gray gabardine.

Went to town to make the deal on the blouse and watched a parade leading a Chinese prisoner to his death on the outskirts of town. He had been caught cutting down the copper wire on the city telephone poles, one of the biggest crimes in China today.

When I got back to the barracks, Fritz Wolf and Matt Kuykendall came over and we got in a good bull session about the graft in China. And, man, is it something else! The powers to be are making money head over heels. Everyone seems to get his cut—"cumshaw." War profiteering is running amok. Some of the guys in the AVG are making a few bucks on the side in various black-marketing schemes. The Old Man fired several of the guys yesterday that he caught red-handed.

Jim came in and told me about escorting seventeen Chinese bombers to Hanoi from Mengtzu. It was a completely screwed up mission. They were way off course. As they approached the general area of Hanoi and encountered anti-aircraft fire, they jettisoned their bombs and turned back. Their formation flying was terrible.

January 23, 1942

Talked to Colonel Wong of the Chinese War Area Service Corps this evening. We discussed the general conditions in China. Some will purchase a truck fully loaded with material of "you name it" in Rangoon for about two hundred dollars U.S. gold. After it is driven up the Burma Road to China by some trusted hiree, it will be sold for twenty thousand dollars U.S. gold. Many Chinese are getting rich in this manner. If the Japs take the Burma Road, there will be another road built further inland from Calcutta through Tibet to China. Trucks are decreasing in value, but their spare parts are going sky high. The smart people who own good automobiles are tearing them down and selling the parts as spares.

He also said that he expects Russia to enter the war later on against Japan.

January 24, 1942

Glad to be back on duty today. Had a test flight on my No. 5 and worked in it with a combat training flight for John "Blackie" Blackburn. No problem with him, even though he has never done that before.

Another report from Rangoon. A Jap raid on the city resulted in the AVG shooting down nineteen Japanese planes while losing only three planes. Bill Bartling and William "Black Mac" McGarry made crash-landings in Burma and got back okay to base. Allen Christman was killed. He had to bail out once before. I guess his number was up. War is a nasty business.

Still another report later in the day from down south. A second Jap raid resulted in their losing fifteen planes! Every one of them was shot down with no AVG losses. Has there ever been anything done like this before in aviation history? I do not think so.

The Third Squadron escorted another Chinese Air Force bomber raid against Hanoi with same results: poor navigation and bombs thrown away.

I began to feel bitter about us just sitting here with the guys down at Rangoon fighting their hearts out, but I felt a lot better by midnight. Twelve pilots in the First Squadron are going to Rangoon tomorrow. We drew cards to determine who would go. Jim's draw was bad—he stays. But George and I are going!

*   *   *

The first taste of battle—just three engagements over China and Burma—demonstrated our ability and training as fighter pilots. During that first week of action the AVG destroyed fifty-five enemy bombers and fighters while losing only five Tomahawks. Unfortunately, two of our colleagues were killed, but at the same time approximately two hundred enemy airmen were either killed or captured.

We were shattering the myth that the Japanese Air Force was invincible.

4. *The Battle of Rangoon*

While the First and Second squadrons were defending Kunming, the Third Squadron was engaged in combat a thousand miles south—the Battle of Rangoon.

The odds for success were not favorable. Olie Olson's Hell's Angels had twenty-five pilots and sixteen P-40s to fight alongside the RAF, which had a few Lysander bombers and twenty Brewster Buffaloes. The Japanese, however, had about 150 bombers and fighters based at several airstrips in Thailand.

The Americans and British waited nervously, and then on December 23 the Japanese launched their first attack against Mingaladon Airfield and Rangoon. The first wave of bombers attacked without detection, dropping their loads on the docks and heading back to base unmolested. But not on the second strike; thirty bombers escorted by twenty fighters clashed with the RAF and AVG. In the brief but frenzied battle the Japanese lost six bombers and ten fighters. The British lost five pilots and their Buffaloes, and the battle marked the first combat deaths for the AVG. The youngest member of the group, Henry Gilbert, was shot down while attacking a bomber, and Neil Martin's plane exploded while being riddled by four enemy fighters.

The Japanese returned on Christmas. This time sixty bombers and thirty fighters headed for the city, but before reaching targets they were met by twelve P-40s reinforced by sixteen Buffaloes. One observer stated that the battle looked like "rowboats attacking the Spanish Armada." Nevertheless, the allies proved victorious. Olson radioed Chennault that it was "like shooting ducks. . . . We got 15 bombers and 9 fighters," while losing two planes and no pilots, since they bailed out safely. The RAF contributed by shooting down seven more, but lost six pilots and nine Buffaloes.[1]

---

[1]Chennault, *Way of a Fighter*, Chap. 9. Also consult Robert B. Hotz, *With Gen-*

Both sides needed rest and reinforcements. Stung during daylight raids, the Japanese staged some night attacks during the next few weeks while resupplying their air power in Thailand. On the other side, the Hell's Angels had only eleven P-40s left, so during the first week of the new year Chennault replaced them with seventeen planes of the Second Squadron led by "Scarsdale" Jack Newkirk.

The Panda Bears harassed the Japanese attempts to rebuild their airforce by conducting a number of strafing raids into Thailand, especially against airstrips at Mae Sot and Tak. On one attack they destroyed twenty-four planes, three trucks, and many buildings. The AVG became such a nuisance that beginning on January 4 the Japanese mounted a three-day fighter sweep to eliminate allied fighters near Rangoon. The enemy destroyed only a few P-40s and killed none of our pilots, while the Second Squadron shot down thirty enemy fighters.

Meanwhile, the Japanese Army pushed into Burma. The British Army retreated, and on January 23 the Japanese commenced five days of air attack against Rangoon. Six major assaults resulted in heavy casualties for Japan.[2] The AVG and RAF knocked down fifty planes, and the Flying Tigers lost only one pilot, the third killed in action, Allen B. Christman.

Newkirk radioed Chennault in Kunming that the spirit of his Second Squadron was running high, but that was not the case with his equipment—the group was down to just ten P-40s. The Old Man sent our First Squadron, and on January 25 twelve of us arrived at Mingaladon.

*   *   *

---

eral Chennault, chaps. ten and eleven, for descriptions provided by other members of the AVG.

[2] It is interesting to note the Japanese reports of these events. Concerning their attack against Rangoon on December 23, their War Department admitted that four planes did not return to base but claimed that the force shot down fifteen Allied planes. Instead of the loss of twenty-four fighters and bombers on Christmas Day, they reported nine lost while smashing forty enemy planes in a dogfight and eight more on the ground. They claimed losing no planes on January 4 while shooting down six Americans. Finally, they noted destroying five Allied fighters on January 29 and eight more on February 6, bringing their claimed tally to eighty-two in the skies over Rangoon. *Japan Times and Advertiser* (Tokyo), December 25, 27, 1941, and January 9, 13, and February 7, 1942.

January 25, 1942

Before taking off from Kunming, Sandy got us together for a briefing for the flight to Rangoon. He also told us we were definitely going into the USAAC. We may be offered regular commissions. Our inducted rank will be based to a great extent on Chennault's recommendations. Further, our CAMCO contract will be honored for the remainder of the full year, which means several thousand dollars for me.

We took off and flew formation to Lashio, Burma. There we had a good lunch at the CNAC club and also met some U.S. Army officers who were doing some surveys on the Burmese railroad. After a long wait for refueling we got off for the last lap to Rangoon.

We broke off in our usual echelon for landing. My approach and touchdown were perfect, but suddenly I heard my right tire blow. I can not remember fighting an airplane as much as I did that one to keep it on the runway, and I finally got it stopped about fifty feet off the runway with the tire completely shredded. I considered myself lucky, but the guys called it great work. In any event, I'm proud that I did not bust up No. 5 before getting in a position for some real combat.

I noticed a B-17E parked across the field. Damn, it looks good! In a talk with the USAAC crew I learned that its performance is about like that of the B-17B, which I flew at Langley, Virginia. Moreover, it has defensive guns all over it. Supposedly there are quite a few of them now in Singapore.

The Mingaladon Airfield here at Rangoon has been bombed quite a bit. Right in the middle of the field are two burned-out aircraft—a Brewster fighter and a small Moth trainer. The one big hangar has two bomb holes in the roof, but it is still in use. There is no doubt: here is war.

Bob Little picked me up at my plane and gave me a quick drive around the landing field area. He was driving a new jeep, and I marveled at it. First one I had ever ridden in. Looks like most of us will get our own jeep from the Lend-Lease storage area just off the port docks of the city.

After a quick scotch and soda with the RAF pilots at their club, we formed our first opinions about the British fighter pilots. They are quite a raucous bunch—"bloody" this and "bloody" that. My first impression is that they are sissified dainties, but others say they are gutsy guys.

We drove into blacked-out Rangoon and had a fine dinner at the Silver Grill, which is one of the favorite hangouts.

January 26, 1942

We have been organized into two squadrons for tactical reasons. The First is called red yellow and the Second is blue green. We operate as four separate flights of four P-40s, when that many are in commission. I don't know how long the planes will last; they are taking a beating.

At the sound of the RAF siren we scramble off and climb madly to twenty thousand feet, then patrol an area east of the field. Seeing no enemy, and hearing the radio call from the tower of "free beer," we roar back to the airstrip. Then we land, park, and again take up an alert posture.

We had four scrambles today. Up and down. Up and down. I soon developed a violent headache, and I am sure it was from the rapid descents.

The RAF supposedly has an early-warning radar deployed a few miles east of the field, and that is the source of our air-raid alerts. How good their identification is I do not know, but apparently it is not so sharp.

The takeoff procedure is a hell of a mess. The RAF has three or four Brewster Buffaloes and two or three Hurricane fighters, and we have twenty P-40s on the field. The wind direction does not matter when the scramble order sounds. The Brewsters dash off down one runway, and the Hurricanes take off in the opposite direction a few seconds later. In the meantime, our First Squadron is getting into the air on another runway which intersects the RAF runway in the center of the field. Then come the blue green flights down the same runway but in the opposite direction. The Blenheim bombers are dispersed and remain on the ground.

I keep wondering how long good luck can hold. If we get our timing screwed up, there are going to be a lot of fighters in a tangled mess at the intersection of the runways. And when vultures get involved on the runway trying to consume the remains of a dead dog, things get even more hairy.

In our last scramble today the Japs came in at a lower than usual altitude, and our squadron was too high. The Second Squadron tangled with them and got four. But Louis Hoffman failed to return from this fight. He was shot down—the only loss. We felt very bad about him. He was probably the oldest pilot in the AVG, an ex-Navy man with a wife and children back in the States. A damn good pilot, too. I had practiced dogfights with him many times before. He was found not too far from the field, badly mutilated.

Finding adequate quarters in Rangoon for all of us turned out to be a problem. Billeting requests were radioed throughout the city for the citizens' help and cooperation. A Danish oil man, Mr. Jensen, East Asiatic Company, Ltd., has agreed to billet George and me. We showed up at his residence tonight about 7:00 P.M. A very neat and comfortable home. He turned out to be most genial and helpful. He fixed us up with two good beds in a bedroom of our own on one side of his house. His wife and children had already evacuated to Madras, India. His number-one boy calls us "master" and waits on us hand and foot. Mr. Jensen gets a small "feedback" for taking care of us.

George and I had scotch and sodas with Mr. Jensen out on his front lawn tonight—relaxation and pleasant camaraderie. The air-raid siren gave us about five minutes of warning. The Japs were trying to bomb the field to wipe out our aircraft. We watched all of this and even saw the reflections of the bursting bombs against the low-hanging clouds. Later came the rumbling sound of the bombs. What a show. We have no night-fighting capability. Even if we did, we could not do anything here but watch.

After all the excitement abated, we had a wonderful vegetable dinner and retired.

January 27, 1942

We were up at 6:00 A.M. and had a quick breakfast. Mr. Jensen's number-one boy fixed me a little Thermos bottle of coffee to take to the field. Off we went in our jeep in the dawning light of a new day in this war. I thought to myself how I liked this life.

We merely lounge around in the alert shack reading or playing acey-deucy, a game from the Navy. A scramble startles us into action, and I mean "startle." No matter how experienced, a scramble alert, horn, ring, or siren really shakes you up! Our alert shack is actually a bomb-riddled RAF barracks that still has enough roof to shade us from the hot sun. We have lawn chairs and some cots. Every pilot takes his choice.

We had two alerts this morning and I took off once ahead of Sandy, the squadron commander. He said nothing over the radio about his plane being "out," so I rolled on the runway and took off. No contact with the Japs.

We have our lunch buckboard-style while on alert. It is not the best in the world, but it is adequate. We closed shop a little early tonight and I had barely finished my bath in our billet when the Jap raiders came over. Last night they did little damage, but tonight was a different story. George and I, Mr. Jensen, and another Dane, Mr. Mather, heard them come in. There were three of them. They dropped bombs on the field and on the city from about ten thousand feet. One bomber returned over the city and dropped lower and lower. We tried to followed him with our eyes as well as our ears in the darkness. We could hear his engines clearly right over us and on the way out to the field from the city, but we could not see him. Suddenly we saw tracer bullets darting across the sky.

"Damn, George! A night fighter!" I screamed. The bomber burst into flames immediately and turned down into a short dive and burst into a ball of fire no more than a mile from us. George and I, in mutual understanding, turned and shook hands. Across the street we heard some neighbors clapping their hands in glee. What a show!

We sat in our lawn chairs and reveled in the success of the RAF night fighters. A neighboring Dane came over with an RAF wing commander who was billeted with him. We talked at length about the war situation. George retired, but I stayed up and Wing Commander Barnes and I developed a close comaraderie. He is the first Britisher I have met who was teed off at his homeland about putting as little as possible into the war effort and expecting to get a lot out of it. He and George had argued the merits of the Hurricane versus the P-40, and that was the main reason George gave up in disgust and went to bed. In spite of his preference for the Hurricane over the P-40, we got along fine.

January 28, 1942

George and I were scheduled for a day off, but we had to get up to drive Bob Prescott out to the field for alert duty. Also, Hoffman's funeral was scheduled for 8:30 A.M..

About the time we got to the RAF headquarters on the field, the air-raid siren sounded. We hurried across the field to our alert area. The flight scrambled, and I picked up John Dean in the jeep and drove over to RAF operations. We stood around hoping to hear the radio chatter of combat, but again no Japs.

We returned to our alert area. While sitting there in the jeep, Tom Cole frantically directed our attention to a flight of three aircraft diving on the field from the east. Man, did we scramble for the nearby ditch. It turned out to be Sandy Sandell with two wingmen. We cussed him and climbed out of the ditch.

As soon as the flight landed, we attended Hoffman's funeral. George and I were picked as pallbearers. God! What an experience. He had not been embalmed, and the stench was sickening. His coffin was covered with an American flag. We had to delay the rites in order to lengthen the burial hole; the coffin was too long. We finally laid him to rest in the Rangoon cemetery and with the permission of John Dean (his best friend) George and I got some pictures of the grave. I thought George would cry.

We decided to drive to Rangoon and try to forget it. At the Silver Grill we ordered strawberries and ice cream and spent twenty minutes trying to get two British girls to take a ride with us in our jeep through the city. We struck out completely. We stopped at Coombes's jewelers and shopped for stones. I bought some star rubies, three star sapphires, and several pieces of beautiful green jade. I think I paid about 175 rupees for all of the gems. We took pictures of the huge, gold-plated Shwe Dagon Pagoda and enjoyed the sights of the main part of the city. Some parts were very modern and reminded me of Singapore. People recognized us immediately. Everyone in Rangoon loves the AVG pilots.

We drove back to the field. Lo and behold, there had been some action! The guys had shot down seven Japs. Damn it to hell! My day off. Will I ever see action?

I learned that Sandy Sandell had a narrow escape when a badly damaged Jap fighter tried to ram him on his takeoff. The Japanese pilots always try to take out one of our aircraft as a last-ditch effort when they know they are going down for the last time. They are either fanatics or real heroes, I am not sure which.

Bob Neale, who is really the vice squadron leader of our First Squadron, seems to be under strain here. He is glum, glum, glum. Bob is an ex-Navy pilot with a wife back home. A really great guy, and a close friend.

While having a drink after dinner on the veranda of the RAF

Officers' Club, we watched the RAF Blenheim bombers taking off for a night raid on Bangkok, which has been taken by the Japs. One of them lost an engine on his roll and decided to abort the takeoff. He could not stop and ran off the end of the runway in a big wide swooping ground loop. No one was hurt, but another valuable aircraft was lost.

January 29, 1942

We had to get up early this morning and drive to a remote air-strip—Johnnie Walker (we named all our outlying strips after some brand of liquor).[3] There we dispersed our few remaining aircraft the night before. The overnight loss of a P-40 to a lucky Japanese night raider at Mingaladon would have been unforgivable.

In the early morning haze we drove through rice paddies and semijungles along dusty roads in our jeeps. Finally, our headlights picked up the dim outlines of the P-40s. In a matter of minutes we had the engines warmed up. No crew chief to help here. The pilots do it all. Checked everything, a complete preflight. The crew chiefs were scheduled to go to the main airport and await our arrival, after which they topped off the tanks and took care of last-minute checks. Just as there was sufficient light to see the end of the strip, we took off and headed for Mingaladon, some five minutes away, and settled down on the big runway for the routine of standby alert.

Two alarms this morning, but we never saw a thing. The third one, however, proved to be something else—a real battle!

Eight of us were on alert. All of us got off in rapid succession and climbed up to nineteen thousand feet in a loose formation. The RAF surveillance radar at Rangoon continually passed information that "bandits" were in the immediate area at certain locations with refer-ence to the city.

Suddenly we spotted a swarming beehive of Japanese I-96 fighters about ten o'clock low. We dove in. I was breathing hard as I charged my guns. Gunsight switch on. I was almost vertical in a dive. The Jap fighter I picked out began turning tightly in a horizontal plane. I missed him by a mile. Aware of their maneuverability and tactics to get on our tails, I continued my dive on down a few thousand feet further. As I started pulling up I partially blacked out. I realized then that I had

---

[3] Johnnie Walker field was a few miles north of Rangoon.

the throttle full up against the firewall and I was getting detonation in my engine. No one on my tail, so I stole a peek at the air speed indicator—over 400 MPH. Using this speed I climbed back up to eighteen thousand feet.

There they were! This time I picked one that was flying straight and level, but as I closed in, he turned sharply. I missed again as I rammed on past. Circling back, I found myself a bit more at ease. I would have to do better than this.

I could see no other P-40s for the moment—only I-96s. I was a little more relaxed and approached a twisting, rolling Jap. I drove a burst into him. He had to be damaged as I flew past and he started off into a gentle dive. No more attention for him, however, for I had to keep my head on a pedestal looking around. Too many in the area—couldn't let one get on my tail.

The fight was now taking form. No formation, just a swarming mass of a few P-40s and a hell of a lot of Japs twisting, turning, diving, and maneuvering to get position. I found myself on the rear quarter of another Jap. I bore in and fired. He started downward towards a cloud. I stayed above in anticipation that he would come back up out of the cloud. He did, climbing back up and leveling off squarely in front of me. He must have been within two or three hundred yards as I closed in and opened fire with all six guns. He made no effort to turn; it was probably too late. My tracers tore into his cockpit and engine. Suddenly I was right on him. I had to raise my left wing to get over him as I zoomed past. His cockpit was flaming. I squealed in delight, laughing aloud. Enough for him. "Got one! There you are, Hoffman, old boy!"

This fight was not over—plenty of Japs everywhere I looked. I wheeled sharply to get back into the melee, and realized that the swarming formation of enemy fighters was retreating eastwards. I firewalled everything and closed in for at least one more encounter. There were some on the fringe of the circle, seemingly isolated. I started in. When they thought I was completely committed, they pulled up in an Immelman. Now we were head-on. I squeezed the trigger. Damn! Only my thirties fired. No fifties! And no time to check them. As we passed each other, I saw smoke trailing from one of the fighters, and he disappeared in a dive down into some clouds. I was satisfied that he could never return home.

I was reluctant to let them get away. After my routine dive of 350 to 400 MPH, I pulled up sharply and started back into the mess. I kept trying to recharge my two .50-caliber guns: the butts protrude out from the top of the instrument panel just opposite my shoulders. I finally got one working. I was now closing in on a loose V formation of three ships. The Jap leader waggled his wings and started a gentle turn to the left with his number-three man staying with him. Number two was on his right wing and began falling back and easing off to the right. Their tactics were obvious. Feinting at the leader and his wingman, I rolled sharply towards the right wingman and tried to line up on him. He whipped around and down, and I fired wide and then dove on down through and past.

An undercast of clouds now began to drift in, and I decided to call it a day. After all, I was getting too far eastward from our field. Nearing the field, and after checking with the tower, I did a slow roll across the runway as my first victory roll in my life. I then landed and taxied towards the alert area at the opposite end of the field.

While taxiing past a revetment, I saw quite a crowd around one side of the enclosure. Closer observation revealed a crashed I-96 fighter. The Japanese pilot had apparently been shot out of the air, and he was making a last suicidal attempt to crash into an old RAF Blenheim bomber which was sheltered in the revetment. He had missed it by only a few feet.

An RAF airman held up a leather helmet with the pilot's head still in it and with parts of his throat hanging down in a bloody mess. With his other hand the airman pointed two fingers skyward in the usual V-for-victory sign. I returned the V-sign and taxied on. I could not, however, return his broad grin.

Later I walked over to examine the crashed Jap plane more closely. I picked up a charging handle for his machine guns from the smashed cockpit. I don't known what the Japanese letters on it mean, but I decided to keep it to remind me of my first successful aerial combat against fighters.

The Japanese I-96 fighter reminds me of the U.S. Army Air Corps P-26 pursuit ship: low, single-wing, fixed and faired landing gear, and open cockpit in which the pilot's forehead is about even with the top of the windshield. Painted a slate grey color, it has two yellow stripes encircling the rear fuselage just forward of the tail and the red chevron V-sign in between the two stripes.

There must have been at least thirty-five I-96 fighters. We figured that we got at least sixteen of them. I think I shot down two. At least now I have done something. Matt Kuykendall took hits in both wings and miraculously missed being killed when a Jap bullet grazed his forehead, knocking off his goggles. His oil tank was hit, and he was forced to land early in the fight. This was our only damage. Unbelievable!

The rest of the day was quiet. At 6 P.M. we dispersed the flyable aircraft to the outlying strip. George Burgard nearly let his ship get away towards the end of his roll and had to give it the gun and go around.

Thirty-six miles of weaving, dusty road and we were back at our quarters. How tired I was—all tension had left my body. Mr. Jensen, our Dutch host and landlord, congratulated me after hearing the exploits over a scotch or two. I retired. I thought to myself how content I was now that I had done something in this war.

January 30, 1942

The air-raid sirens went off last night about 3:15 A.M. and the "all clear" was not sounded until about 4:00 A.M. Nothing happened.

I have gradually been taking over the jobs of operations and engineering officer for the squadron. It seems that someone has to start pulling things together. Everyone is doing what he prefers to do, and even the scheduling of who is on alert is getting confused.

Rumors are rife that we may go back to Kunming tomorrow, but I doubt it. The RAF were supposed to deploy a unit of Hurricane fighter aircraft here, but I see no signs of them.

A mission was planned to hit the airfield at Moulmein, Burma, just to the east of Rangoon. The idea was to keep alive the threat that we could hit it at any time, thus discouraging the Japs to use it as a forward base. Our squadron declined to go; we want to conserve our planes. The Second Squadron sent over three ships, and Tom Cole failed to return. I have lost count of how many guys we have lost in combat, even as few as they are.

January 31, 1942

Had a tough time staying on the right back roads to Johnnie Walker field this morning; the fog and mist were like pea soup. Even after getting to the field, we had to delay takeoff for an hour or so, hoping the stuff would lift. When we decided to chance it, I went on instruments the second my wheels left the ground.

Upon landing at Mingaladon we were sent right back up because of suspected Jap bombers. I was told the "bandits" were about ninety miles out, so I climbed to the west to twenty thousand feet before turning back to the east. Red Probst was my wingman. Bob Smith said his plane was missing too badly to try taking off.

I got a glimpse of an aircraft about my altitude far to the east and started after it. I took my eyes off it for a second to check my instruments, and when I tried to spot the plane again I could not find it. Damn it to hell! I'm sure it was a Jap, and he was probably heading for Moulmein. I got the news that the Japs had bombed Toungoo, our old base. By this time I figured all would be clear at Rangoon. My radio quit working and I could not confirm a thing, so I returned to base. To my surprise there were continuing reports of Japs on their way, so up I went again. All of this flying without any refueling was draining my fuel tanks. I stayed aloft as long as I could, patrolling at twenty-one thousand feet. With low fuel I barreled back to the base and landed quickly. This time all was clear.

After lunch we scrambled again. I grabbed a Second Squadron P-40 and took off. No Japs. The RAF control center had mistaken fourteen incoming Hurricanes as the enemy. I am losing faith in the RAF so-called radar warnings. Their identification capability seems practically nonexistent.

The AVG was written up as "The Wonderful Knights of the Air" in the local Rangoon paper today. I suppose it was part of Leland Stowe's work, since he had been doing a lot of interviewing of the bunch the last few days.

Got paid today, but my seventy-five-dollar-per-month increase didn't appear. Also my insurance deductions remain screwed up.

Got in a little early tonight and found that Mr. Jensen had arranged a party. About eight couples were there, all Danish people from his company and all equally genteel. The party was really a lawn party, and drinks were running freely. I was not holding back myself. One of the younger couples, the Hansens, were most pleasant, particularly since she was so charming and attractive. We danced a lot, and I really relaxed for the first time in a long while. She asked to see Doris's picture, and of course I folded it right out of my wallet.

February 1, 1942

Sunday and a day off. It is beautiful. Unfortunately, last night was beautiful, too—a full moon and the Japs took advantage of it. We had four air raids. Their targets were Mingaladon and our satellite dispersal fields. They were determined to knock out the AVG.

I tried to sleep through the noise of the sirens and bursting bombs, but it was a fitful night. I refused to run to the bomb shelter every time.

Bob Prescott came by with the jeep this morning and told of the Jap bombs getting Mickelson's P-40. Also, Bob Neale's No. 23 got some shrapnel damage in the tail section. Really no other damage. I think I'll ask Sandy Sandell for permission for some night alert duty. With a good moon, I believe I could get some of those guys.

Had a sorry breakfast at the field mess and heard that the Japs are driving on Singapore. Moulmein fell last night. The British cannot stem the tide, and I wonder if they are waiting for the Aussies or the Americans to do it for them.

Five more mechanics came in from Kunming and told us that the story now is that we will not go into the U.S. Army Corps until July 15. I wonder. . . .

Took a jeep ride into town this evening and ran into some technicians from the American Mission in Rangoon. Their story is that there are some eighty-two thousand tons of war materials for China in Rangoon right now, and their job is to get it rolling up the Burma Road as quickly as possible.

We decided to make a visit to the Shwe Dagon Pagoda, the largest in the world and covered completely with gold leaf. (It is a terrific navigation mark for the Rangoon area when in the air.) Upon entering, we were told to remove our socks and shoes; one must be barefoot while in the pagoda area. It is full of little idols and small temples, a lot of gold and ivory. Many Buddhas everywhere and in many sizes, and one can see Burmese peasants bowing and praying. We bought flowers and some kind of long, slender sticks which were set afire at one end. We placed them at the feet of one of the larger Buddhas.

In the late afternoon Mr. Jensen took me to the local country club, the Kodine Club. We went swimming and relaxed a little. Our dinner was interrupted by the air-raid sirens, but we went ahead and ate. We are getting used to the Japs at night.

February 2, 1942

Had a meeting today with Jack Newkirk, the commander of the Second Squadron. Jack is really the overall AVG "boss" here. He says we are on a military basis from now on, whatever that means. Also some six or eight Hurricanes will be turned over to us. I am not sure who is going to fly them. Not me, I hope. I assume there has been some high-level planning going on between the British and the Chinese and the RAF and Chennault. Rangoon must be held and defended if the Burma Road is to remain open and if supplies are to get to China. Reports indicate that we are to get some more P-40s, this time the late-model E. Even more importantly, a U.S. Army induction board is coming down from Chungking. This means that we are going into the U.S. Army Air Corps.

Ran into a couple of riverboat pilots who happened to be at Moulmein when it was evacuated ahead of the incoming Japs. They said only sixteen hundred Japanese troops took the place. The British decided to give up and pull out. The airport is badly damaged by bombs with eight-foot holes in the landing strip. To advance further, however, the Japs will have to move north to cross the Salween River.

February 3, 1942

Orders came in directing the Second Squadron back to Kunming. This will leave only our First Squadron here to help the RAF fight the Japs. We will have the whole show as far as the AVG is concerned. Tex Hurst decided to quit and is going back to Kunming with the Second Squadron. Jim Cross should be coming down now that the remainder of the First Squadron in Kunming will be coming to Rangoon.

Had a scramble about noon and climbed to twenty-three thousand feet to patrol the area. No Japs again. Old No. 5 is purring like a kitten. I always feel much more confident in my own plane.

The RAF headquarters here clued us in on the Southeast Asian situation. The Japanese have some 735 aircraft in Indochina, Thailand, and Malaya. We have destroyed about one-sixth of them. If we only had more forces here! I definitely detect a growing mistrust and lack of confidence in our pilots here toward the British. Tension is getting worse. Last night some of our pilots went on a spree in town and were beaten up badly. Red Probst was fined one hundred dollars gold.

February 4, 1942

Had another frustrating ride out to Johnnie Walker field this morning. The natives get in the middle of the road with their oxcarts and pay no attention to us even though we sit on the horn. Finally, in desperation I pulled my pistol and fired into the air. It worked quite well.

Had a couple of alerts this morning. On the last one I was at twenty-three thousand feet and flew over Moulmein to check the area. No Japs. Not a sign of life on the river, in the town, or on the railroad. It's a strange feeling to be over enemy territory for the first time.

Tomorrow is a day off, so George and I got a bottle of Black Label scotch at the RAF club and decided to go into town for a night of relaxation. Met Bob Little at the Silver Grill, and he was having a gay time. We watched the dancing and some of the Anglo-Asian girls, who were beautiful. Bob Layher and Hank Geselbracht joined us. George and I threw in the towel about midnight and took off for home.

February 5, 1942

The Japs were over again last night, but their bombing was very poor. A few native huts were destroyed.

Some of our guys escorted the RAF Blenheim bombers on the Moulmein raid today and succeeded in doing some heavy damage to the Japs' supplies.

February 6, 1942

The Japs really laid on a big bombing effort last night. I nearly fell out of my bed, the bombs were so close. I thought they knew exactly where I was and were going just for me! It was the first time I got a bit scared of bombs. There were four raids in all. Not much damage in town; it was obvious they went for our planes at the field when we saw the damage that morning on arriving at the parking area. Made me wonder just how much they knew about our dispersal plans at night.

A Hurricane fighter was standing on its nose near a bomb crater in one of the runways. It was one of the two ships that went up last night. They got two Jap bombers, but upon landing one did not see the crater and dropped his left wheel in the hole. The enemy hit the runways about ten or twelve times. The natives had the craters filled shortly after sunup. The job was really no great deal, since the material was packed gravel and laterite.

Later on we scrambled against a raid and tangled with about thirty-five enemy fighters. We had six P-40s and two Hurricanes. Pappy Boyington did not see them at first, and I waggled my wings at him. His flight followed me, and we tore into them. I caught an I-97 fighter in my sights at about five hundred yards and let go with all guns. He suddenly did a snap roll: why, I will never know. My firing engulfed him. As I closed in, I misjudged my speed and had to pull up and away drastically to keep from hitting him. I am positive his career had ended! There were too many other enemy aircraft in the area to stay glued to him, so I made several passes on other ships but did not get in many effective bursts. Too damn excited, I guess. I saw tracers coming at me several times, but I received no hits. I had to dive out once when a Jap got too close on my rear, and when I leveled off and climbed back up, I lost the enemy fighters.

Turning eastward, I scanned the horizon. I picked up a lone I-97 and started after him. My first burst turned out to be only one of the thirties. What in hell happened to my two fifties? I charged and recharged both fifties and got them working. In I went again, and in my concentration I did not see another Jap who had come down on me but overshot me. He pulled around to get on my tail; I dove away. Just as I did, I got a glimpse of another P-40 whizzing past me—No. 23. That was Bob Neale, and I was glad, for I figured one of us would get the Jap. Bob and I fought that little devil some five to ten minutes. He must have known he was done for, but he was a game little guy, and he would turn eastward in an attempt to get away every chance he had. Bob started one of his attacks, and as he closed in, the Jap pilot turned sharply and ended up flying straight at me. All my guns were firing as we barreled on at each other head-on. He started pulling up and I followed as long as I dared, then broke off in a screaming dive out. He flipped around in an amazing turn and followed me down. I had my throttle jammed fully forward—one glimpse at the instrument panel showed 52 inches of manifold pressure. I hoped the engine would stay together. But what the hell! It was either the engine or me. Looking back I saw Bob's ship on the Jap's tail. That was some comfort. I was in a vertical power dive and skidding like mad, since I did not bother the rudder trim. Bob told me later that the I-97 turned out to be duck soup. I set him up for Bob, and the unintended cooperation paid off. I ribbed Bob about getting half the bonus. He just grinned.

On the way back to the field, I was feeling low. With all that fighting I had only one probable. One AVG flight accounted for seven certains and five probables. We are still far superior in the tallying of kills. My personal count is now two down, two probables, and one damaged.

One Hurricane nosed up on landing to keep out of a ground loop, and John Croft overshot and tore a landing gear off in the overrun boonies. No other damage for our side. A Second Squadron flight escorted some RAF Lysander light bombers over to Moulmein for low-level bombing later in the day. They got no resistance on their mission.[4]

February 7, 1942

Man, they did it again last night, and hard! The Jap bombers got a Blenheim and a Hurricane on the ramp and set two buildings afire. Many bomb craters on and off the runways. It really makes for a ticklish approach and landing to miss all the craters. Wind direction isn't even a factor. You just pick the best area of the two intersecting runways to land on. They again made four raids during last night. They are beginning to disturb our sleep!

We received a great shock today! Sandy Sandell was killed in an aircraft accident. I actually watched and was horrified. What a loss to us and what a shame to lose a man like that while we are engaged with the enemy. Sandy was up on a test flight of his P-40. He had been having some trouble with the controls of his ship and was checking it out thoroughly. On one pass near the field he went into what looked like the start of a slow roll, but he was awful low—some five hundred feet. He rolled all the way over on his back and that was far as he got. He lost altitude very quickly and went right in. We don't know whether he had control problems or what.

Bob Neale was made the new squadron commander, and Pappy

---

[4]That same day the commanding officer of the RAF in Burma, Air Vice Marshal D. F. Stevenson, sent the following telegram to Chennault, who put it up on the bulletin board: "Today the First American Volunteer Group destroyed its one hundredth Japanese aircraft in the defense of Rangoon. I take this opportunity of expressing to Colonel Chennault, their commander, squadron leaders Sandell, Newkirk, and Olson, and to the fighter pilots and maintenance crews the deep admiration of the RAF Burma for this remarkable piece of air fighting" (entire telegram reproduced in Olga S. Greenlaw, *The Lady and the Tigers*).

Boyington the vice squadron commander. I am running operations and happy about it, but not at the price of losing a man like Sandy.

After dinner tonight I sat out on the lawn in the moonlight and just looked at the stars and wondered about everything in general: life, death, love, Mom and Dad, Doris, and my being in Rangoon, halfway around the world and involved in war where people are shooting at each other and trying to kill each other. And what for?

February 8, 1942

No raids last night. Wonder what the Japs are up to? Quite busy most of the morning improving scheduling for alert, aircraft parking, and pilot and airman procedures. I frankly don't see how we have done so well fighting a war without a better understanding between the people in the outfit.

Went on an escort mission to protect some Blenheim bombers while they hit the enemy at Pa-an, Burma. I believe they bombed the wrong side of the river, but that was not my mission, it was the RAF's.

Made the usual trip to Johnnie Walker field this evening, but on my way back I was talking with a Gurkha officer. He said there was only one British brigade defending the west bank of the Salween River. They might slow the Japanese down, but they will never stop them.

February 9, 1942

Had a long session with Bob Neale this morning about the outfit, pilots, men, and organization. Bob is an ex-Navy bomber pilot—a medium-built, jovial guy from the state of Washington. He has a wife back home, a situation that most of us are not concerned with, being single. He is well liked by the pilots and men and is a fine pilot. We are close. We agreed that I should draw up an emergency evacuation plan for the squadron, and I started work on it. We are just not too sure how long the Japs will be kept from swarming into Rangoon.

We learned this evening that Bus Keeton got a Jap bomber at Toungoo the other day. Good old Bus; great for him.

There were three escort missions to Moulmein today, and the bombers did some good this time. As a matter of fact, we even got rumors that the British recrossed the river at Moulmein and took some territory from the Japs. Sounds good; maybe things are beginning to look up! The RAF Hurricanes are dropping incendiaries at night, and while the Japs are fighting the fires, the British Army crosses the river in raids.

I'm beginning to wonder why the Japs have stopped coming over at night—and even less than usual during the day. I am itching for some more action.

February 10, 1942

More work today in putting the finishing touches on our evacuation plan.

Jim Cross came by, and it was good to see him. He told me that a lot of the fellows at Kunming are planning to quit. An undercurrent of unrest is prevalent all over the place. Some of these guys are just plain prima donnas, and others are just plain scared. Yet to a certain extent I can't blame them. Hell, I get scared at times too. I think the problem up at Kunming is that they are not in action and they are bothered by boredom, not being in on the war.

February 11, 1942

Fog held us up at Johnnie Walker field until about 10:30 this morning. Sat around and did paperwork until an alert put us in the air about noon. No Japs; just one of our reconnaissance missions returning. Damn! Why shouldn't the radar control center know that?

Had a run-in with John Dean about scheduling and had to control my temper to keep from having a fight. Being the operations officer is not an easy job in this outfit, particularly under this strain.

On the evening dispersal flight I got a scare flying No. 3. The engine was missing badly. I "coughed" it in to a safe landing.

Tonight Bob Neale took Bob Little and me to a dinner at the RAF air vice marshal's quarters. There was an unusual number of the higher-ups at the party. Between drinks and dinner we learned a lot about what the war situation was in our area. One rumor was interesting: an American B-17 outfit was due here on 20 February. We are supposed to get more fighters. Things look bad for Singapore; Japs are already on part of the island. The worst news was learning that many Japs have crossed the Salween River just northeast of here. I wonder how long we can hold out?

February 12, 1942

Today I took a flight of six P-40s and six Hurricanes to patrol the

Pa-an area in case Jap bombers tried to bomb British and Indian Gurkha troops there.

Still more work in running operations, and Bob Neale is beginning to depend on me more and more. We consult on all key decisions. Tonight, for instance, we decided to disperse the planes in the far corners of Mingaladon and not fly them to Johnnie Walker field. It is the only way we can beat the morning fog problem and have P-40s on early scramble alert at Mingaladon.

Heard from home today by cable. "Everyone is fine." That was a real lift. I feel much better, since I had been worrying about them lately.

Several of us went on a binge tonight—we needed it! Bob Little, Bob Neale, George, and a few others tried to drink the RAF under the table. I really blew it, although I had a hell of a good time! Fritz Wolf, in his drunken drawl, bent my ear about "rank" in the AVG. Hell, there is no such thing. Following that, both of us got friendly as ever and decided to tell all the RAF where to get off. George kept saying our comments were "out of this world." I finally lost my cookies in the men's room and just barely caught Bob Little pulling out in the last jeep from the hotel entrance by screaming at the top of my lungs and barreling the natives off the sidewalk as I ran for the car. The last thing I remember is the ride home and looking in driveway after driveway trying to find our own home. I'm glad that I have the next day off.

February 13, 1942

Oh, never will I do it again! What a hangover!

Bob Little finally talked me into going over to the golf course, but play was interrupted; Bob Neale called me to the field. He wanted me to write up a detailed report on Sandy Sandell's crash, finish the excavation plan, and prepare a routine report on operations to send to the Old Man in Kunming. When I got to the field, Bob was in a dither. Seems like things are in a mess. Bob may be the commander here in Rangoon, but it seems like I'm doing all the damn work. Everyone comes to me. But what the hell! I guess that is the operations job. Bob is a gung-ho guy.

February 14, 1942

We received quite a writeup in the local gazette today. According to them, we are "lean, bronze giants with gleaming teeth!" Even Churchill was quoted giving some plaudits for the AVG.

We listened to an RAF intelligence officer briefing us on the east Burmese front around Pa-an. One British battalion was surrounded yesterday but was freed by a bayonet charge by supporting Gurkha troops. The Japs fled the field, leaving their arms. But as usual, at the end of the report we learned that the British are making another "strategic retreat."

I led six Hurricanes in my No. 5 P-40 this afternoon to escort some Blenheim bombers. Our target was Martaban. The bombing was fair, but we saw no fires as we circled to return. Tonight I dispersed my ship to the satellite field.

George and I were invited to another home in the neighborhood, where several of the pilots were billeted. Practically all of our pilots were there, and many of them had local girls. One was a real doll—an Anglo-Eurasian. I danced with her several times. The greater part of the well-to-do families have evacuated Rangoon, and there are not many desirable girls remaining in the city; at least we haven't found them. The ones we do find that are worth dating get so much attention they rapidly become arrogant and snobbish.

Needless to say, there was a lot of drinking, and many of the guys really got stewed. Jim Cross was feeling no pain. He surprised me by saying he had decided to go back to the States. Jim is homesick, obviously, and probably weary of the strain. But who the hell isn't? I believe Johnnie Farrell has talked him into the idea. Johnnie already has put in to resign and go home. Jim got awful cantankerous and was in a fighting mood with any one who would risk it. We finally got him settled down enough to go home. I'm thinking a lot about Jim's decision before falling asleep, but I guess that is his business.

February 15, 1942

We are waiting for Bill Bartling this morning, but he didn't show, so George, Dick Rossi, and I went on out to the field. About five other pilots didn't show up on time for alert, and even old Pappy Boyington was real late. Bob Neale was furious, and he and Pappy had a hell of an argument. I guess last night's party was a bit too much.

Pappy Boyington is turning out to be a different man from what I had earlier thought. He is an ex-Marine flyer and an exceptionally fine fighter pilot from what I have seen. He has a lot of experience in fighter aircraft, probably more than or as much as anyone in the AVG. And I am sure that was the major factor that led to his being selected as vice squadron leader. He has led a lot of flights, but he does not seem to care to do anything on the ground. I thought he would be very active and probably even get into my operations area more. Even before this morning's argument, Bob Neale would come to me on everything, and he ignores Pappy altogether. I believe the drinking party last night finally brought everything out in the open.

Actually, Bob Smith was too tight to get in an airplane this morning, and I took him off the alert roster. Jim is also in a pouting mood this morning. I hope the outfit snaps out of it; otherwise we will not be fit to fight the Japs.

Bob Neale called a meeting just before noon, and I briefed everyone on our emergency evacuation plan. Everyone is tense as hell, especially Bob. I really cannot blame him, and I think he knows more than he is telling me. It was also announced that Jim and George are to be made flight leaders. That was a shot in the arm for old Jim, and it changed his outlook considerably.

I tried to get a nap in the afternoon, but Bill Bartling awakened me and wanted to get an administrative order published. I also learned a truck of ammunition was lost. There are so many things like that around here that I am beginning to wonder just what is happening.

February 16, 1942

I began again this morning trying to analyze my feelings. My nerves are okay, I finally concluded, even in spite of dreaming every night about fighting air battles. The thing to do is just stay as busy as possible.

Heard Singapore fell to the Japs yesterday. I just wonder if the Japs will now start concentrating on Rangoon. The briefing yesterday on the evacuation plans was timely indeed.

Escorted the bombers to the Moulmein area, where they bombed a little village, Mutpun. Several fires resulted. A flight of RAF Hurricanes went out to strafe a Japanese elephant train, but they couldn't find it. The Japanese have apparently taken over the local domestic animals for supply transport.

The guys have begun to kid each other about evacuation and finding Japs in our cockpits in the morning runups and have been betting on who will be the last to leave the place. Actually it is relieving the tension and is a good thing. Underneath, however, all of us realize the danger of our position here.

Mr. Jensen told George and me that he and his business associates have decided to evacuate tomorrow. They will go north to Hsi Paw for a while. From there they will make further plans.

February 17, 1942

We gave Mr. Jensen a warm send-off this morning and thanked him over and over for his kindness and consideration.

Bob Neale and I had a long discussion this morning about the possibility of Jap paratroopers hitting the field. Many of the guys have started speculating on this danger. I let Bob know my doubts about the Japs trying that right now. Their lines are not near enough for an overland dash across the river to join up. We had heard that they did use these tactics a few weeks ago on the island of Sumatra.

Took Bob Smith on my wing to rendezvous with the Lysander bombers and hit the Japs in the village of Bilin. We never saw the bombers, nor did we see any bombing. This seems to be happening more and more. I suppose the RAF is having some of the same problems we are having in the AVG.

February 18, 1942

Had an alert this morning and climbed to twenty-two thousand feet to patrol the area for incoming Japs. No sooner had we throttled back to cruise when we got the order on radio to "snapper," the code word for "land immediately." I still don't know what the foulup was. On the landing Red Probst blew a tire and nosed up No. 45. That leaves us with twenty-three aircraft.

Bob Neale is hot under the collar about a couple of the flights getting off one at a time rather than in pairs. The guys know better, but that is another case where Bob or Pappy ought to get on them, but they do nothing about it and hop on me. I'll get them straight about it tomorrow at the briefing.

Had dinner at the men's billet area they call the 18-Mile Ranch. With Mr. Jensen now gone we have to eat someplace else. The stories

I picked up from the men are incredible. On the docks at the port are all kinds of equipment, merchandise, and food that are beginning to pile up. Some of the men have begun to go down to the docks, drive their truck up to a pile of whatever they are interested in, speak in a commanding voice, and direct the Burmese laborers to load the stuff onto their truck. Then they merely drive off with it. Not only are our men doing it, but so are local people. The men say that is where they learned the trick. The men have caches of canned fruit, rifles, shotgun shells, soap, radios, and whatnot. John Dean picked up three more jeeps for the men yesterday the same way. Hell's bells! No wonder war costs so much!

Organization in the city seems to have gone haywire. It must stem from administrative officials evacuating. No one seems to be in charge at the docks. Thievery is rife all over the city. Of course the local citizens do not condemn us for picking up things at the dock. They say we should have it rather than letting it pile up for the Japs to get later on.

George and I dropped by to see Charlie Sawyer and Ed Leibolt at their billet home, and their owner also had evacuated. On the way to town we picked up Ed's Burmese girl friend and went to the Silver Grill for a party. George picked up a girl there and we went back to our quarters.

Since George and I shared the same bedroom, I lay awake for quite a while listening to George and his girl across the darkness of the room. The noises of their fun damn near ran me nuts. I rolled and tossed. One thing was certain: I was not interfering with George's play. God! How lonesome a man can get. I finally fell asleep, thinking of Doris, after the noise died down.

February 19, 1942

Same old routine—alert duty—alert duty! Same old afternoon—more alert duty! No Japs; not even any alert scrambles.

Heard the Japs and British Army are really tangling over to the east at the Bilin River. We got wind of a wild rumor that over ten thousand American shock troops would land here tonight. It's amazing what one will believe when in a tense situation.

George went down to the docks and made a swoop for us. We both now have good British radios to take to China. Tried out my radio tonight. San Francisco comes in loud and clear. It was good to hear the words "United States." The news was heartening, particularly aircraft production figures and plans for an air force of over 240,000 officers alone, not to mention the airmen.

February 20, 1942

Got bad news this morning of the Japs crossing the Bilin River. Makes things more binding now for us—more tense.

There are indications that the RAF may be getting ready to evacuate. Some of our airmen are leaving tomorrow to go up north to the town of Magwe on the Irrawaddy River. Another RAF airport is situated there. Dick Rossi says a forty-eight-hour notice is being posted all over the city suggesting that the civilians evacuate Rangoon. We are prepared to leave also, but we will stay as long as we can.

February 21, 1942

Arrived at the field this morning to find that Stephen Kustay, one of our armorers, had been in an automobile wreck last night. Doc Richards is fixing him up, bad cuts on his face.

Flew a patrol over the city this morning. Another flight took off for Bassien in an attempt to pick up what was thought to be a Jap bombing raid. No luck. The worrisome part of the Bassien flight is that the city is due west of here, and there are reports that some Jap paratroopers hit the place yesterday.

Bob Neale told me to take a flight of six to escort some Blenheim bombers on a raid of the roads northwest of Bilin. With no Hurricane cover, we really got in a tangle on this one! We cruised over the enemy lines at about sixteen thousand feet, and I gradually eased down to twelve thousand to stay closer to the bombers. I was concentrating too much on the bombers and ground targets and failed to see the Jap fighters that came in about two thousand feet above us. Suddenly I saw them just before they came within gunnery range. My flight had broken up, for the others had seen them earlier. I split-essed and shoved the throttle full forward. The Japs didn't follow.

I climbed back up to altitude and started back into the fray. The first one I got my sights on was approaching head-on! Both of us were blazing away. He veered off in a gentle diving turn to the right. I think I got him, but I was too busy to follow up. There were about thirty Jap fighters, and slightly below them were about twelve bombers. At first I thought they were ours, but they turned out to be Japanese. We were outnumbered too badly to attack the bombers, and I had lost them anyway, so I started after the enemy fighter formation. Several attacks, but no good ones. The maneuverability of the I-97 is amazing—how they can turn! Reminded me of my P-12 days at Kelly Field in advanced training.

During the entire fight I saw only one other P-40. That made it a bit lonesome. I suddenly noticed antiaircraft puffs all over the sky, and I didn't know whether they were British or Japanese. I had been fighting for some ten minutes, and the Japanese had turned to the east. I headed back for Rangoon.

Johnnie Farrell got one, but he also got a bullet through his canopy that resulted in his having a serious cut very close to his right eye. He is okay. George thinks he got two. Smith says he got one and maybe another one. Jim didn't get any, and damn it, I can't say I got any either! At least I received no hits again.

I wonder how long this can last? It's a bit tough to continue to fight outnumbered as we are, but the guys still barrel right on in. I figure we got six and lost none. I now have two certains, three probables, and one damaged.

George told me that he had tried to warn me by radio of the Jap fighters above us on the first pass, but as usual the damn thing was not working. We can't maintain these small commercial radios and have worked out some visual signals.

I hadn't even finished my combat report when Bob Neale barged over and told me to take five more ships and cover his flight of six—we were going back to the same area. I was eager as hell and was hoping we would see them again, since I didn't fare too well before. The Blenheims bombed the area, and then Bob went down with his flight to strafe the Japanese columns on the road. I counted over fifty trucks in the column heading northwest towards Kyaikto, which is the British Army headquarters. The British were retreating across the Sittang River towards Pegu. No Jap aircraft turned up, and after about an hour we returned to the field. Upon landing, Bob directed me to go right out again with three more P-40s to strafe.

I asked, "What about top cover?"

"None," he came back.

What the hell, I thought, as I looked at him. I had just given him top cover. There was no time to argue. I ran for my plane, and off I went. Bob Prescott failed to get off, and Jim turned back with a bad engine. Bob Smith and I went on.

Bob Neale had told me of a Blenheim that had been damaged and had bellied in near Moulmein that the RAF wanted strafed and set afire. I looked all over the area but could not find it. I headed north to the main road on which I had seen so many trucks in my previous mission. This time I was at treetop level, and then I found the Jap motorized column. I strafed it from one end to the other. Some vehicles already were on fire and bombed out from the previous RAF bombing and Bob's strafing. I saw many horses standing idly along the road; obviously the riders had long since taken to the jungles to avoid the strafing. I circled to come back down the column again, and Smitty was right behind me. I came close to the treetops in my porpoising and jinking to get in bursts at choice targets. Once when I thought I may have nipped a tree with my prop, I received some ground fire. They hit my right wing with a burst but with no real damage. I saw tracers pass me several times. The thought of being hit from above by a patrolling Jap fighter bothered me constantly, but fortunately I saw no other ship except Smitty's P-40.

I buzzed over a burning village and then back south to search again for the grounded bomber. A little more relaxed now, I took my time. I finally found it in an open area near a small inlet. I riddled it in three or four strafing passes, but it would not catch fire. On my last pass I noticed several natives and a small dog scampering from the nose of the ship. I pulled away and started home.

Then my ship started shaking violently. It sounded as though the engine was missing badly. I pulled up in a gentle climb and started out over the bay towards Rangoon. I was determined to get back to friendly soil if I had to swim to it. I throttled back and switched to a full rich mixture. I had my canopy rolled back, my oxygen mask off, and my helmet removed. I was ready to ditch or bail out. The vibration lessened considerably, and the engine began to smooth out. I nursed the plane back to the field and set her down on the runway with a great sigh of relief. When I cut the engine in my alert space, I sat there and looked across the nose of the fuselage to reflect and take a deep breath.

I saw the problem immediately. There was a one-inch hole right through the middle of one of my prop blades. Somehow a .50-caliber bullet went right through the blade on my last strafing pass on the ground bomber.

I had really been in combat—a lot of it, all kinds, and all day. I had seen war at its worst. That Jap column had been wrecked by .50-caliber slugs tearing the trucks to bits. I saw one Japanese on his horse ducking for cover and I had grinned as I passed over to get a bead on a truck down the line. I'm sure I would have gunned him down just like a truck had I been in the right position. What a business. Like beasts. No thought for life whatsoever. Instead, a feeling of hatred for the Japanese that becomes deeper day by day.

On our way to quarters tonight we could see towering flames of a huge fire on the docks on the Irrawaddy River in downtown Rangoon. Apparently the British are destroying the dock area in preparation for evacuation of the city. We passed several Indian infantry units on their way to the front and many trucks filled with supplies.[5] The sight I liked best was the column of light tanks rumbling up the road. I wondered how long we would hold out.

I wish it were possible to pull all my thoughts on paper, those which run through my mind when I get in battle like we were today. It's so funny to say I am not afraid. I don't have time to be afraid. I just try to shoot down an airplane without getting another one on my tail. My stomach and neck muscles are going to be strong by the time this war is over.

February 22, 1942

Bob Little came by to pick us up this morning. "We're on one hour's evacuation notice, so bring all your junk," he warned, so we piled our personal belongings and that precious radio in the jeep and headed through the fog for the field.

The guys had worked all night in changing my prop and checking out my engine. What a bunch! And what those few can do in such a short time with so few parts. I am continually amazed at the mainte-

[5] Before Rangoon fell on March 6, 1942, the British had to burn 972 trucks, five thousand tires, and a thousand blankets of American Lend-Lease supplies so they would not fall into the hands of the Japanese. Charles F. Romanus and Riley Sunderland, *Stilwell's Command Problems*, p. 84, vol. II of their *The China-Burma-India Theater*.

nance our gang achieves with practically no equipment. They really contribute to the guts of this outfit!

The citizens of Rangoon are leaving by the thousands. Our hosts at the billets tell us to take anything we want when they leave. They consider it lost and would rather we have it than the Japanese. Some of the pilots have radios, beautiful carvings, food, liquor. One guy plans to take a refrigerator with him. How he'll get it on his jeep is beyond me.

While on his way to the city, Bob Smith was stopped by a Dutchman in a truck who loaded him down with brandy, rum, beer, and other types of liquor. He gave Smitty the address of his store in the city and told him to take anything he wanted. No wonder a war ruins a country.

All of the convicts, lepers, and insane are being turned out of their institutions and given freedom. Looting is out of all reason. Jim Cross came across an insane woman on his way to the field this morning. It was hysterical to hear his telling us of the wide berth he gave that woman. Last night Bob started to stop on the road to give some white hitchhikers a ride, but his host told him to drive on—the two were lepers.

Went up on a scramble this morning but saw nothing. We are sending Jim and Mickey Mickelson up north to Magwe, about 250 miles away, with Edgar Goyette in three of our P-40s. Their mission is to work out of that field with four RAF Hurricanes and patrol the Rangoon-Prome highway if and when we evacuate.

Got quite a kick out of one of George's stories today. In his last engagement with the Japs he was so excited that when attempting to turn up his gunsight rheostat, he tore it off its mount.

We were listening to the San Francisco newscast when several of the men came in and said they had heard rumors that the Japs had cut the Prome road already. George drove over to check with Bob Neale and learned that there was no truth to the rumor.

February 23, 1942

We followed our latest routine this morning and toted all our belongings along with us to the field. We could leap off any minute now and abandon the place. The road is filled with evacuees going north. Looting is completely out of hand. Many of the men are getting their share also. We have at least a hundred cases of various kinds of liquor, box after box of cigarettes, toothbrushes, talcum powder, cheese, canned goods, anything that might be of use in China. I saw one jeep loaded with cases of sherry. Also could not help watching starving dogs eating the dead carcass of a cow alongside the road. No one to feed the once-loved pets.

Our alert area is at the end of one of the runways adjacent to one of the main roads going north. We sat around watching the stream of evacuees all day. Sent six more planes up to Magwe today along with many of the maintenance men in jeeps and trucks.

We decided to keep thirteen P-40s here, but that quickly dropped to twelve today when Dick Rossi attempted a takeoff, didn't make it, and purposely ground-looped his ship at the end of the runway. That one was washed out. Also, No. 13 is a lemon, so that leaves us with eleven. I keep wondering how long those will hold up without any spares. I hope the Old Man knows everything about our predicament here. We are depending on Bob Neale to keep him informed.

We have been escorting bombers all day trying to slow down the Jap penetration; also a lot of strafing. An RAF flight ran into three Japanese observation planes and wiped them out of the sky.

The guys are really getting jumpy and irritable. I can understand some of it; I'm a little touchy myself.

Seems like everyone has some excuse to get out of doing something that has to be done. I'm glad I'm running operations and scheduling. I can schedule the reliable ones, even though their rotation for the chore isn't due. It is the same old story. In a clutch about ten percent of a group seem to be the reliable ones and do most of the work. It sure as hell is true when the most fierce combat crops up.

February 24, 1942

I understand that General Wavell has told the RAF commander to throw all his air strength into the battle for Rangoon. This includes the AVG, for our mission is the same. After all, China and the Old Man want the Burma Road defended as long as possible.

The Japs are still trying to cross the Sittang River. The British have already blown up the bridge. When they did, there were still two British brigades on the east side of the river. Many of them got across by swimming the river. The local RAF station commander told Bob Neale and me that we would be involved mostly in direct air support.

Bob, George, and three others went over to strafe the airport at Moulmein. They got three bombers and a fighter that were on the ground and left them burning.

I took a flight of four to escort bombers against Kyaikto, with four Hurricanes as top cover. After the bombing I dropped down with my flight to check a small airport in the area. Nothing on the airstrip, but on the road nearby I came across a small Japanese supply column. We practically obliterated them. Some oxen were pulling two artillery caissons, and after our first pass the road was smeared with blood, dead oxen, and riddled caissons. God, what a mess! Man, what those .50 calibers will do! It was a sickening thing to think about at the moment, but those thoughts are fleeting. We returned to Mingaladon.

Our air warning net is nothing more than a radio direction finder now. It hardly gives us time to get off the ground, and that is the greatest of all fears.

We got a message from the Old Man at Kunming wanting six trucks of food and military supplies. What in the hell is he thinking about? Or are they that hard up? Anyhow, he should be worrying about getting some better aircraft replacements down here for these worn-out crates. Maybe he is; I don't know.

February 25, 1942

Fog again this morning, and we had to take off in it from John Haig to get the ships over to Mingaladon.[6] What a mess. John Haig is a single sod strip with Hurricanes and P-40s parked at both ends. No control tower whatsoever. Fog so dense that we could see about halfway down the strip, and here we were taking off directly at each other! We had to be alert to stay on the right side of the narrow strip on the takeoff run and quickly get to the right a bit more as our wheels left the ground. I still don't know how we did it without killing someone, but we did.

We do things over here that would surely draw court-martials at home. Also we are flying aircraft that would be condemned back in the States.

We're sending Bill Bartling to Kunming with complete poop on the situation here for the Old Man. We want some P-40 replacements

[6] John Haig airstrip was a few miles northeast of Rangoon.

that will not drop 200 RPM on one-magneto check before takeoff. Some of the pilots have gone to Cairo, Egypt, to pick up P-40E replacements for us. Hope they bring them here. But I have an idea that Chennault will re-equip the Third Squadron with them and rotate us and replace us with that squadron.

Heard a rumor today that an Axis submarine hit some coastal city in the States. Good, maybe that'll wake 'em up at home.

Went up about noon on a scramble with Bob Little. At about fifteen thousand feet Bob wagged his wings, indicating he had seen the enemy, and started off in a dive. I followed him. Apparently Bob Neale with Bob Prescott on his wing broke away from us, because Neale also had picked up another formation of Japs. They got four of them, and Bob Little and I never got in the fight. Made me feel bad.

We escorted the bombers to Moulmein again and saw no Japs again.

Still another alert about 4:30 P.M., and this time we did see the Japs—about forty fighters and twelve bombers. We had eleven P-40s and eight Hurricanes. One additional aid we had in this fight was good radio communications. Previously we had been putting the heat on the communications airmen, and they turned in a major effort. I had Blue Flight, Bob Neale had Red, and Bob Little had White. I had better radio contact with Orphan, our ground control, so I acted as the air commander.

We were climbing to the west all out, for we knew our warning was short and we didn't want to get hit from above right after takeoff. Orphan came on: "About fifty bandits headed towards Bassien."

"Roger," I replied and then relayed it to the others. We turned towards Bassien.

Then Orphan again, "Bandits southwest of field—twenty miles!"

I headed back even though I was still climbing, and in my excitement I forgot my communications relay job. By the time we got back near the field, Neale's and Little's flights were several thousand feet above me. About the time I caught sight of the Jap bomber formation, Neale came on the radio: "Come on over here. Here they are!"

I thought "Where in the hell is 'here'?" and started in on the bombers. There were fourteen in perfect V formation. Suddenly I caught sight of that usual cluster formation of Japanese fighters directly above the bombers and changed my mind. I had to get some more altitude and speed.

I made my first attempt on one of the fighters, head-on. He caught fire before I closed in so close that I had to pull up to miss him. I looked for another while I reached up and gave a pat on the charging handle of the .50-caliber guns.

Again I was involved in a head-on attack. The Jap fighters were as aggressive as we were. We headed straight at each other, each with all our guns blazing. At the last second he pulled up and I did the same thing at the same time. (It is more natural concerning G-forces to pull up than push over.) I reacted unconsciously as I shoved forward on the stick violently. My seat belt was damn tight for combat, but my head still hit the top of my canopy. We shot past each other, him above me. I rolled and pulled violently to the left, straining my head over backwards to pick him up. He, too, was in flames. Yeow! Two in less than three minutes!

I made several more passes, but never really got positioned well enough to get in a good burst. Suddenly, from nowhere, a Jap I-97 pulled up right ahead of me, apparently completing a loop. He then rolled over right side up. He obviously had aimed to attack me from below and misjudged, ending up ahead of me. All I had to do was squeeze the trigger. I did. Damn! Nothing happened! I yelled at the top of my lungs and cussed and cussed. There was no time to charge the guns, for I was practically eating up his tail. I shot above him and to the right and then shoved over in a shallow dive, staying in a tight turn. I took a minute to recharge my guns, and some of them started working, at least the fifties. I looked back and saw a fighter on my tail. A violent split-S and that got him off.

Pulling back up to altitude and turning back into the melee, I saw another P-40. It was John Blackburn joining on my wing. Blackie and I saw a lagging flight of three Jap fighters off by themselves. We bore in on them.

I took on one of the wingmen. He had two white stripes painted around his fuselage just ahead of his rudder and elevators. He and I started fighting separately. I lost sight of Blackie and assumed he was in an individual fight. It was the I-97's horizontal quick-turning capability against my hit-and-run, higher speed in the vertical plane. Neither of us was having much luck getting the other lined up for a good close burst.

I finally caught him at the top of a climbing turn. I poured on my thirties, all four of them, into his fuselage from a rear, left quarter position. Damn, my fifties had stopped again. He went off in a partial spin. I followed him as he sped toward the ground. He was done.

I flew eastward hoping to pick up a straggler. From nowhere Bob Little barreled in on me from the right and took up a wing position. I grinned to myself and gave him a thumbs-up sign, and then we sighted a flight of five Jap fighters. We moved in and started jockeying and maneuvering for position. I got a reasonably good bead on one. I was boring in, and then suddenly felt my plane quiver and rumble. I looked back: two Jap fighters right on my tail! The usual split-S maneuver again. Straight down to "400 MPH indicated" and I pulled away from them rapidly.

I was over Moulmein Bay, and my engine was acting up. Bob found me and rejoined on my wing, and we headed back to the field.

As we neared Mingaladon, we made a diving pass and did victory rolls before coming in on a landing pattern. Just as I started down with my landing gear, Orphan came on: "Two bandits northwest of the field." Up went my landing gear and back up to fifteen thousand feet. Finding nothing in the area, we returned and landed quickly.

The Jap bombers had hit the field, all right, and the airmen were adamant that one Jap fighter came down and made a strafing pass. Several Blenheim bombers were badly damaged with bomb fragments. One Lysander was still burning, as were several small maintenance shacks.

Everyone was excited and jubilant. They yelled and roared when I claimed three and maybe a fourth. Although outnumbered by three or four to one, we got nineteen and probably eight more. The RAF Hurricanes got six. That makes our total for today twenty-five certains and probably ten more. On the other side, one of our guys, Ed Leibolt, did not return from the melee, but we are hoping he got down okay and will show up later. This is the best day yet for the AVG.

We dispersed six of our ships, and it was a good thing, for the Jap bombers came over strong this evening. Had a good meal at the Ranch.

Bob Neale told us he got the word from the Old Man to evacuate on March 1.

February 25, 1942

Checked the bomb damage this morning and found only a few hits on the runways, but the RAF lost two Blenheim bombers—charred ruins.

Bob Neale took a flight to strafe Moulmein. They caught four Jap fighters on the ground and got them all. It must have been fun, and I was teed off that I didn't get in on it.

At about 10:30 I took Dick Rossi on my wing, and we started searching for Ed Leibolt's aircraft. We could find no trace of him, so started back for Mingaladon.

On our approach we saw the alert crews dashing out to their aircraft, and it was obvious they were scrambling. We circled the field and joined them. We had barely reached eighteen thousand feet when we spotted a formation of fifteen Jap bombers and some twenty or thirty fighters. I had joined Bob Little's flight, and it appeared to me that he had not seen the bandits yet. I pulled up to him and waggled my wings pointing off to the left: away we went. We had to get a little more altitude to come in from above the fighter escort. While climbing I found myself engaged with four fighters. I took a quick peek to my rear to see if anyone was with me. Hell, I was by myself!

I attacked, and I was head-on with one of the fighters. We barely missed each other. I turned to see if he was on fire. He wasn't, and he was easily turning inside me. Immediately, two others were on my tail. I half rolled and went into a vertical dive—everything forward. Pulling out and up again, I got into position to make another attack. He saw me coming in and went into a left turn. I led him a lot and squeezed the trigger. His ship straightened up a little, and then started off in a steep spiral with smoke trailing. I pulled up in a shallow climb to follow him.

My speed had fallen off, and when I looked back I saw two Jap fighters smack-dab on my tail. Their guns were spitting smoke. Again, quickly into a split-S with full throttle. They followed. All I could do was hunch up behind my armor plate and wait for my acceleration to pull me out of their firing range. None of the bullets hit my fuselage, but I got a few in the left wingtip. When I got out of range they pulled away.

Climbing back up, I could find no more enemy. John Blackburn joined on my wing, and we returned to the field.

We lost none, but Jim Cross got a good burst through his windshield, oxygen bottle, and left cockpit. Flying metal cut his cheek, and he got several shrapnel pieces in his shoulder. The poor guy was as pale as a ghost. I thought of how unlucky the guy was. We were sending three P-40s to Kunming that afternoon, so I scheduled Jim to take one of them. He was glad to do it.

I now have six to my credit, two probables, and some damaged. I hope to get those bonuses at five hundred dollars per ship. Wow!

In one day our squadron in all the melees accounted for twenty-three certains and eight probables. This is the new record for the AVG. How proud we are!

I developed quite a headache this afternoon and spent a lot of time juggling aircraft and pilots to keep an alert crew standing by. We are out of spare tires; if one blows, then that ship is lost. The last oxygen is in the bottles in the ships, and that's it. Other spares are practically gone, and some have already been sent up north. We are just hanging on. We'll stay here, however, until we can get the airmen out.

We felt better when three P-40s suddenly showed up in the traffic pattern from Kunming. One of them quit on the approach, but the pilot got it on the runway okay. Wonder how long this can go on?

Again we dispersed the ships to John Haig field and went to the Ranch for supper. We listened to the Japs bombing the field while we ate. The men are really getting edgy. Bob Neale said he had heard rumors that the Prome Road had been cut by the Japs. He wasn't sure, but it certainly gave rise to the question about leaving now rather than waiting for the first of March.

We drove on back to our quarters and tumbled into bed. Before we fell asleep we heard another wave of bombers trying to knock out Mingaladon as an operating field. I wish I had a drink of cold water and a hot shower.

February 27, 1942

Bob Neale woke me up with a hard shake about 12:30 A.M. to tell me the RAF started pulling out. Their warning gear had already been dismantled and moved: no warning system anymore, what there was to it: He said we will pull out at daybreak. I coaxed him not to wait.

Off to the Ranch. We got the men up. They got necessary personal belongings and prepared to pull out in a convoy of jeeps and trucks according to our evacuation plan. A small, specialized group went to the field and worked the remaining hours of darkness to get the remaining P-40s in shape to fly out at dawn. Miraculously, they got Jim's riddled No. 78 ready.

I dozed a little in the early-morning hours in my jeep, but the mosquitoes soon got the best of me. A cot in the alert shack was a bit more comfortable.

As daylight came we found that the runways were still in good shape. We packed what we thought would be needed up north and drove over to Haig field to wait for takeoff time for Magwe.

Antiaircraft fire appeared off to the east, and we saw a Jap bomber formation high and heading towards Johnnie Walker satellite field. Fortunately, they never spotted us. Thank God! We had quit using Johnnie Walker for dispersal.

Bob Little took off with his flight for Loiwing, China, just across the northern Burma border. After making a lunch of cold canned pork and beans, I took off with three others and headed for Magwe. Goodbye Rangoon!

Bob Neale and Smitty stayed for a while longer, as Bob wanted to be the last to leave. I don't understand, but Bob said something to the effect that maybe Ed Leibolt would walk in. Bob is quite upset about losing Ed.

*   *   *

At a time when the Allies were retreating in Europe, Africa, and Asia, the men of the AVG were becoming famous as the Flying Tigers. Time *glamorized many of the pilots, reporting that Matt Kuykendall landed with a bullet crease in his forehead and then proclaimed, "Now I'm mad," and that after shooting down eight enemy planes John Newkirk radioed his wife: "There were not enough of them to keep us busy."* Collier's *wrote that the enemy was advancing in the Far East and that only "one obstacle stood in the path of swift, easy victory. The Burmese heavens were full of 'sharks.'" The events at Rangoon gave Americans a feeling of pride which* Time *captured by writing that the battle proved that "man for man, plane for plane, anything labeled U.S.A. could whip anything labeled Made-in-Japan."* [7]

[7] *Time,* February 9, 1942, p. 26; January 12, 1942, pp. 25, 30; *Colliers,* July 4, 1942, pp. 16ff.

That seemed to be true, for during six weeks defending Rangoon the AVG had thirty-one encounters with the enemy and destroyed 217 planes, probably destroyed 43 more, and lost only four pilots and sixteen P-40s. With the help of the RAF, allied pilots destroyed approximately 300 Japanese planes.

Prime Minister Winston Churchill placed the confrontation in perspective by stating: "The victories of these Americans over the rice paddies of Burma are comparable in character if not in scope with those won by the R.A.F. over the hop fields of Kent in the Battle of Britain."[8]

[8]Churchill's statement is reported in *Time*, February 9, 1942, p. 26, and in Chennault, *Way of a Fighter*, p. 131. Concerned about the survival of their own island, the British press had little praise for the AVG in Burma; an exception is found in *The Times* (London), February 28, 1942, p. 4.

5. *The Raid on Chiang Mai*

Rangoon fell on March 6. Losing the port meant the end of the supply route, the Burma Road, which endangered the military situation in China. The British were concerned, for now the Japanese threatened India. The enemy began storing supplies for an invasion and even training dissident Indians, who they hoped would help them win the last great eastern colony of the British Empire.

Burma was a gem, a key element in Japan's strategy. By capturing all of it they would sever the British and Chinese armies. Also, Burma was a major rice exporter and possessed resources, such as tungsten, manganese, and oil in the north at Yenangyaung, needed for continued expansion.

In March, therefore, the British combined plans and forces with the Chinese in an attempt to contain the Japanese in southern Burma. Under the command of Lt. Gen. Sir Harold R. L. G. Alexander, the British and Indian troops established two defense lines, one west and another north of Rangoon. The generalissimo deployed Chinese troops to positions east of the city and placed them under command of Lt. Gen. Joseph W. Stilwell.

Alexander, Stilwell, Chennault, and Chiang Kai-shek faced a powerful Japanese military machine in Southeast Asia. The Japanese army was larger, better equipped, and reinforced with ample air support. Fourteen enemy air force regiments were based in Thailand and southern Burma, meaning that about 450 enemy planes confronted a dozen RAF bombers and thirty AVG fighters, which were based at Magwe in central Burma.

Faced with such odds and realizing that one battle could wipe out a large portion of his pilots and planes, Chennault shifted tactics during March. He ordered raids on Japanese airfields, hoping to surprise the enemy and destroy planes on the ground.

The first strike was on March 19 against an enemy strip 10 miles from Moulmein, or about 250 miles south of Magwe. The Japanese never suspected that the AVG was able to hit targets so deep in their own territory, so the field was lined with twenty fighters. William Reed and Ken Jernstedt surprised them, making six strafing runs without receiving antiaircraft fire. When they left, fifteen planes were burning. The pilots then turned toward the field at Moulmein and destroyed three bombers and a transport. In all, the raid destroyed nineteen planes, meaning that Reed and Jernstedt recorded the highest number of kills on one mission of any pilots in the AVG.

The next day the British ordered a raid. RAF bombers struck their former base, the aerodrome at Mingaladon. They surprised the enemy, who left fifty planes exposed on the field. Some Japanese fighters got off the ground and damaged a few Blenheim bombers, but nevertheless the British destroyed a dozen enemy fighters and sixteen bombers.

The Japanese responded swiftly and forcefully. On March 21 they initiated a massive attack against Magwe. For twenty-five hours, 266 enemy planes pounded the airfield. Two waves of bombers struck first, destroying many Hurricanes and Blenheim bombers. A few hours later they attacked again, leaving the field smoldering and fatally wounding two members of the AVG, pilot Frank Swartz and crew chief John Fauth. The attack on Magwe eliminated the bombing capability of the RAF in Southeast Asia.

Chennault and his men were enraged, and he called Bob Neale and Jack Newkirk into his office to discuss plans for retaliation. The Old Man knew the headquarters of the Japanese Air Force in Southeast Asia was at Chiang Mai, Thailand, and he selected it as the primary target with a secondary objective a smaller base some twenty miles southeast at Lampang. An overnight stop at the RAF airbase of Namsang, Burma, would permit a predawn takeoff the morning of the strike. Chennault asked for volunteers to fly ten P-40s and appointed Neale air commander because of his familiarity with that part of Burma and Thailand. When Bob told me of the plan, I quickly volunteered for the raid on Chiang Mai.

*   *   *

February 27, 1942

On the way from Rangoon, we flew low and patrolled the Prome Road, which runs north to Magwe, Burma. We saw our men in convoy and buzzed them to let them know we were with them. On the first pass they scattered like madmen for the roadside ditches. I grinned and thought of the names they were calling us.

Coming into the field at Magwe and getting in the traffic pattern, I saw just about every kind of airplane imaginable. The RAF air vice marshal greeted us and suggested we park our ships in the RAF Brewster Buffalo dispersal area. George and Black Mac McGarry took off for some more patrol work over the convoy.

Blackie Blackburn and I got a jeep and drove to a small town, Yenangyaung, about thirty miles out of Magwe. We had heard that there were quite a few Americans there, oil people. Also there was supposed to be a fairly good American-style club there. We met several oil people who were very nice to us, and we took a swim in the club pool and had a few drinks. Apparently we were right in the middle of an oil field. The horizon was broken in all directions by towering oil-well derricks.

We were late getting back to the field at Magwe. I was thirty minutes late for a meeting in which I was to meet the head RAF officers. I was greeted and reintroduced to Air Vice Marshal D. F. Stevenson, commander of the RAF in Burma, whom I had met upon my landing. We had a very pleasant dinner and exchanged views about the war in Southeast Asia. I departed about midnight and went to the pilots' mess, where I found my empty bunk and turned in with my clothes on. What a miserable night. It was much chillier than Rangoon, and the mosquitoes had a feast.

February 28, 1942

An English breakfast was something new to me compared to what I had been eating in Rangoon. The tea just didn't grab me.

I caught a ride to the dispersal area with an RAF pilot who flies women and children out of here to Akyab, India, in a BT-9, the basic trainer I had flown years ago at Randolph Air Field. How he gets two women and two small kids in that two-seated aircraft amazes me. I think he takes one of the small children in his lap.

Our spare P-40 tires and oxygen have arrived, but engine spares are still en route. George and Black Mac showed up about nine, and we worked out an alert schedule. I took off for the local polo field, which was set up as a camp for our airmen. They had completed the trek from Rangoon and were tired, dirty, and sweaty. Their morale was just about rock bottom and they were threatening to quit. I got them together and gave them a pep talk to try to cheer them up, but I have to admit that it was difficult to find subject matter that would fit.

Had a scramble alert about noon and cruised around for about an hour—no Japs. Our alert shack is a tent, and the field is nothing compared to Mingaladon—a very dusty long runway. Hot as hell during the day, and it reminded me of a field in West Texas or Arizona.

The RAF headquarters called a meeting and reviewed our operations plans for the next few days. Our AVG contingent has the primary mission of local air defense.

While at the meeting I got a phone call from Snuffy Smith, who was at Myingyan, about a hundred miles to the north. He attempted a landing in an open area after getting lost on the flight from Rangoon. He got one propeller tip and banged up one wheel. He said he could fly it out if he could get replacement parts. He and Bob Neale had no maps when they left Haig field. The alarming part was that he didn't know the whereabouts of Neale. They had gotten separated. I told Smitty to stay in touch. What to do?

Later, I was in the midst of a frustrating phone conversation with an operator who spoke very little English when suddenly Neale's voice boomed in loud and clear: "Charlie! Charlie! That you?"

"Yeah Bob! That you?" I answered, "Where are you? You okay?"

Bob responded: "Yeah, I'm fine. I landed in an open field near this little town of Singu. The plane is okay, but I need some gas. Looks like I'm about forty miles north of Magwe. Get some gas up here, and I can fly it out."

I told him I'd get gas tomorrow and hung up. What a relief. I couldn't help but recall a comment old Bob had made to me when I left him at Haig concerning navigation and no maps. In his jovial style he tried to reassure me about finding Magwe: "Gol'darn, Charlie, you can't get lost. Hell, it's right on the river." Indeed, the Magwe strip is on the Irrawaddy River, but the haze and dust over this barren area together with no maps while flying over the country for the first time is ticklish business.

March 1, 1942

I got in my ship and took off to the north to look for Bob Neale and Smitty. The airmen should have been on their way an hour earlier. I didn't have much trouble locating Bob, since he had told me he had landed in an open area and got away with it. That fact narrowed the areas down considerably. There he was, waving like mad. He had slept under the wing all night, for I could see a cot. Many natives were hanging around. I scribbled a note that the airmen were on their way with gas, dropped it to him on a low pass, and went off looking for Smitty. No luck in locating Smitty, so I went back to the field.

I lolled around in the alert tent the remainder of the day until I got interested in a B-24 that was landing and had the Army Air Corps insignia on it. I drove up to see who it might be and gee, it was old Horace Wade, an upper classmate of mine. How great. We traded stories for quite a while while they refueled his plane. He told me of the aerial combat on other Pacific fronts and said the Japanese Navy Zeros were giving them a hard time. Our pilots in other areas, however, are beginning to fight like we do, and things are getting better. He said men with six months' experience are flying B-17s across the Pacific. I figured it would be that way one of these days, but I had no idea it would be so soon.

Took Wade to lunch at the pilots' mess. While eating we were interupted by an RAF Blenheim trying to abort a takeoff and smashing into the end of the runway. The irony was that I had just been telling Wade about the many RAF crackups on the field.

Wade had brought General Wavell and Maj. Gen. Lewis Brereton into Magwe for a planning conference. Chennault has not come down, and I wasn't invited to represent our tiny AVG outfit. If they are going to do anything they had better do it quick, for the rumors are that the British Army plans a retreat to the Prome area just south of here.

I said goodbye to Wade and again took off looking for Smitty; still no luck!

What I thought were RAF men actually are New Zealand pilots. Good guys, and very much like Americans. They have been flying Brewster Buffaloes and now are being checked out in Hurricanes. One of them cracked up on landing and tore the gear off.

I caught sight of Bob Neale in the traffic pattern and went down to meet him. He nearly overshot his landing, since the haze is so bad that it is difficult to tell the runway from the rest of the field. We got a kick out of razzing him, and I got my two cents in! "Famous last words. It's on a river. You can't get lost." He just grinned at me.

March 2, 1942

Bob and I talked over the situation this morning and I brought him up to date on what had transpired while he was in the boonies. The RAF told me they heard a newscast that Bob has been awarded the British Distinguished Service Order. I told him about it. He sure as hell deserves it.

March 3, 1942

Bob Neale told me to take Blackie Blackburn and fly up to Kunming. We could swap P-40s for better ones. The main reason for the flight, however, was to take a letter to Chennault from Air Marshal Stevenson. I took off. My engine was cutting out at times, and my compass was off. Fortunately I knew the compass problem and allowed for it and just trusted the engine. Found Lashio and landed. While having a snack with tea, I had a chat with a colonel in the Chinese Army. He knew I would see Chennault, so he asked me if I would give him a message. I nodded and he wrote a note urging the Old Man to come to Lashio for some high-level discussion. General Wavell is here, and so is the generalissimo. Chinese troops have moved south into Burma and are headed for Toungoo to stop the Japanese advance. Obviously the British and Chinese are beginning to combine their operations.

Blackie and I took off for Kunming. Hit it on the nose in spite of my compass and went right in to see the Old Man. He was in good spirits and greeted me warmly. There wasn't much to pass on to Bob Neale, however, for we have to wait until after the Lashio conference.

It is like heaven being back at Kunming and having my old room available. The AVG was invited to the theater in town tonight: *They Met in Bombay* with Clark Gable and Jane Russell.

Madame Chiang Kai-shek was there and hailed us as heroes. She is our honorary commander. A very attractive woman and impeccably dressed in her mandarin gown. A real diplomat and a real charmer. She told us we would get our five-hundred-dollar bonuses as promised!

March 4, 1942

Newkirk's Second Squadron swapped a couple of good P-40s for our two clunkers and we started cranking them up. Blackie's air speed indicator was out; I couldn't even get started. What a hell of a note!

It would take a while to get the ships ready, so I went over to the operations office to check weather and see if I knew any of the U.S.

Army Air Corps people gathered around an old DC-3. General Magruder, General Stilwell, several colonels and majors, all U.S. Army, were standing around chatting about the war situation. I introduced myself to General Stilwell and told him about our experiences so far. He was interested in the Rangoon stories, and his mood was definitely pessimistic. He said the situation was bad. General MacArthur's stand in the Philippines and the AVG successes were the main topics back in the States. The hatred of the Japanese in the States has swelled and intensified. And he said: "The Japs shall surely pay. The U.S. is to start their offensive in China, and the defense of Burma will be turned over to the Chinese." More talk revealed that the British would defend India, and seventy-five DC-3's would be allocated to fly army supplies and equipment from Cairo to Chungking.[1]

Our planes were ready, and just as we started taxiing for takeoff, Olie Olsen, commander of the Third Squadron, blocked me in his jeep. Chennault wanted to see me again. The Old Man said the plan is to replace our squadron with Olie's outfit in the Magwe area, and I am to relay this to Bob Neale.

Upon returning I immediately went into session with Bob. We grabbed a jeep and drove to the American club to clue in the pilots and men. While driving, Bob and I talked and concluded that we should try to convince the Old Man to let us stay here. Perhaps he would change his mind if Bob put up a good plea. We then will continue to be in the main action. I had let Bob know of the discontent and low morale of the others at Kunming. They were really doing nothing and felt left out. Our pilots and men took the information with mixed emotions. They seem ready to rotate, for quite a number of them took exception to Bob's idea of staying.

We got in our jeep and started back to Magwe. On the way Bob told me that he had recommended Bob Little and me for the Distinguished Flying Cross. I am happy about that and thanked him.

One last thing before getting into my hammock: when in Kunming I was handed a cablegram from Doris. What a shot in the arm. How wonderful! Hell, I guess I will marry her when I get back.

[1] After this meeting on March 4, Stilwell recorded in his diary: "To airfield to wait for Chennault. Had a talk. He'll be O.K. Met a group of the pilots, they look damn good." *The Stilwell Papers*, p. 49.

March 5, 1942

Bob Neale and I took a gaggle of P-40s over to Namsang, a small RAF airstrip some 175 miles to the east just north of Thailand. We were to refuel there and join up with three RAF Brewster fighters, six Hurricanes and eight Blenheim bombers. The plan was to bomb Lampang airport in north central Thailand, where the Japanese supposedly had set up a major airbase.

The Blenheims came by and headed straight out without circling the field as briefed. The circling maneuver would have given us time to scramble off and rendezvous with them. We took off anyhow and tried our best to overtake them: the haze made it impossible. Trying to do our part, we flew on down into Thailand about halfway to Lampang. Still no bombers and no enemy, either. Back we went to Namsang. Once on the ground we learned that the entire mission was a complete fiasco. The Blenheims had gotten lost and landed at Heho, a small RAF field just west of Namsang. We brought our guys back to Magwe, utterly disgusted.

March 6, 1942

Four of the Third Squadron pilots came in today, and Bob met with them to plan their replacing us; we have given up the idea of trying to get the Old Man to let us stay.

Two reporters had driven over from Maymyo to interview us and write stories for the papers back home. One was United Press correspondent Darrell Berigan, who had been with us a few days at Rangoon. They had two English girls with them, and they were knockouts. They were introduced and I found it hard to talk with Berigan instead of his girl friend.

Col. Charlie Caldwell, one of my old B-17 flight leaders at Langley Field, Virginia, is in Tenth Air Force headquarters in New Delhi and landed here today. He and a couple other bomber pilots are flying in British Fusilier troops and taking Indian troops home.

March 7, 1942

Still at Magwe. We were ready to pull out when we heard the story of Pappy Boyington leading a fight of five P-40s on an escort mission protecting the generalissimo. On the way back to Kunming they got lost, and all five had to make belly landings. One went down very close to the Indochina border. Now there must be some shuffling to take care of these losses.

Had a good dinner tonight with the RAF boys and listened to the stories of the bomber pilots who had been in combat in Libya.

March 8, 1942

We were on alert all day long. The Japs haven't made any attacks on Magwe. The British Army is retreating up the Prome Road. Rangoon has been destroyed to make it as useless as possible to the Japs. I will be glad when the Chinese troops make contact with the advancing Japs.

March 10, 1942

Up and on alert at 7:00 this morning. The New Zealand Brewster RAF outfit pulled out and went to Calcutta. Saw the B-17s coming in and went down to chat.

Bob Neale and I went to the American Club tonight, and we witnessed a pathetic sight: a swarm of evacuees—mostly women and their babies. How pitiful—the worried and panicky faces of those mothers. They're moving through here to Magwe for evacuation to India.

Bob bought a bottle of champagne and we got a little buzz on. On the way back to Magwe, Bob talked to me about the outfit. He says he wants to make me his vice squadron leader. I thought about Pappy and wondered what he would think.

March 11, 1942

Olie Olsen and Fritz Wolf arrived. The Third Squadron now has seven pilots here. Olie told us of the low morale of the guys at Kunming; said it was a mess. Bob Prescott went into Lashio on the way here, engine trouble. Another flight of six led by Duke Hedman got lost and had to belly land wherever they could. Two may be capable of being salvaged. Hell's bells! That makes nine P-40s lost in the last two or three days! Olie said four or five of the pilots are quitting, and some of the men have already resigned.

An unusual event occurred tonight that really stirred us. We were in the middle of dinner when someone noticed a huge fire billow just west of the field. I wondered if it was the damaged Blenheim that had been circling the field for the last hour. It was. The Blenheim was one

125

of a formation that had gone south to hit the Japs near Pegu. The pilot had caught some antiaircraft fire in his head and was killed instantly. The observer was trying to fly the plane and was too scared to try to land it. He had ordered the gunner to bail out, and he had shoved the body of the pilot out with a long lanyard on his chute rip cord to save his body. Then the observer bailed out and the ship crashed.

Dog tired tonight, so I turned in early but could not go to sleep. I guess I wanted to do some soul-searching. I tried to imagine what the reactions of Mom and Dad and Doris would be when they read Darrell Berigan's stories about us and my quotes. I also thought about the recommendation for the Distinguished Flying Cross and felt rather proud. Then I recalled Doris's last wire in which she said she would come over here if she could be with me. I'm going to sleep on that.

March 12, 1942

Leland Stowe, another correspondent, came by to get some poop for a story on us. Says he is going to Russia from here.

This afternoon a Chinese DC-2 came in from Kunming, and out stepped about twenty of the Third Squadron men along with Dick Rossi and Frank Swartz. We are scheduled to leave tomorrow and return to Kunming. Took Dick and Frank with me and hustled some blankets and cots for the airmen.

I learned a lot of disquieting news about the situation in Kunming. Seems like most of the guys have started thinking about making money rather than fighting the war and that everyone is disgruntled about one thing or another. Bob Little is now the group engineering officer. The responsibilities of the squadrons in Kunming have been usurped by the group headquarters—centralized. The airmen have little to do and as a result get restless and irritated, or drunk. Looks like Bob Neale and I are in for tough going when we get there. Matt Kuykendall and Joe Rosbert went on a tear and ended up shooting their pistols in the air. They also beat up one of the Allison engine men. They are now under arrest and confined to their rooms. Pappy Boyington and Bob Layher finally hitchhiked to Kunming after their lost-flight belly landings. They were physical wrecks. George Burgard and Black Mac McGarry took off from Kunming to look for the other flight of five, led by Duke Hedman, and now Black Mac is missing, and so is Bob Prescott, who tried to get to Magwe from Lashio. What in hell is happening to the outfit?

March 13, 1942

All of our remaining airmen and pilots of the First Squadron boarded the DC-2 and took off for Kunming. A very comfortable flight, for I didn't have to worry about navigation. These old Chinese Air Corps boys knew the country like the back of their hand.

Kunming looked like heaven after dusty, humid Magwe. My room is luxury compared to Magwe, and I straightened it up and spent a few minutes telling Jim Cross goodbye for his two-week recuperation leave in Calcutta. I suppose his bad luck and shrapnel wounds are still getting him down.

Took a ride over to the main hostel on the other side of the city to pick up our new AVG insignia that Walt Disney designed for us—the Flying Tigers. The emblem is a tiger with all legs outstretched as though in flight, leaping out of the angle of a blue V for victory. His snarl shows his fangs and his claws. A clever little insignia. Of course it is a cross of a tiger shark (like on the nose of our P-40s), the Asian tiger, and the tiger spirit of a gung-ho American fighter pilot.

General Chennault took Bob Neale and me and several others with Harvey and Olga Greenlaw to the number-one Kunming Chinese restaurant for a big dinner. The food was great.

March 14, 1942

More problems. Heard this morning that John Dean and Carl Brown are on the carpet for something. Never did get the whole story, but I was not a bit surprised. Bob Neale is running into trouble, as I thought he would, in moving me up to vice squadron leader. Pappy Boyington is bound to react, and it may cause some hard feelings.

Went to the movies tonight, and it was *The Shopworn Angel*, a war movie with all of the horrors. Even though we are in the middle of a war, I guess we have not thought too seriously about it: frightening and very, very depressing. As a matter of fact, it got me thinking about when I will stop dreaming of fighting the Japs in aerial combat. Every night I go through this, usually waking up in a cold sweat. Many of the other pilots say they have the same experience.

I noticed a small Chinese boy huddled in a corner of a building entrance as I entered the theater. He seemed to be asleep. I stood there and looked at him for a long time. I felt nothing but pure pity: the poor little guy. When we came out of the theater he was still there, this time with a companion huddled up against him. Both were just children, little kids. They were in rags and filthy. I wish I had dropped some money in their laps. I thought about that scene until falling asleep.

March 16, 1942

Went out to the field and sat around shooting the bull with the Second Squadron pilots. Hear that when we get at least six of our P-40s back in commission, we can operate on our own.

Went to the funeral on the outskirts of the city this afternoon for Colonel George of the U.S. Army Air Corps and three other Americans who were on a Chinese DC-3 that crashed yesterday. Seventeen were killed. We stood at attention as Padre Paul Frillmann, our AVG chaplain, officiated. Four Chinese coffins with the bodies of four Americans. Where we got four American flags, I'll never know. I was glad when it was over.

March 18, 1942

Turned on the radio news as usual and heard that General Douglas MacArthur has flown to Australia to take command of the Southwest Asian area. More power to him.

Heard that the Third Squadron got fifteen Jap planes on the ground at Moulmein at dawn yesterday. William Reed and Ken Jernstedt caught them by surprise and in strafing passes set all of them on fire. Why the Japs park their aircraft the way they do defeats me! They just don't seem to realize the advantages of dispersal. Robert "Moose" Moss got one a few days ago when he caught some Jap boats entering the Irrawaddy River. He started strafing them, and they had a flight of five fighters as cover. He got one of them.

March 19, 1942

While playing cards and losing money I was cheered by the news from San Francisco. The U.S. Army Air Corps and the Australian Air Force dealt some blows to the Japanese Navy—sank twenty-three ships off New Guinea in the Coral Sea! Also, the Russians are going strong, and then all of a sudden the announcer said, "The AVG did it again," and he told about the Third Squadron's strike at Moulmein. He talked it up—terrific![2]

March 20, 1942

I saw a woman tonight at the theater who, without a doubt, was one of the most beautiful girls I have ever seen. She was Euro-Asian and Bob Smith knew her—a Miss Hall. He wouldn't introduce me, but it made no difference. I just stood there and ate her up with my eyes. She knew it and liked it. Maybe I can meet her later some time. I'll have to corner Smitty.

When I returned from the theater and entered my room, there sat Pappy Boyington, Red Probst, Bill Bartling, and Matt Kuykendall—all stewed to the gills. They had gotten into my Dry Sac sherry and scotch and were now drinking my gin. What a riot! After getting tomorrow's alert schedule from Red, I tried to get them to leave. Every one of us in the room was on alert tomorrow morning. Bartling was fairly sober, but Pappy was really feeling his oats and as usual was wanting to fight with someone. He picked out Bartling for some reason or other and told him to slug him first. Bart would not swing at him but stood his ground and told Pappy to slug him first. This was ridiculous! Pappy jabbed out and clipped Bart on the chin. It flew all over me. I grabbed Pappy and pulled him aside. It took all the persuasion I ever had to keep Pappy from powdering me, but I was sober and he wasn't. I ended up telling Pappy off, but I don't think it phased him. Pappy wants to fight me more than any other guy in the Flying Tigers.[3] It didn't register at the time, but I guess the vice squadron leader replacement deal was at the core of the problem. I did a lot of talking and his belligerence finally subsided. I told him that one of these days we would decide who could "knock the other one on his can." Pappy is a powerful man. No telling what would happen. He is shorter than I am but outweighs me by at least thirty pounds. He's built like a bull. I finally got him to leave and go to bed.

[2] The *New York Times* carried the story on page one of the March 19 issue: "U.S. Flyers Raid Moulmein." It reported that "nine Japanese pursuit planes, two bombers and four transports were left blazing."

[3] Boyington wrote in his memoirs about this period of his life: "I was an emotionally immature person of the first order, which does not help peace of mind or make happiness. Frankly, this is what makes screwballs, and I'm afraid that I was one." *Baa, Baa, Black Sheep*, p. 102. He also describes his role in the raid on Chiang Mai on pp. 96–100.

March 21, 1942

A lot of us were late this morning for alert duty, and Bob Neale raised hell. He really got on Pappy.

Bob Neale and I got together with Skip Adair in the evening and discussed the entire Kunming AVG situation. We have lost thirteen pilots since the AVG was formed over here, but very few were lost in actual combat. We now have about 260 people in the Flying Tigers.

March 22, 1942

Magwe was really hit yesterday by the Japs! Some sixty Jap bombers with about twenty Model Zero fighters hit the field in three waves. Olie Olson's Third Squadron got two Zeros. Frank Swartz was wounded, and John Fauth, a crew chief, was killed during the bombing. They had about two minutes of warning.

We were still digesting the bad news when Bob Neale came in and told me to get ready: "We're going to make them pay." The Old Man has directed a retaliatory mission on the Jap Air Force headquarters in Southeast Asia. Neale, Boyington, McGarry, Bartling, and myself, together with Jack Newkirk, the squadron commander of the Second Squadron, and four of his pilots are to draw up plans to hit the Jap airbase at Chiang Mai, Thailand.

At noon we took off for Loiwing, China, en route to Lashio and Namsang, Burma, and then Chiang Mai. My old ship, No. 5, was back in commission, so I took it. Neale is in command. Jack Newkirk led the flight because Bob has never been to Loiwing. We wandered all over the sky until we hit the Salween River. At this point Jack turned south when he should have turned north. I was convinced Jack was wrong and I checked everything I could see. Bob, Bartling, and I came into Loiwing after giving up trying to get Jack to turn back north.

I landed a bit fast and overran the runway extension. A small narrow-gauge railroad runs across the runway extension, and I blew my tail wheel tire on the tracks. It will have to be replaced. Refueling all of us took too long, and Newkirk's flight finally got in late, so we are staying over until tomorrow. What a break for me! My plane will be repaired easily.

Loiwing is really a depot for the Flying Tigers. There is an American Club, and two American ladies act just like our mothers. We sit in overstuffed chairs and eat great food. There are three huge windows which overlook the beautiful river valley and provide a panoramic view of the distant mountains.

Many of the AVG are here on their way out of Burma. F. E. Fox and his convoy are here, and he says there must be at least thirty P-40s here and eighteen of them can be put in commission in a short time with some help and parts.

Finally we turned in—on Simmons mattresses!

March 23, 1942

We were up at 5:30 and rode out to the parking area during a foggy, drizzly dawn. At least we didn't have to worry about a Jap strike in this weather.

Some of Olie's Third Squadron boys came in under the ceiling with the remaining P-40s from Magwe—Fritz Wolf, Fred Hodges, John Croft, and Moose Moss. They told us of the Jap raid there two days ago. Three waves of bombers came over with plenty of Zero escorts. Their bombing was excellent, destroying practically all the Blenheims and Hurricanes. They got six to eight of our P-40s. No warning at all. The dispersal satellite field right out of Magwe was also hit, and the RAF must have lost at least seventy men out there from the bombing.

As usual we got the funniest and most entertaining story out of Moose Moss, a Georgia boy. He told us that he and Hodges ended up in the same ditch trying to hide from the bombing, and Hodges was clawing at the dirt trying to get further under the bank while pushing the dirt under Moose, who was becoming more exposed by the minute! We cracked up.

Fritz was in a ditch by himself, and he said it was the loneliest feeling in the world to be there alone while the bombs fell all around. He said he prayed, and that he was sure he whimpered at times—and he is no baby! The concussion of the closer bombs lifted him off the ground several times. He threw up once.

Frank Swartz and John Fauth were wandering around after the raid waving their hands for help. They were bloodied all over. Fauth's ribs were exposed on one side and part of his lower left jaw was blown away. Swartz had a huge gash under his left jaw and had lost part of a hand. Moose grabbed them and loaded them into his jeep, but as he started off the field he narrowly missed a delayed-action bomblet.

All of the men and the pilots have been deeply affected by that bombing. They have a fear of bombing imprinted in their minds, and I can understand it.

After talking to the Magwe survivors, we got back to our business. Bob Neale and I had a long discussion about top cover. I argued with him at length, since I was depending on the element of surprise for a dawn attack. We could use everybody for strafing.

About 3:00 p.m. we decided to leave for Namsang. We went by way of Lashio and Heho. The weather was as hazy as usual. I flew on Bob's wing, but I kept my thumb on my map for my own navigation. Upon landing we dispersed our ships in two groups, one at the end of each of the two intersecting strips. We lined up five trucks on the left side of each of the two runways. In between we made arrangements to intersperse lanterns. These were to be our predawn takeoff aids.

We ate at the RAF mess. Then at the barracks we had a last-minute review of our plans. We will rise early.

March 24, 1942

A Burmese native woke us at 4:05 and we got into our clothes quickly. As I was pulling on my shoes an RAF officer burst in and shouted, "All right, you curly-headed fellows, it's time!" It was chilly, and we were kidding and gabbing just to keep our spirits up until we got to the breakfast table.

By 5:25 we were in the cockpits warming up the planes. There were ten of us. It was pitch dark, and some had never taken a plane off at night. Since there were no lights for reference, we parked an old truck at the far end of the grass strip and turned on the headlights. This was our aiming point for takeoff.

Bob Neale, our leader, took off and I followed him. It was 6:10. When I pushed the throttle open, the blue exhaust flames whipped around the lower sides of my windshield and trailed along the fuselage to the rear of my vision. I aimed at the truck lights and felt my way along the grass strip until the wheels felt light. A little bit of back pressure on the stick, and I was free of the ground. I couldn't see a thing. I went on instruments. My basic reference was my rate of climb indicator. As long as it showed "up," I felt reasonably assured. A few seconds later I relaxed and looked up for Bob's navigation lights. There his plane was, slightly to the left and above me. I followed and wondered how in hell those other guys will make it to rendezvous over the field at ten thousand feet.

Our plan called for me to fly Bob's right wing in number two position, for I had flown over the area before and had reconnoitered Chiang Mai Airfield. Bob had never seen the base. Pappy Boyington and Bill Bartling were numbers three and four, and then came Eddie Rector and Black Mac McGarry as a top-cover element of two ships. Jack Newkirk was leading another flight with Hank Geselbracht on his wing, followed by his second element of Frank Lawlor and Bus Keeton. They would attack a small field south of Chiang Mai at Lampang.

Bartling, who had never flown an aircraft at night, was to join up with Boyington. As he approached ten thousand feet and cuddled up next to his flight leader, he saw the number 7, Bob Neale's P-40. He dropped back and I slipped into place. Pappy was close behind, and soon we were in formation making a last circle around the field just as dawn was beginning to break across the eastern mountain tops. We couldn't pick up Newkirk's flight, so we struck off, as planned, on a course of 150 degrees.

The early-morning haze hid any landmark that would have been helpful, but I could not miss the deep Salween River gorge as we passed over it. I estimated a ground speed of 230 MPH, and figured Chiang Mai Airfield at 7:12.

About 7:10 and for some five minutes prior to that I had decided that the towering mountain to our left front was the identification point. The airfield was at the southeast edge of that mountain; I remembered it well. I edged in close to Bob's right wingtip, and he sensed that I was trying to tell him something. Radio was taboo on this mission. Yet we were abreast of the mountain and Bob was still looking forward, so I waggled my wings—almost touching his—and pulled forward with a slight throttle burst tapping my head with my left hand. I took over, and Bob, understanding readily, fell back on my left wing.

I nosed downward in a gentle left turn and hoped I was right. At about six thousand feet, and as the haze thinned, I saw the field and outlines of the hangars. I flipped on my gun switch, and another thousand feet lower I fired my guns in a short burst to check them and let the other guys know this was it—the main Japanese Air Force of Southeast Asia!

I positioned myself to cross the field the longest way, seeing a line of parked Japanese I-97 fighters. I pulled back slightly, preparing to strafe the entire line. Now it was clear: we had caught them flat-footed without any warning.

I made my first strafing run firing everything into the I-97s. At the end I remained low and turned sharply to the left. I got a glimpse of Bartling's plane zipping past, just to the rear. After turning 270 degrees I was in a position to strafe another line of parked aircraft. These were sitting practically wingtip to wingtip. Hell, I hadn't seen this many aircraft in years. Seemed like the whole Japanese Air Force had tried to crowd into this one little field. I couldn't miss.

I squeezed the trigger again. Damn it! My fifties wouldn't go! I charged them quickly; they caught. I steadied my aim and strafed the entire line of ships. I was so low that it seemed as though my prop tips would clip the heads of Jap pilots who by now were trying to get into their cockpits. Other men, evidently maintenance people, were lying flat on the ground nearby. Props were turning on some of the fighters, but not a single aircraft was taxiing. As I completed my second run, I looked to the area I strafed first: three aircraft were in flames.

I turned sharply to the right to better assess the damage, and just at the right time. Tracer bullets flew all around; it was obvious they were meant for me. The antiaircraft defenses had come to life, but they still were frantic and disorganized. Puffs of black smoke appeared about a thousand feet above the field, which made me wonder about Ed Rector and Black Mac McGarry, who were assigned the job as top cover. I craned my neck searching for enemy aircraft in the air: none!

I lined up for my third pass. This time the direction was northwest. I turned too quickly and didn't line up well. I aimed poorly and fired. Ricochets did some harm, but I wanted a better finale.

I extended my third pass a little longer so I could make another 270-degree turn for a final pass, this time down the original line of aircraft of my first pass. With more time and better light I could do a better job. A large Jap plane stood out from the others; perhaps it was a reconnaissance ship. I settled on it as my primary and let go. As I bore on it, firing, it seemed to shake itself to pieces. With only inches to spare, I pulled off and raked other aircraft with my fire. God only knows how many planes were damaged or destroyed in that pass.

Only seven or eight minutes had passed, and I had seen only one P-40, Bartling's. Banking again, I caught a glimpse of three aircraft to my upper right. I choked! Were they Japs? Nope! Three P-40s pulling off the attack.

To hell with pushing my luck. Seldom does one get two passes, much less three or four, in a strafing mission. I pulled up to join the other P-40s.

The antiaircraft puffs were more numerous now, but they were way above me at this point. I looked back at the field as I rounded the southwest corner of the mountain, and it did my heart good. What satisfaction!

The resulting destruction of the successive passes in that ten to twelve minutes of aerial attack is too much to describe. The entire airfield seemed to be in flames as we headed back to Burma. We apparently caught them as they were preparing a major concentration of aircraft for a big strike against us in China. It was a mission accomplished exactly according to Chennault's plan. How proud he would be. Hell, I was!

Heading back, I soon found three of the guys on my wing—Ed Rector, McGarry, and Bartling. Constantly on the alert that we were not being followed by some Japs, I continually looked around. It was this worry that drew my attention to one of the P-40s wildly wagging his wings and dropping back and lower. Something was wrong. I circled around and came along next to Black Mac's ship. He was losing altitude rapidly and slowing down. Neither Ed nor I could stay with him even at greatly reduced throttle. He kept heading west, and we kept steering him northwards. The Salween River was just ahead, separating Thailand from Burma, and we wanted him to get to the other side of that landmark. He rolled his canopy back, and his ship started trailing smoke.

Suddenly his aircraft rolled over, and Mac bailed out about a thousand feet above the treetops. His plane nosed down sharply and crashed in a ball of fire. Mac's chute blossomed open and he drifted downward. He hit in a small glade on a large plateau some three hundred yards from his burning plane. He was okay—up on his feet and waving at us. We circled him.

In an effort to help him in some way, I drew a circle on the map indicating where I thought he was and wrote 7:41 A.M. near the circle. Buzzing him the last time, I dropped the map right on him and then headed northwest towards Namsang. He hit the ground about twenty-five or thirty miles southeast of the Salween River and has some rough, mountainous jungles to go through to get to the river. If he can make the river, he'll be fairly safe.

I spotted the RAF field at Namsang. We landed and found Bob Neale and Pappy already there. Bob was stunned when I told him of Mac's predicament. The RAF commander of the field promised the fullest assistance to locate and rescue him.

We were ecstatic over the success of our strike and spent the refueling time congratulating each other. Yet I couldn't get Mac off my mind, and I still was a bit concerned about the possibility of a follow-up Jap strike on us. When all planes were refueled, we took off and headed west to Heho, the small strip on which Jack Newkirk's flight had planned to recover after their attack on Lampang. There were no P-40s at Heho, so we headed on towards Lashio, where Ed Rector landed to report Mac's situation to the British Army headquarters. The rest of us flew to Loiwing.

We made a screaming dive and buzzed the field in a victory formation pass. Then in a sharp climbing turn to string out for landing, I was startled by a loud bang followed by a staccato noise. I pulled the throttle back, sure that my engine had blown up. A quick check of all instruments, however, showed all normal. I started examining all exterior parts of the aircraft, and there it was: a ripped and torn refueling flap on my inner left wing panel. What a relief. How horrible to end up such a terrific day with a crash landing at the home base.

Once on the ground we got together and assembled the AVGers at Loiwing to recap our experience and critique the mission. We found additional good news—and also additional bad news. Jack Newkirk's flight of four had rendezvoused after takeoff at about six thousand feet over the field and then headed out. This put them in the Chiang Mai area a few minutes ahead of us. For some reason or other, while flying down to attack Lampang, they decided to strafe the Chiang Mai railroad depot. Then, after finding no Jap aircraft on the field at Lampang, they started back up the railroad and strafed secondary targets all along the way. They were having a heyday of a time at first, arriving close to the Chiang Mai field some twenty minutes after our attack. They then encountered fairly heavy antiaircraft fire. The Japs had recovered in the area. Jack Newkirk, according to Geselbracht and Lawlor, had apparently spotted what appeared to be a Japanese tank or armored vehicle and went down to strafe it. He never pulled out. We don't know whether he was hit and couldn't pull out or he waited too long to pull out. He crashed and left a ball of fire along the road for some two hundred yards. He must have hit the ground at 275 MPH.

Lawlor and Keeton confirmed the damage at Chiang Mai. The smoke boiled upwards several hundred feet over the field and covered the entire area. It looked as though the entire airfield was in flames.

Our critique was interrupted by the air-raid siren, and we ran for the ditches while Bob Prescott, Fritz Wolf, Roy Hodges, Moose Moss, and Bob Brouk took off in our refueled aircraft to repel any possible Jap attack on Loiwing. Again our fears were unfounded—no attack.

At the clubhouse Mrs. Davidson fixed us lunch, and Chuck Hunter, the Allison engine man, gave us a drink—which we needed by this time. Bob Neale prepared a message for the Old Man in Kunming.

Soon we were in the bar—the whole gang—celebrating the day's work. It's surprising how quickly one gets over the horrible loss of his buddies in wartime and revels in the successes of the day. Everyone was laughing and enjoying the moment. Yet Jack was gone and we weren't sure of Black Mac. It makes one wonder about the nature of human beings.

There had to be at least fifty Japanese aircraft on Chiang Mai Airfield. I am convinced that we must have destroyed at least twenty-five or thirty of them. Wingtip to wingtip, the exploding, fiery debris from one aircraft would have destroyed adjacent planes. Indeed, this was a great success for the AVG and the Allies. But can the AVG afford to lose such men as Jack Newkirk and Mac McGarry and two P-40 aircraft in these times? We wonder. . . .

*   *   *

Casualties were mounting. Frank Swartz and John Fauth died after the Japanese raid on Magwe, and William McGarry wandered in the jungle for twenty-eight days before he met another human—Thai officials who arrested him and put him in jail in Bangkok. Fortunately, the Thais never gave him to the Japanese, and he sat out the war until early 1945, when American agents cooperating with members of the Thai resistance freed him and flew him to Kunming.

Nevertheless, the raid on Chiang Mai was a complete success, even better than the pilots had thought. Stalling the Japanese advance, it gave valuable time to the British. Air Vice Marshal Stevenson wrote Chennault, "Many thanks for the breathing spell furnished us by your magnificent attack." The raid was received more enthusiastically in the American press. New York Times headlines ran, "U.S. Fliers in Burma Smash 40 Planes," and continued that pilots of the American Volunteer Group "caught the Japanese pilots as they were running to the cockpits of their planes and pumped 3,500 rounds of ammunition into both grounded planes and personnel. Seven Japanese planes were seen bursting into flames and the remainder were riddled with machine-gun bursts." It was a great day for the AVG, and for the Allies.[4]

[4] *New York Times*, March 25, 1942. For an account of the raid and Jack Newkirk's death, see *Newsweek*, April 6, 1942, p. 20.

6. Shot Down

The raid on Chiang Mai halted the Japanese advance, but only temporarily. The Allies were forced to continue evacuating Burma. Early in April the enemy smashed General Stilwell's Chinese division and British troops north of Toungoo, opening the way for a Japanese advance into northern Burma and threatening southern China.

The task for the AVG was enormous. To meet the enemy, Chennault deployed Olie Olson's Third Squadron and eventually Tex Hill's Second Squadron at Loiwing, close to the Chinese-Burma border. He kept the First Squadron in reserve at Kunming.

The Japanese Air Force had recovered from the Chiang Mai raid by April 8, and twenty Zeros attacked Loiwing. Their raid failed, thanks to the early-warning system located in northern Burma. Along with a few RAF pilots, the Third Squadron got off the field and destroyed ten enemy fighters while losing only two British Hurricanes and two P-40s parked on the airstrip. Two days later five Zeros slipped through the warning net and struck the field, damaging nine P-40s. But the planes were hit superficially and back in action later that morning when the enemy struck again, this time with twenty-seven bombers. Fortunately, heavy overcast prevented the bombers from finding the field. Later that day, enemy fighters returned and were engaged by the Third Squadron. Olson's pilots shot down eight Zeros and then returned to their headquarters and put up a sign: "OLSON & CO., EXTERMINATORS—24 HR. SERVICE."

The Japanese relented in the air, but not on the ground. They continued their drive north, and this dismal military situation was one reason for a rising mood of pessimism and declining morale within the AVG. There also were other reasons. Some men were tired of combat, war-weary, while others who had not been at the front were bored and restless. Included in this latter group were men who had volunteered for the AVG to make money or get out of the military, not to risk their lives. Also, some pilots disliked escorting British Blenheim bombers, which flew so low that P-40 escorts became easy targets. Finally, another issue put the men on edge. It had become general knowledge that the AVG would be disbanded on July 4, but no one knew if they would be sent home or inducted into the Air Corps and ordered to remain in China.

Bad attitudes were becoming commonplace by April. Chennault reported that his files were packed with citations for men not maintaining physical condition, not being at their duty stations, or being drunk and disorderly. In fact, twenty-two pilots and forty-three crewmen had been kicked out of the group, most of them receiving dishonorable discharges.[1] By May only fifty-two pilots remained in the AVG.

Declining morale became more serious as Stilwell retreated in Burma. As theater commander he ordered Chennault to have the AVG conduct low-flying reconnaissance and strafing attacks—"morale missions" to boost the spirits of his demoralized Chinese troops. The Old Man and his pilots thought that these flights were a waste of precious fuel and ineffectual. Air-control communications did not exist between pilots and ground troops, and visibility was poor. Forest fires, fog, and clouds produced a smoky haze that made identification of the enemy almost impossible unless the pilot flew so low that he became an easy target. At times mistakes resulted, and friendly troops were strafed instead of the enemy.

The Old Man found himself in a dilemma. He disagreed with Stilwell and agreed with his pilots, but in April he was inducted into the U.S. Army Air Corp as a brigadier general, and his superior was Lieutenant General Stilwell. At the same time, he had a contract to fulfill with Chiang Kai-shek—to use his few planes to defend China against the Japanese Air Force. It is significant that most AVG personnel involved in daily combat were not aware either of the high-level bickering or that Chennault now was in the USAAC and had to take orders from Stilwell.[2]

This was the situation in mid-April at Loiwing when the pilots received orders not only for more "morale missions" but also for another strike against the Japanese air base at Chiang Mai. The mood was

---

[1] Chennault reported problems with his men in *Way of a Fighter*, p. 155.
[2] Discussion between Bond and Charlie Older, January 6, 1983.

becoming alarming. R. T. Smith of the Third Squadron recorded in his diary on April 17: "To top matters off the Chinese army, and of course the British, are being pushed back in Burma. Now they intend to hold the line and want us to give them air support. Our twelve ships against the whole damn Jap Air Force. It seems mighty futile to all of us and we're wondering what's taking the U.S. so damn long to get something over here. At this rate our morale won't be very good fast! Phooey!"

Under these circumstances Chennault left Kunming and flew to Loiwing. On April 18 he scheduled a meeting with the Second and Third squadrons. He informed them that he was a brigadier general in the USAAC and that he took his orders from Allied headquarters, that the situation was becoming grave, and that the pilots would have to fly more morale missions. Specifically, he ordered the Second and Third squadrons to escort Blenheim bombers on another raid against Chiang Mai. The Old Man said, "You have no choice." Otherwise, he would expect their resignations.

Chennault's blunt and threatening attitude took the men by surprise, and after the meeting they began to discuss the situation in increasingly defiant tones. Tempers flared, and a few became outraged and rebellious. They disliked such missions and remembered that Newkirk and McGarry had been lost in the first Chiang Mai raid. They drew up a petition which noted the overwhelming numerical superiority of the enemy air force, and dwindling numbers and poor condition of their own P-40s, and the fact that continuing the morale missions was dangerous and unreasonable. It concluded that unless some changes were made, they would refuse to fly and would tender their resignations. Of thirty-four pilots present, twenty-eight signed, and they gave the petition to the Old Man.

Chennault immediately scheduled a meeting for the next day, April 19. He told the men that he would not accept resignations. Any refusal to fly would be considered desertion in the face of the enemy, and, furthermore, those who would not fly were showing a "white feather." Being accused of cowardice was too much for one pilot, who rose and took vehement exception, especially considering the group's record and the size of the enemy forces. Chennault quickly retracted the statement but stood firm: the men would have to obey orders.

Tex Hill, a staunch supporter of the Old Man, then took the floor.

He felt that he was in a dilemma, disliking the missions but being a leader in the AVG. He stated that the war was no longer a matter of personal considerations, for that ended when Japan attacked Pearl Harbor. The United States was at war, so the AVG contracts were meaningless. He volunteered to lead anyone who would fly the mission.[3] Five others volunteered, and the rebellious spirit of the group quickly dissolved. Chennault tore up the petition and dismissed the pilots.

The affair had much more impact on Chennault than on his men. Seven years later when he published his memoirs, he still was angry and labeled the episode the "pilots' revolt." Actually, the men thought the morale missions were foolish, and as Pete Wright noted in his diary, "did not want any more taking orders from Stilwell." Perhaps R. T. Smith best summarized the men's feelings when he went back to his room and wrote that the pilots expected Chennault's behavior, "but we at least showed him what we thought of some of the missions and tactics employed. So he and all of us are forgetting the whole affair and carrying on as usual."[4]

The Chiang Mai mission scheduled for the next day never took place, since the bombers failed to rendezvous with the P-40s. It was a good thing. On April 19, Dick Rossi noted in his diary: "Of the 4 Tomahawks that were to strafe, two had oil trouble and would have had to come back, one was not filled with gas and would have had to return. The fourth plane burned out the generator and couldn't have fired its guns if it did get there." A few days later, on April 23, Madame Chiang Kai-shek ended the issue by informing Chennault that the AVG no longer had to fly low-level reconnaissnce or morale missions. In the future the group would be used for its original purpose—to defend China from the Japanese Air Force.

Meanwhile, the Japanese Army continued advancing. On April 20

---

[3] Discussions between Bond and Tex Hill, January 10 and 31, 1983.

[4] Chennault, *Way of a Fighter*, p. 156. Discussions between Bond and the following pilots who were at Loiwing: Charlie Older, January 6, 1983; Dick Rossi, December 14, 1982, and January 13, 1983; Pete Wright, January 16, 1983; Robert Hedman, February 12, 1983; Bus Keeton, January 6, 1983; and R. T. Smith, January 13, 1983. Discussion between Bond and Jim Howard, January 13, 1983. Pete Wright and R. T. Smith diaries, April 18, 1942.

it occupied Lashio, forcing the AVG to demolish the CAMCO factory and repair facility a few miles away at Loiwing, including burning sixteen unsalvageable P-40s. Five days later General Stilwell and his British counterpart, General Alexander, agreed that the only hope for survival was to evacuate Burma and retreat to India. Alexander boarded a plane, and Stilwell began his famous walk out of Burma.

Then the Japanese Air Force attacked. They had been waiting for April 28, the day before the emperor's birthday, so they could inform him on the next day that they had a present—knocking out the Flying Tigers. Chennault surmised that they would attack and was prepared. He had sent a reconnaissance mission into northern Burma, and it reported heavy activity at enemy airstrips. On the twenty-eighth a large flight of bombers and fighters attacked Lashio and Loiwing. The Japanese did succeed in damaging the airfield at Loiwing, but only after a tremendous sacrifice. By the end of the battle the Second and Third squadrons had not lost one plane while shooting down twenty-two enemy aircraft.

The Japanese Air Force again had been stung, but their ground forces continued to advance against a disorganized and demoralized Chinese Army. On April 29, Japanese tanks rolled into Lashio. By May 1 they crossed the Chinese border and occupied Loiwing. The enemy was on the Burma Road heading north, and no army stood in the way.

The enemy's advance forced the AVG to begin operations out of Paoshan and Yunnanyi while maintaining headquarters at Kunming. The Old Man ordered Bob Neale to deploy a flight of our Second Squadron to Paoshan, just northeast of Loiwing. After being stationed in Kunming and also ferrying new P-40Es from India to China, I was eager to see some action.

*   *   *

March 25, 1942

Fred Hodges flew in from Kunming and told us that the Old Man wanted us back there immediately, so we took off and hit Kunming right on the nose; the navigation problem is dwindling.

After arriving, we critiqued Harvey Greenlaw, and I presume that he filled in the Old Man about our success at Chiang Mai. At the end of

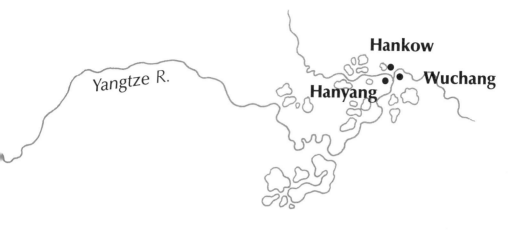

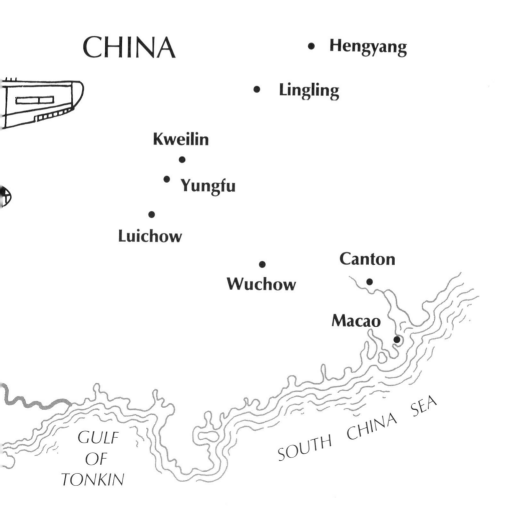

Hankow

Wuchang

Hanyang

Yangtze R.

Changsha

CHINA

Hengyang

Lingling

Kweilin

Yungfu

Luichow

Canton

Wuchow

Macao

GULF
OF
TONKIN

SOUTH CHINA SEA

the meeting he told us that tomorrow there will be a meeting to discuss our induction into the U.S. Army Air Corps. Here's hoping I can find out about a regular commission.

A few of the new P-40s arrived a few days ago. They are E models with six .50-caliber guns in the wing roots outside the propeller arc and hydraulically rechargeable from the cockpit. The plane is a little faster and has a longer range. In a discussion with George McMillan and the others who had ferried six Es back from Africa, I learned that they liked them very much even with a belly tank slung underneath.

Tonight I heard the news from San Francisco. Lo and behold, they announced the results of our raid on Chiang Mai!

March 26, 1942

Went to the main hostel this evening for the meeting to talk induction. The Old Man ran it. He wanted to know how many were for the idea of being inducted on the spot. It lasted for about an hour. I asked one question: "General, what's our chance of getting a regular commission if we are inducted right here in Kunming?"

He quickly replied: "Charlie, there has been nothing said or done about that."

The consensus is that most want to resign from the AVG and go back to the States immediately or stay in the AVG and go home at the expiration of their contracts. General Chennault implied that he would be able to get replacements, but it wasn't clear whether he meant more AVG volunteers or AAC personnel. There was no doubt that the Old Man's first and foremost desire is to keep us together as his AVG.

Upon returning to my room I found Jim Cross, who had returned from Calcutta. He had a fine time and seemed in much better spirits. Said those folks down there have no idea a war is going on, the way they act. Evening clothes and parties all the time and American generals and colonels all over the place. Jim also got George Burgard in a worrying mood. Rumors have it that his old girl friend has gotten married to some officer at MacDill Field. I guess I must quit ribbing George about his women.

March 28, 1942

Spent hours shooting the bull with Tex Hill, Second Squadron leader, about how we might get back to the States if we did elect to leave: through India or maybe Russia? We are not sure, for the ad-

My plane, No. 5, was out of commission, so I scrambled in No. 31 for my first taste of combat over Kunming in December, 1941. A Japanese bomber tail gunner scored a hit in my horizontal stabilizer; this type of damage was repaired overnight by our superb ground crew, who riveted aluminum patches over the holes.

Chinese laborers building the runway at Kunming. (*Courtesy, Jim Cross*)

Representing various flying "uniforms" and sidearms are (*left to right*) Joe Rosbert, myself, Ed Leibolt, and Louis Hoffman. We are on alert duty in December, 1941, at Kunming Airbase. (*Courtesy, Larry M. Pistole*)

My No. 5 P-40, which was destroyed in April, 1942, during Japanese strafing raids at Loiwing, China. All we had for aiming the machine guns on the early P-40 models was the single iron gunsight just forward of the canopy windscreen.

In the P-40 preparing to take off for a mission.

Chennault with his pilots reviewing Kunming's air defense positions and possible Japanese bomber approach routes in early January, 1942. *Standing, left to right*: Carl Brown, Jack Croft, myself, Ed Leibolt (hands on knees), Louis Hoffman, and Olie Olson. *Kneeling, clockwise from left*: Matt Kuykendall, John Dean, Joe Rosbert, Chennault, and Sandy Sandell. Clifford Groh is walking up in the background. (*Courtesy, J.J. Harrington*)

Alert shack at Kunming Airfield. (*Courtesy, Jim Cross*)

Hostel 1, home of the Second and Third squadrons, in downtown Kunming. Chennault also resided here. (*Courtesy, Jim Cross*)

Left: This snapshot taken at Kunming in December, 1941, shows the "blood chit" sewn on the back of my USAAC flight jacket. In Chinese it states: "I am an aviator fighting for China against the Japanese. Please take me to the nearest communication agency." *Right*: Trying to learn Chinese from my tutor in January, 1942, at Kunming.

Emma Jane ("Red") Foster (*left*) and Jo B. Stewart, AVG nurses, visiting a Chinese temple in Kunming in early 1942. (*Courtesy, Emma Foster*)

Pilots at Kunming Airfield in early March, 1942. *Left to right*: Bob Neale, George Burgard, Bob Little, myself, John Blackburn, and Black Mac McGarry. Unfortunately, McGarry was shot down a couple of weeks later during the raid on Chiang Mai.

A self-portrait taken at eighteen thousand feet while on patrol over Rangoon in February, 1942.

Clare Boothe Luce took this picture at Kunming Airfield during her visit in April, 1942. Sitting on the P-40 (*left to right*) are Mortimer Snerd Shilling, Bill Bartling, Joe Rosbert, Pappy Paxton, and Frank Adkins. Standing below are myself and Bob Little.

Some of Olson's Third Squadron and Hill's Second Squadron pilots in front of the alert shack at Loiwing Airfield in April, 1942. *Left to right*: Herbert Cavanah, Tex Hill, John Petach (profile in rear), Bill Reed, Olie Olson, Moose Moss, Parker DuPouy, Bob Prescott, Cliff Groh, and an unidentified man sitting in the rear. (*Courtesy, Larry M. Pistole*)

Left: Outside the barracks at Kunming in May, 1942, just a few days after being shot down for the first time at Paoshan, China. The dark discoloration on my face and hands is from the gentian violet salve used to treat the burns. *Right*: In dark glasses and bandaged after being shot down for the second time, June 12, 1942. *Left to right*: Bob Neale, Bus Loane, myself, an unidentified USAAC fighter pilot who had just arrived in a group to replace the AVG, and John Dean.

John Hennessy and the Beechcraft he piloted for Chennault and other AVG staff. (*Courtesy, John Hennessy*)

vance of Japs is going strong, and no one is certain about the security of India. The Japanese Army is pushing the newly grouped Chinese back north from Toungoo. The Old Man seems to think that if the Chinese can't stop them in Burma, we may just have to sit here and wait the outcome of future action.

Checked out in the P-40E. My first landing was raunchy, but I love the way it handles even though it feels a bit heavier in the air. What I loved the most is the sound of those six fifties firing out front. What a swath they cut in the target on the lake. Look out, Japs!

March 29, 1942

There is very little enemy air activity along the Toungoo front. If Jap bombers do come over to bomb the Chinese lines, the formation is small and there is no fighter escort whatsoever.

The Old Man keeps complimenting Bob Neale on the mission at Chiang Mai.

A couple of New Zealand Army men showed up at our hostel. We had a long talk with them when we learned that they had been in a Japanese prison in the Hong Kong area and had escaped. One had crawled through the surrounding fence and the other had escaped through a sewer. The latter, however, first had come up through a sewer hole in the backyard of the Japanese naval district headquarters. Naturally he went back in and crawled to the next opening. Their food in the prison was rice and water, and many of the prisoners were wracked with dysentery and diarrhea.

March 30, 1942

Started reading Hemingway's *For Whom The Bell Tolls* and I am enjoying it. Bob Neale and I sat around trying to concoct another Chiang Mai type of mission. Possible targets could be Hanoi or Rangoon. We have got to get back in this war someway. There is a morale problem in Kunming when we cannot be involved in fighting the Japanese. We decided that we were fully capable of pulling a night strafing mission against the Japanese at Mingaladon Field in Rangoon and also the satellite fields. We know them like the back of our hand, and with a full moon we could do it. We could launch it from Magwe.

March 31, 1942

What the hell, nothing to do, so went out to the field to chat with the guys on alert.

In the afternoon I went to the main hostel and drew another two-hundred-dollar gold draft. This is payday. On the way back to our hostel I came up to a roadblock in the middle of the city. One of our airmen had hit a Chinese child in the street and had broken his leg. It is very easy to do, for the Chinese have no appreciation of the speed of an approaching automobile. They will walk right out in front of it.

Heard the news tonight, and the heartening note was a report that the newer B-17Es are taking a toll of the Japanese Navy Zeros in the Southwest Pacific.

April 1, 1942

April Fool's Day. It is like all the others: dull.

Flew another P-40E and now feel more familiar with it. Sure enough, I discovered that when the three guns on just one side are fired, the plane goes off into a slight skid.

Went to the Nan Ping theatre in town and then returned to my room with the intention of working out details on a raid on Mingaladon Airfield at Rangoon. About the time we got started, Matt Kuykendall staggered in and then Mickey Mickelson dropped in, also stewed to the gills. There must have been a party in the hostel area that I did not know about. Mickey wanted to change outfits and become a part of the First Squadron. John Hennessy came in—obviously from the same party. He pilots the Beechcraft transport for the Old Man or for any executive mission required for the AVG: a real fine guy. He and Mickey commiserated for a while and finally left swearing that they were going to resign and go home, but I know that they are not about to leave the outfit.

Heard that Lashio was bombed twice today by the Japs. The bombers had good Zero escort. Olie Olson's squadron is having a hard time in the area because of heavy haze. Pappy Boyington and Moose Moss damaged two P-40s yesterday. Pappy's was on takeoff, but it wasn't his fault. The engine just quit. Never heard what caused Moose's accident.

April 2, 1942

Quite restless today, so I went down to the field alert shack and chatted with one of our doctors, Major Tom Gentry. He just returned from Chungking and said that some of the AVG would be going there soon.

Tonight the AVG pilots were invited to a dinner by the governor of Yunnan Province. We arrived about 7:30 and parked in a huge garden area in the hills overlooking Kunming. We walked down a path covered with pine needles and lit by Chinese paper lanterns. In the reception hall a Chinese colonel introduced me to the governor, who was receiving the AVG pilots. A short man of medium build, with shaved head, horn-rimmed spectacles, unusually bulging eyes, and a broad smile, the governor is reputedly one of the richest men in China. We stood around and chatted, sipping Dubonnet wine and absinthe—wow, too potent for me!

We walked into a huge dining room and sat down at tables of our choice. I sat between Willie Fish and Frank Schiel. During dinner we were entertained on an elevated stage at the far end of the dining room by Chinese opera. The food was Chinese, but we ate in American style. The champagne and soup were delicious, but not the Chinese wine. We were at a table along the outside part of the banquet room, and many of us were passing our glasses of rice wine through the windows to the eager hands of the Chinese guards stationed outside.

The governor toasted President Roosevelt, the United States, and the Flying Tigers. Skip Adair responded for General Chennault, who was in Chungking meeting with Chiang Kai-shek. George McMillan gave the governor a Flying Tiger insignia and made him an honorary member of the outfit.

C. E. Smith, our adjutant, Pappy Paxton, and Bob Little put on a skit in Chinese costumes which was a scream. I am not sure how the Chinese took it. Red Probst, having had a lot of rice wine, decided that he should be in the skit and ended up on the stage. This made things more riotous.

Red was sitting at the Greenlaw's table next to Olga, Harvey's wife. When Red left for the stage, Bob Little took his seat next to Olga, and she seemed pleased. She is a very exotic woman.

At the end of the dinner the band gave their best rendition of the "Star Spangled Banner."

April 3, 1942

Heard that Erik Shilling got lost in that Burmese haze yesterday and never saw the Rangoon fields. That means that we have no intelligence for any raid against Rangoon. Luckily, Shilling did get back to Loiwing.

149

John Hennessy had another forced landing in his Beechcraft. That guy is one damn good pilot. With all the trouble with that airplane, and with forced landings in this country, he is still healthy and alive, and the aircraft is still in one piece. He really deserves credit.

Heard KGEI, the San Francisco news, tonight. The announcer talked about an American fighter pilot who shot down three Japanese aircraft around Java. They called him an "ace." I wonder what they would call Bob Neale—he has fourteen to his credit.

April 4, 1942

Drove over to the main hostel to have Doc Everett Bruce clean my teeth. He said I had three small cavities and must come back Wednesday to get them filled. Spent some time with Jo Stewart, just gabbing. She is a terrific person, loved by all of the men.

Rumors are that we probably will get some P-38s and then escort AAC B-17 raids against the Japanese.

April 5, 1942

The weather is getting nastier and nastier. Jap bombers would never find Kunming in this weather, and if they tried we would never be able to find them.

Got a wire from the Old Man, who is in Chungking. He said we should expect a Jap raid today; actually, I think he was just getting us on our toes for his arrival with the generalissimo. They are having a big pow-wow here tonight about something. I believe it pertains to Burma. The Chinese are not stopping the Japanese advance into northern Burma. They are outnumbered greatly by the Japs.

God bless John Hennessy. On a stop at Lashio he personally went into the post office and swiped all of the Kunming-bound mail, and many of us got letters from home. How wonderful.

April 8, 1942

Went over to the dental office, where Doc Bruce filled my teeth. God, that tooth grinding is worse than combat!

General Chennault called a special meeting tonight of all the AVG members in Kunming. He was really hot under the collar. First time I have seen him that way. Apparently two crew chiefs beat up a couple of the pilots, and he was not going to stand for any more of the wild stuff. He is kicking the two crew chiefs out of the outfit.

He also told us that we would not be inducted into the AAC, and a new law had been passed in the States that prevented any of us from resigning our jobs in the AVG.[5] This stunned me. It sounds more like threats and warnings than facts, but I am worried.

April 10, 1942

This morning I was ordered to get a patrol in the air to escort a Chinese DC-3 leaving Kunming. The generalissimo was on board, and the warning net had reported three unidentified aircraft. As I was about to take off, I was informed that five enemy aircraft were over Yunnanyi, just west of Kunming. I climbed to twenty thousand feet, and on a turn caught sight of a group of planes. I turned into them and turned on my armament switches. Fortunately I recognized them— Bob Neale's flight. He and his flight also had scrambled.

Heard tonight that Olie Olson's Third Squadron got seven Jap planes over Loiwing yesterday. But other news was more alarming. The Japs strafed the Loiwing field early this morning: no warning whatsoever. The alert pilots were actually on their way to the field when it happened. About ten P-40s were shot up—some badly. My No. 5 was there, but they tell me it will be back in commission in a day or two.

The San Francisco news tonight was bad. The Philippines have fallen. God, what a shame! A nation like ours unable to help a force of 36,000 Americans repulse an overwhelming invading force of 135,000 Japs. No wonder a military man can learn to hate his adversary and question the competence of his own government.

At least there was one bit of good news. The Royal Australian Air Force and the U.S. Army Air Corps have gained air superiority over New Guinea.

April 11, 1942

George McMillan told us in our daily briefing that we have received information from our Chinese spies in Hanoi that the Japanese have eighty aircraft in that district and maintain a night patrol of eight fighters. Perhaps our Chiang Mai raid made Christians out of them concerning dawn raids. Mac also said Bob Neale's outfit was to provide

[5] No such law was passed.

seven pilots to proceed to Karachi, India, to pick up seven P-40Es and ferry them back to Kunming.

Bob told me to lead the flight and to take Bob Little, Matt Kuykendall, John Dean, Bill Bartling, Joe Rosbert, and Pappy Paxton. My friends George and Jim were greatly disappointed that they were not selected to make the Karachi trip. One of our passengers on the DC-3 out of Kunming is Clare Boothe Luce, who for days has been interviewing members of the AVG.[6]

Just before taxiing out we had quite a scene in getting two Chinese passengers off the plane. They had slipped past the security people and were trying to get out of China. Our transport pilot, an old veteran in China, said it happens all the time.

Our first leg of the flight ended at Lashio. The Japs had bombed the place several times, but there was not a great deal of damage on the field. The railroad station, however, was a mess, and several boxcars were burned and demolished. We waited for the refueling and in the meantime ran into Tex Hill, Peter Wright, and Jack Croft, who were flying P-40Es on reconnaissance missions out of Lashio and Loiwing.

An American DC-3 landed, and when the pilot got off, he turned out to be Lieutenant Lanning, an old friend from MacDill. He gave us cartons of cigarettes and told us that if we left the AVG, Pan American Airways would snap us up quickly at $750 a month. I am making a mental note of this. Things still are uncertain for my future.

We took off just before dark and made a night flight to Calcutta. That was just fine by me, for I was concerned about Japanese fighter interception. I dozed all the way, and after landing and clearing customs we grabbed cabs and headed for the Great Eastern Hotel. It is some sight after the long stay in China and Burma. The people seem unaware that a war is going on. Bob and I are in the same room, and we turned in early while the others went out to make a night of it.

April 12, 1942

We slept late and had a wonderful breakfast. Later we ran into two USAAC officers and Harvey Greenlaw. I thought he was in Lashio, but

---

[6] Luce later described the pilots as the "most wonderful bunch of kids that ever drew the breath of life," and she urged that their kill ratio should become the benchmark for all American pilots. *New York Times*, May 3, 1942.

I suppose he is here trying to borrow some equipment and men from the AAC.

Talked to an AAC lieutenant colonel named Homer L. Sanders about the P-40Es. He says that they only have four of the planes in all of India and that practically all of their planes were lost when the aircraft carrier USS *Langley* was sunk.[7] He and his pilots are eager to get into the war, but there seem to be problems concerning the command relationship between the AAC and the AVG. It all seems confusing.

We rode out to Dum Dum Airport and barged into the operations office. We talked about the war situation. There are a lot of aircraft on the field: Hawk 75s (a version of the P-36), Brewster Buffaloes, Hurricanes, Lockheed Hudsons, and many DC-2s and DC-3s. A Jap raid here would make history—be like Chiang Mai. We learned that a large convoy of ships with a small aircraft carrier and a cruiser were sunk outside the harbor when they attempted to sail out south around India. If the Japanese Navy is that powerful right outside Calcutta, it appears that things don't look so good for India.

Bob and I went by the hospital to see Frank Swartz. His hand is much better; he lost only the tip of his right thumb. His neck is still in a brace, and skin grafting is being done every few days. His mouth is a little crooked across his face. I felt sorry for him; we did everything to cheer him. He was like a little kid, showing happiness to see some of the old gang and talking to us. Soon he will return to the States for more plastic surgery. While in the hospital I ran across my old Rangoon RAF friend, Squadron Leader Cotton. His bullet-ridden leg is healing rapidly. I looked across the room to see another RAF pilot who was badly burned and wrapped in heavy gauze from head to foot. The surprising thing about him was his cheerfulness in spite of his condition. How I admire him. It is so depressing seeing terrific men in such pitiful conditions.

I was glad to get out of the hospital and into the hotel bar. After a drink or two Bob Little and I decided to take a nap. We got up too late to get with the rest of the gang, so we went to the Grand Hotel. We ran into a few New Zealand bomber pilots from Magwe days, and after a

---

[7]The USS *Langley* was sunk in February, 1942, with thirty-two P-40s on board. Actually, ten P-40s from the convoy reached India. Romanus and Sunderland, *Stilwell's Mission to China*, p. 92.

few drinks we left for the Club 300, a very swanky night spot with lots of slot machines. We had a gay old time, and by midnight Red Probst and Pappy Paxton showed up. Always the comic, Pappy got out in the middle of the dance floor and put everyone in stitches with his singing and dancing. The manager actually was delighted with our merriment and gave us drinks on the house.

April 13, 1942

Bob and I needed some clothes, so we hiked off and bought quite a few things, including bush jackets. Then we dropped by the army-navy surplus store and got a few things for our buddies in Kunming and some perfume for the two nurses. Ended up at noon having a lunch of hamburgers and milkshakes—what a treat!

April 14, 1942

Attended a luncheon, where we found Bill Bartling and Joe Rosbert with a couple of chorus girls. They had met the girls at a floor show the night before, and they made arrangements for dates for Bob and me. We were told that departure would be early tomorrow, so we decided to have a last fling. We picked up the girls about 8:30. My date was a buxom blonde who was filled out more freely on the bottom than on the top. She proved to be fun anyway. They went backstage to prepare for their acts, and we sat in the front row and watched. The show lasted until about midnight, when the girls got off and we headed to a nearby club. We did not get in, for all clubs are required to close at midnight, so we left for Joe's hotel room, since he had booze and a phonograph. We drank and danced. I took my buxom blonde home about 3:00 A.M., returned to my hotel, and told the desk clerk to wake me in an hour.

April 15, 1942

I didn't even go to sleep. I stayed up and started packing. Just before dawn we gathered in the lobby and checked in at the ticket counter of the British Overseas Airways Corporation. We are leaving by flying boat. Rosbert still had his chorus girl hanging on his arm. Obviously, he did a lot better than any of us!

April 16, 1942

We arrived at Karachi. It is a large port and many ships are in the harbor. Two stand out prominently; they have large red crosses painted all over them.

We glided over the bay and landed smoothly on the water. At the customs waiting room we ate tea and cakes.

It was good to see American servicemen, the U.S. Army. There are a fighter group and a bomb group at the field. P-40Es, B-17s, and B-24s were all over—also quite a few P-43s. I was delighted to learn that the P-43s are destined for the Chinese Air Force. One of the seven P-40Es allocated for our gang is out because of a cracked wing, so I got them to agree to let me check out in a P-43. I got a kick out of it, a P-43 leading a formation of P-40Es. It is a nice little plane. Climbs like a scared angel and easily outruns the P-40E, particularly at higher altitudes, since it has a turbosupercharger. Bob Little also checked out in one while the other pilots became familiar with the P-40E.

The RAF station commander briefed us on our routes back to Calcutta. He called us the "seven wild men" because of what appeared to be no air discipline. During our checkout flights all of us buzzed the field before landing. The U.S. Army has no control over us, so we couldn't get into trouble. The AAC fighter boys envied the hell out of us, and their commander told us that if we fought the Japs as hard as we fought each other, we'd do great. Maybe he has something there. . . .

April 17, 1942

We tried to get breakfast at the tent area, and what a mess. Hell, the USAAC is in a bigger mess than we are in the AVG.

We got our weather briefing and lined up for takeoff about 9:00 that morning. The haze was terrible and checkpoints were few and far between, but we made it to Jodphur. After lunch we were in the air on the leg to New Delhi, Tenth Air Force headquarters. I had heard that Col. Charlie Caldwell was there—a wonderful guy who had checked me out in B-17s at Langley Field. I got ahold of him as soon as we landed and made arrangements for the whole gang to stay in the Imperial Hotel. What a layout. We had dinner with Charlie and another colonel, and we chatted until the wee hours about our AVG experiences. I also asked what our chances were to get regular commissions. They only could speculate; they really didn't know.

April 18, 1942

Had a hard time getting the P-43 started, but after replacing the battery we took off for Allahabad.

On the way we couldn't restrain ourselves from buzzing the beautiful Taj Mahal at Agra. I circled it at a low altitude and took some snapshots. Pappy Paxton reported his fuel pressure acting up and returned to New Delhi. I forgot to switch fuel tanks and was startled out of my wits when the engine quit. Thought I would never get it going again, but I did. I was concerned about Pappy Paxton until receiving a message that he would be forty-five minutes behind us.

Our last leg was to Calcutta. I had been briefed earlier on the approach air corridors, and I stayed within them, but I admit I overdid it a little. I dropped the flight down to five hundred feet above the Hooghly River and gave the city a good buzzing! Normal entrance altitude in that corridor is two thousand feet.

After landing we dispersed the planes and caught a cab for the Great Eastern Hotel and then went over to the Elite Theater to see if the same girls were available. My buxom blonde friend had a date, so I asked Joe's girl to get me another. It was too late. Bob's girl also had a date, so we went back to the hotel, got with Pappy Paxton, who just arrived, bought three bottles of champagne, and proceeded to have a good time right there.

Pappy got chummy with the orchestra members and sang songs for them to the great delight of the customers; what a clown! After we closed up the place, several of the orchestra members took us to the Puerto Rican Club, where we continued our spree. The club was really a dive and very rowdy, with many drunken RAF types. Quite a few Spanish gals. I suppose they came with the Puerto Rican name. I gave up, but Bob ended up with some gal we kept calling "Heddy."

April 19, 1942

Up and felt awful. Went out to the field and began checking out the aircraft when Bob joined me. I looked at him and he just grinned. I can only assume last night still was flashing through his mind.

Ed Goyette arrived with a P-43 from Karachi. Also, a Chinese pilot was ready to go to Kunming in another P-43. Since I had already picked up an American ferry pilot in a P-40E, we will be leaving Calcutta tomorrow with a flight of ten. I wired the Old Man to let him know.

While I was lounging around the China National Aviation Corporation operations office, Chuck Sharpe offered me a job with CNAC at eight hundred dollars a month. He said I'd end up clearing about twelve hundred. It is enticing, I have to admit, but I turned it down for the time being. I asked him to let me think about it for a while.[8]

April 20, 1942

Since Ed Goyette and the Chinese pilot were flying P-43s, I had them on my wing. Matt Kuykendall and Bob Little had flights of the P-40Es. We entered Dinjan from the north. The towering Himalaya Mountains were to the north—majestic snow-covered peaks. We gave the field a healthy buzzing before landing. Goyette ground-looped during his landing because of a locked brake and tore up the wingtip, the prop, and one landing gear.

We hired a bus to take us to the AAC encampment, where we ran into seven AVG mechanics who had quit and were on their way home. They described a pessimistic picture of the setup at Kunming and talked as though everyone was quitting. It was depressing.

April 21, 1942

The Chinese pilot reported that he had a bad fuel leak in his left wing. It was dangerous, too dangerous to fly. The fuel was leaking from the wing and running back across the turbosupercharger right under the cockpit portion of the under fuselage. I told him to leave the plane until it could be repaired and come on up in the DC-3 tomorrow with Goyette. That nearly killed the Chinese pilot. He had fallen in love with the plane, and it was like taking candy from a baby. I could see wounded pride in his face; I felt for him. He asked me to see that he would be sent back to India so he could fly it home to China.

[8]CNAC ordered planes in 1941 through Lend-Lease and began receiving them in February, 1942. By July it had ten transports, and the next year it reached its maximum fleet of twenty-five. In March, 1942, Japan closed the Burma Road, and CNAC began service over the Hump with daily flights in June. Owned jointly by the Chinese government and Pan American, CNAC had a contract with the U.S. government to fly essential military and civilian supplies, including mail and passengers. By mid-1942 the CNAC's role was being eclipsed by the American Ferry Command of the U.S. Army Air Corps. This group had seventy-five transports flying over the Hump by October, and in December it was renamed the Army Transport Command. Young, *China and the Helping Hand*, pp. 247–52.

We took off for my first flight over the Hump. Fortunately the weather was fine, and we cruised through at twelve thousand feet. I contacted Loiwing, and to my surprise they directed me to change course and land there rather than continue on to Kunming. As soon as we cut our engines upon landing, the mechanics started grabbing the belly tanks off the P-40Es. The Old Man greeted us—it was good to see him again—and filled us in. The group is doing patrol work over the Chinese lines in North Burma. They already have knocked down several Jap planes. Bob Brouk landed on one mission at Namsang and was caught on the ground by a Jap fighter. He has one leg shot up fairly badly. John Petach had a forced landing near the front and had to destroy his plane before leaving it for the Japs. Bill Reed got lost on one flight and had a forced landing, but he can fly it out as soon as they get some fuel to him.

The pilots were enthralled with the looks of the P-43, and I gave them a short rundown on the way it handled. When we took off for Kunming I demonstrated its climb capability compared to the P-40E's. I was off the ground in half the distance. Arriving at Kunming, we gave the field a healthy buzz. The guys welcomed us warmly and everyone wanted to fly the P-43.

I went over to operations and reported to Skip Adair. He told me Pappy Boyington had submitted his resignation from the AVG, and now I was vice squadron commander of the Adams and Eves. I felt proud and thanked him warmly. Also, we have heard that we will be taken over by the USAAC by the Fourth of July.

At dinner I saw Pappy come in completely looped and staggering. Bob Neale said he had been that way for six days and nights. I feel sorry for him. I can imagine his dislike for me. Oh well, what the hell.

April 22, 1942

My birthday; twenty-seven years old and here I am on alert again.

Japanese reconnaissance planes have been coming as far north as Mengtzu. Today I sent Bob Little and two others down into the area hoping to knock down a couple of them, but they saw nothing.

April 23, 1942

I sat on a board of inquiry today to hear a case about one of our crew chiefs. He struck a doctor at the French Hospital in the city when the surgeon refused to perform an abortion on his wife. We made the decision to fire him and throw him out of the AVG. We also dropped two other airmen as deserters when they overstayed their leave in Calcutta.

April 24, 1942

One of the Chinese P-43 trainee pilots crashed right after takeoff this afternoon. He pulled the mixture control back to full cutoff instead of pulling the turbo control back off full power. Goyette checks them out on the aircraft and said that several have killed themselves.

Went to the Kunming Nan Ping movie again and in the middle of *Room Service* with the Marx Brothers panic suddenly broke out in the theater: air raid! How they got the word, I'll never know, for I heard nothing. It could have been flashed on the screen in Chinese, but I didn't see that either. In any event the theater emptied in nothing flat, including us, but there was no raid.

April 26, 1942

We had a little excitement today. Early this morning the warning net reported activity south of Mengtzu. A little later Poseh was bombed south of here. Then the report came that nine Japanese bombers were sixty miles northeast. We rushed to the planes. I was a little slow in getting it started and as a result decided to risk a takeoff with a cold engine. I got away with it and climbed to fifteen thousand feet. It was like old Rangoon days; I was really excited. The Japs had decided to make another try at Kunming. Then ground control came on the air and ordered "spike" (land at once). The "Jap bombers" had turned out to be Russian-built Chinese bombers coming from the north to land at Yunnanyi.

The Chinese bombers have been assigned the mission of close support for the Chinese front in Burma. The way they take off and land, however, I'm afraid they'll never make it. It may be the plane, but I am inclined to think it is the pilot. It is a sideshow. The majority of the takeoffs narrowly miss becoming bad ground loops, and others get wingtips on landings time after time. We really sweat them out.

April 28, 1942

Arrived at the alert shack at the usual time this morning and turned the light on to get things lined up. Raymond Hastey was snoring away on one cot, and right next to him was his girl friend, a luscious little Eurasian that he had managed to get up here to Kunming when we evacuated Rangoon. For a moment I didn't know what to do. Then I walked over to the bulletin board where I post the names of pilots for the following day's alert duty. I took a red pen and added her name to the roster right under Hastey's name. I don't think Hastey will ever live that down. The guys cracked up when they saw it.

The same old dull day here, but it was a different story at Loiwing. The combined remnants of the Second and Third squadrons got in a real hassle when the Japanese attempted to hit Loiwing with bombers and fighters. First reports indicated they got fifteen Japanese for sure and lost no one, but it is not official.

This afternoon Blackie Blackburn took off for his check ride in a P-40E and never returned. We fear he may have mushed into the lake on a gunnery dive, for he was supposed to do a little of that during the flight. Bob Neale made a short flight looking for signs of Blackie's aircraft around the lake, but darkness forced him in early. We will lay on a search tomorrow morning.

Tomorrow is Emperor Hirohito's birthday, and we are anticipating a big effort by the Japs. I put eighteen aircraft on alert for tomorrow. I hope they try to come up.

April 29, 1942

We were ready for them this morning, but the weather was awful. Later it cleared, and Bob went out for another look for Blackie. He located a slick out in the middle of the lake, and we fear the worst.

Col. Robert Scott had come in with Col. Caleb Haynes, and we had quite a session. Scott brought us up to date about what is going on in the States.

Met Ajax Baumler tonight and traded stories. He is an ace from the Spanish Civil War and is now in the USAAC. He thinks we will probably be inducted into the service on July 4.

April 30, 1942

Same old alert and same old rainy weather. Bob Neale got a large boat and went out to check the oil slick area for Blackie's ship—no luck.

Our guys are being pulled out of Loiwing. Tex Hill's Second Squadron is coming back here, and Olie's Third is to stay at Mangshi. At least that is the latest order of one BRIGADIER GENERAL CLAIRE L.

CHENNAULT, United States Army Air Corps. The Old Man has been inducted!

We hear that Col. Caleb Haynes's secret mission is to get General Stilwell out of Burma.

May 1, 1942

All of the pilots and planes from Loiwing came barging into Kunming. It was the first time I have seen over twenty P-40s in the air since training days at Toungoo. They were an ugly-looking bunch— dirty and unshaven. We did all we could to help them get their junk unloaded and off to their barracks. Of course during the unloading and reloading we discussed their fights with the Japs at Loiwing. The consensus is that they would prefer to fight the Model Zero rather than the I-96 or I-97.

May 2, 1942

Around the middle of the morning Bob Neale came in with the news that eight of us were to go to Paoshan, just north of Burma, and work with the Chinese bombers in supporting their troops in Burma. Initially Bob said the general wanted a good navigator to fly down within a few miles of the Indochina border in a BC-1 to pick up Cliff Groh, who had an emergency landing in his P-40. Bob wanted me to do it. I refused because of the risk and not knowing where I'd get refueled so I could get back. He finally agreed that it was a stupid idea. After discussion he said I would go with him to Paoshan and lead the second flight of four. I jumped at the idea. Off we went.

The Paoshan field is not too good, just a grass aerodrome, no runways, but adequate to land on and take off from in a P-40. After landing we quickly refueled and waited for the Chinese bombers to appear overhead. They finally appeared, nine bombers in a loose formation heading south. We scrambled and took up a position to escort them. The weather was bad, and we were in and out of cloud banks. The bombers were supposed to hit a bridge just below Katkai, Burma, and we actually found it. To my amazement they flew right over it without dropping bombs and headed on down to Lashio, where they attempted to bomb the railroad yards. One bomb hit within yards, but no fires resulted. We then headed back toward Paoshan.

On the way Bob called me on the radio, asking something about my flight. I couldn't understand him and asked him to say again. His voice rose in a loud harangue which was even worse than before. I blew my top and picked up my mike: "If you don't holler in the goddamn thing I might be able to hear you!" He came back in a quiet manner, asking if my men were with me. After landing at Paoshan, we laughed about it.

It was growing dark, so we dispersed our planes and started across town to our hostel. What a ride. The city streets were choked with refugees streaming up from Burma to get away from the Japs. We had to fire our pistols in the air to get them to move so our jeeps could get through. What a pitiful sight.

Our hostel turned out to be an old monastery. Every room was on another level from the others, since we were right at the base of the surrounding mountains. We finally found the dining room and sat down to soup without even washing.

May 3, 1942

We had to drive through Paoshan to get to the field. All along the way we observed hundreds of coolies having their morning call to nature, right alongside the road. How funny it looked.

At the field we worked up a good cribbage tournament waiting for the Chinese bombers. The weather was not too good and they cancelled.

We decided to crank up and make a reconnaissance flight over Loiwing and Wanting. We saw nothing and were on our way back to Paoshan when I saw Bill Bartling pull off Bob Neal's wing abruptly. Then Bob's guns burst with fire. What the hell was happening? No radio response from Bob, so I assumed he was testing his guns against a mountainside. Upon landing I learned differently. Bob told us that all of a sudden a Jap reconnaissance plane just floated up right in front of him. All he had to do was squeeze the trigger. He shot him down in two bursts. Except for Bartling, the rest of us didn't even see the Jap! Bartling was teed off because he was the first to see the enemy plane and didn't get one shot since he was slightly behind Bob.

May 4, 1942

Bob Neale's plane was hit by some return fire from the Jap reconnaissance ship, and Mickey Mickelson showed up sick this morning.

Bob decided he and Mickey would go to Kunming and pick up a replacement for Mickey and another P-40.

Later we heard some noises overhead and stepped out of the alert shack to find two Japanese reconnaissance ships high overhead. Bartling and I took off in hopes of catching them. By the time we got to eighteen thousand feet they were gone.

On the way back to the field I heard Bob Neale on the radio. He was returning from Kunming and near Paoshan. A few minutes later both Bob and Mickey showed up over the field: Mickey was feeling better.

Bob Little and I were cleaning our pistols when Neale yelled for us to man our ships. We dashed out to the planes, and by the time I had started my engine I looked up and saw the Jap bomber formation high above heading toward our field. Looked like about twenty-five bombers at eighteen thousand feet. Neale started shooting his pistol in the air to get everyone's attention; then he ran for the ditch. My engine had warmed up, and I sat there in the cockpit with my hand on the throttle. I paused a second. Hell, I can make it! I shoved the throttle open and headed straight across the field. I had not gotten into my parachute or put my helmet on. I didn't even have my seat belt on, and my canopy was open. My only thought was to get airborne and beyond the edge of the field before the bombs hit. My speed built up unusually slowly, and suddenly my tail literally jumped off the ground. Damn, I had not even put up my flaps, which was pre-takeoff procedure. I had quite a lot of field yet, so I put them up. I leaped forward and just did manage to clear the rock barricade at the far end of the field. I turned to the left and got into my flying gear as I started a maximum climb. I could see the bomber formation clearly now. They skipped the field and were bombing the city.

I wasn't climbing nearly as fast as I expected. Something was wrong. I had full throttle and RPM. Oh, hell! I forgot to raise my landing gear in all the haste and excitement. I got it up and then started gaining on the bomber formation. They were now in a wide sweeping turn to head back south after dropping their bombs. I cut across and pulled up in a steeper climb. In the meantime I stole a quick look at the city below. The bombing was almost perfect—right in the middle of the city.

I looked around for possible enemy fighter escort and saw none, but I did pick up a second wave of about the same number of bombers. I had a better chance against them, since they were trailing the first wave. I positioned myself to concentrate on them. They were at eighteen thousand feet and in a single vee formation. I got about a thousand feet above and off to the right. I made a diving left turn and pulled up into the right rear quarter of the outside flank of the formation. I closed in on the outside bomber and squeezed the trigger. My bursts completely enveloped the fuselage, but I saw no smoke or fire. The two adjacent bombers immediately started streaming a bluish white smoke to attract me to them as "wounded" aircraft. We had been briefed about this trick, but this was the first time I had seen it. I wasn't about to take that bait. The bomber on the extreme flank end pulled away a bit, and this made it even more obvious.

I continued my rear right quarter attacks. On my third attack I saw his right engine disintegrate and ignite into a flaming torch. He went down and through the overcast. I turned on the bomber at the tail of the vee, but suddenly my guns quit firing. I had become too engrossed and had been firing long bursts, by far too long. Recharging the guns produced no results. Hell, I was out of ammunition!

I pulled away sharply and made a diving 180 turn to head back. Now, where am I? I had chased some fifty enemy bombers down across northern Burma and had only gotten one. I was downright disappointed in myself and in my gunnery. I had them all to myself and there was no enemy fighter escort.

There was nothing to do but return to Paoshan. I spotted the Burma Road bridge over the Salween River and felt better about my position. I knew where I was, had sufficient fuel, so I relaxed and changed my course slightly to head directly to the field. I began evaluating the flight, filled with remorse that I didn't get more Japs. The field appeared, and I tried to pick up our ground station on the radio. Several calls brought no reply, and I was now in a steep dive towards the field. I leveled out and did a slow roll as I crossed over the alert area. I tried the radio again with no results and decided that they were probably in the ditches. I thought I'd make a wide turn around the city to examine the bomb damage while spreading out my traffic pattern.

What a sight. Before, the city had been spilling over with evacuees, and now they were jammed all over the place. The Japanese bombs had caught them without any warning. Fires engulfed the city. Many buildings and houses were blown to bits.

After one last look I concentrated on my landing approach. I slowed down and moved the lever for the flaps and landing gear forward. Suddenly I heard several loud explosions. The noise stunned me. I immediately concluded that my landing gear hydraulic system had blown up. I had been having trouble with it operating correctly the last several days but couldn't find anything wrong with it. I decided to try to recycle the gear lever. When I reached down, I cried out in pain. I had stuck my left hand into a raging fire!

I swung my head around and looked to my rear. There they were. Three Jap Zeros right on my tail and firing like mad! The explosions were their rounds of ammunition hitting my armor plate behind my seat. The bullets had gone through my fuselage tank, which still had a few gallons of fuel in it, before impacting the armor plate. The fuselage tank had exploded, and the fire was whipping into my lower rear cockpit and then up around my legs.

What a stupe I had been. I had become so engrossed with the bombing scene below that I had made the fatal mistake that a fighter pilot should never get caught doing: I didn't suspect enemy fighters in the area.

The Japs had laid this attack on a little differently. They knew our situation from the two reconnaissances flights that preceded the bombers. They decided to forego the fighters as bomber escorts and hold them off and away from the field with the hope of catching all of us when we returned—low on ammunition and gas.

For a split second I considered giving up, but something wouldn't let me. I leaned forward as far as my seat belt would permit, closed my eyes because the fire had begun to engulf me, and reached over with my right hand to grasp the canopy crank and rolled it fully back. I unhooked my seat belt with my left hand and put both hands on the stick to make the ship climb abruptly and roll over one-half turn to the right. I took my hands off the control column and reached for the right side of the cockpit to get out of the seat.

The airstream grabbed me as the upper part of my body protruded outside the cockpit. It dragged me out. I had forgotten my earphone connection to the radio plug, but the force of the wind tore it loose. I knew I was out of the airplane and opened my eyes. One second the blue sky and the next the ground. I was tumbling. I looked down to find the metal ring to pull my parachute and jerked it wildly. I felt a tugging and then a violent jerk. I was in the parachute straps, floating.

Suddenly I became terrified. Those dirty bastards will strafe me like they did Henry Gilbert at Rangoon. Automatically I started praying—out loud. I prayed devoutly to God with my eyes closed, and then opened them to look for the Zeros. Fortunately, they had pulled away and were heading south.

Looking down, I saw the ground rushing up at me. I would hit backward if I didn't do something, so I tried to kick around in my harness, and I did get about halfway around when I hit. I fell across some large clods of earth in a rice paddy. The parachute gradually floated to the ground beside me. I sat up and realized that I still had the rip cord ring tightly grasped in my right hand.

I landed in a Chinese cemetery, about a mile and a half from the field. I quickly came to my senses and punched the release on my parachute harness. The straps fell away, and I ran to the closest burial mound and used it as a barrier against possible strafing by a Jap fighter. I squatted there watching the remaining Japs make passes on the field.

I felt a burning sensation on my neck and shoulders and suddenly realized that my scarf and flying suit were on fire. I hurried to a small stream flowing through the cemetery and laid down on my back and wallowed in the water. My head ached. I reached up to rub it and felt something wet and drew my hand away to look at it. It was blood. Christ! I looked down at my hands. They were badly burned, and the skin had been torn loose in several places. Blisters were forming. My face and neck and upper shoulders were scorched; my eyebrows were gone. Pain was setting in.

There were many Chinese in the cemetery crouching behind the burial mounds. I motioned for one of them to come over to me. He reacted warily but did start walking towards me. He had one hand behind his back. I went through the gestures of picking up a telephone and calling while uttering the usual Chinese greetings, "Wau. Wao. Whoo. Wa." I did not have my flying jacket, on the back of which was sewn the Chinese flag and directives written in Chinese to help us. Nevertheless, he seemed to get the message, smiled lightly, and then brought his hand from behind his back, revealing a large rock. He was

166

ready to give me the works, thinking I was the enemy. He motioned for me to follow him and led me off to a cluster of huts. We entered one, and a group of Chinese peasants looked at me without any emotion. Fortunately, there was a telephone.

It's amazing what one can do in an emergency with sign language. I got them to understand that I needed an American doctor. A Chinese man got on the phone and got the word back to our AVG hostel. Eventually Doc Richards appeared in the doorway.

The agony of my burns had me on the verge of passing out. I wanted to die to get out of the pain. I would lie down, get up, walk around, lie down, get up, hold my hand in the air to reduce the circulation and throbbing pain, cry out aloud, and pray.

Doc took off my clothes and examined me. My helmet had too long rips in it. Apparently the armor plate in the P-40, which tapers off at the top to resemble the narrowing shoulders and head of a man, had barely kept all but a couple of bullets from hitting me. Otherwise I would've been killed. Two bullets barely missed the armor plate and ripped past my head close enough to cut my scalp and bring blood. My eyelashes and eyebrows were gone. My face was blistered on the left side. Around the hairline of my neck was an open wound of burnt flesh where the helmet plug to my aircraft radio had dug into my flesh when I forgot to unhook it upon bailing out. My shoulder blades were heavily blistered, and one blister ran down the middle of my back about six inches. My right thumb was blistered, and my left hand looked terrible, third-degree burns.

Doc gave me a shot in the arm and a couple of capsules of something, and I sat down for a minute to let the stuff set in. Then he started pulling the skin off the blisters. He looked at the USAAC ring on my left hand and said that it had to come off. I just peered back as the dope began to grab me. Nevertheless, when he pulled off the ring and the burned flesh on my finger, I nearly hit the ceiling. Then he started pouring peroxide on the open, raw places. That put me on the verge of convulsions, but fortunately the dope began to take hold. He smeared gentian violet all over the upper part of my body and very heavily over the burned portions. I became a gooey mess.

Doc asked me if I could walk, and I could. My socks were wet, since I had lost my boots. A Chinese gave me a pair of sneakers, and we walked out toward the jeeps. My flying suit had been tied at my waist to keep it off my burns on the upper part of my body. On the way through the rice paddies to the jeeps, Bob Neale came up and told Doc Richards that Benny Foshee was in a bad way from bomb shrapnel. A Chinese doctor had wanted to amputate one of Benny's legs, but he would not have it and kept yelling for Doc Richards. I urged Doc to go on and take care of Benny.

We met Bob Little at a main junction in the city, and we tried to joke about the whole deal. By now the dope had taken over and I couldn't feel a thing. Bob Neale, Bob Little, a Chinese interpreter, and I drove through the city towards the hostel, an eight-mile trip. Neale and Little had to fire their pistols into the air to get space for us to drive by the panic-stricken natives on the main road.

I shall never forget the horrible sights as we made our way through the bombed-out city. We drove past what had been shacks, homes, buildings, and factories, and now they were either leveled or still burning. There were bodies lying everywhere, in and under charred debris. Some were completely dismembered, and others were burned so badly the teeth were showing from fleshless faces. I saw one body with no leg, arms, or head, and another with the skull half gone. Once Bob Little had to get out of the jeep to move a timber from our path. When he heaved it aside, a human head rolled across the road. The air was filled with the smell of burning flesh. Once you smell that odor you never forget it. One very pitiful sight was a wailing Chinese mother on her knees in the middle of the road with her dead child in her arms and her dead husband at her side. Had I not been under the influence of the dope I would have up-chucked right there. Many times I thought Neale and Little would vomit. None of us said a word during the trip.

When we arrived at the hostel, we learned that Benny Foshee had died before Doc Richards could get to him, apparently from loss of blood. Doc Richards was busy sewing up the buttocks of an airman. A bomb splinter had ripped him open. The hostel had taken two bombs, and the place was a mess.

Everyone told me they had watched from the ground as I was shot down. Doc Richards and Bob Neale had fired their pistols at me to warn me that the Zeros were on my tail. They also said the Japs had been firing at me while I was over Paoshan. Joe Peeden, a mechanic, said my plane hit and bounced for a hundred yards and then burst into a ball of fire.

They all congratulated me on being alive, and I went to the hostel. My number-one boy shook the debris off my bunk, and Doc gave me some sleeping pills. I thanked God I was still alive, lay down on my blistered back, and fell asleep.

7. Old Hard Luck Bond

In May the Japanese Army advanced into southern China. The situation was perilous. The enemy controlled all the seaports, and now were marching up the Burma Road, meaning that the only way of supplying China was by air from India "over the hump" to Kunming. The city had to be saved, for if it fell, the alternative route was an overland trek from the Soviet Union, an impossibility at that time since the Germans were attacking and the Red Army was retreating towards Moscow and Stalingrad. Most experts agreed that if Kunming fell, then China would be forced out of the war and Japan would be able to turn its energies toward India, Australia, and, ultimately, the United States.

There were two obstacles between the Japanese Army and Kunming. One was natural: the Salween River, which flowed down from the Himalayas and carved a mile-deep gorge through the mountains of southern China. On the southwestern bank, the Burma Road twisted and turned twenty miles along cliffs to decline one mile towards the only point of crossing. On the northeast side, the road continued its tortuous path up hills slanting towards the Plateau of Paoshan. A bridge had gapped the powerful river, but the Allies destroyed it to stop the Japanese advance; the awesome task for the enemy was to ferry men and material across the Salween.

The other obstacle was the AVG. Chennault based most of the group at Kunming, leaving only five P-40s at Paoshan. The enemy attacked on May 4, the day I was shot down, and on the next day they struck again. Flying in two waves, one from southern Burma and the other from Chiang Mai, enemy fighters and bombers rendezvoused south of Paoshan and were met by nine P-40s, some stationed there and others from Yunnanyi. In the ensuing battle, the AVG lost none while destroying eight fighters. The bombers never got an opportunity to drop their payloads and scurried back to Burma.

At the same time, the Japanese Army started building a pontoon bridge across the Salween. To prevent the completion of that bridge-head, Chennault needed dive bombers, and just two weeks earlier I had returned from India with a flight of new P-40Es, which, unlike the older P-40s, were equipped with bomb racks. Many of our pilots had trained as dive bombers in the United States Navy. One of them was Tex Hill, and on May 7 he led eight Flying Tigers to the river, where they surprised the enemy. They hurled bombs into mountainsides, causing landslides and trapping the Japanese. Then they strafed, demolishing pontoons and supplies. For the next four days the AVG attacked, bombing and strafing, and by May 11 enemy traffic was heading not north but south on the Burma Road. As Chennault later wrote, "The AVG had staved off China's collapse on the Salween."[1]

These attacks, however, were not accomplished without tragedy. Bob Little, a pilot in our First Squadron and a very close friend of mine, was killed on a dive-bombing mission. While diving at the enemy, he lost a wing, either from antiaircraft fire or because a bomb in his wing rack predetonated. He was a workhorse in the squadron, always doing more than his share, and it was a personal loss for me because his boyish personality and sense of humor were a great boost for my morale. He was a fine person, and his death was a great loss to the AVG.

Meanwhile, the Japanese began to regroup and change their strategy in China. Blocked from advancing in South China, they prepared to attack the middle of the nation, especially along the Hankow rail-road and up the Yangtze River. This meant that in June, Chennault redeployed the AVG north to protect Kweilin and Chungking and began preparing for an air war over central China.

But before that move, and before the monsoons, the Old Man decided to make one last strike from Kunming. On May 12, Tom Jones, the vice commander of the Second Squadron, led an attack against Gia Lam Aerodrome in Hanoi. As with the Chiang Mai raid, the pilots surprised the enemy and strafed planes on the ground. Fifteen planes

[1]Chennault, *Way of a Fighter*, p. 167. The *New York Times* wrote on May 11, 1942, that after one attack on the Salween, "At least twenty trucks were left burning and sixty to eighty others were riddled with bullets."

were left burning, and twenty more were damaged. The raid was a complete success except for the unfortunate fact that antiaircraft fire killed John Donovan.[2]

Also during May and throughout June a noncombat issue—the uncertain future of the AVG and our possible induction into the USAAC—was becoming pressing. Although officials in Washington had authorized induction a few weeks after Pearl Harbor, there were no discussions of the issue until late in March, when Chennault conferred with the generalissimo, Madame Chiang, Stilwell, and the newly appointed commanding officer of the USAAC in the China–India-Burma theater, Brigadier General Clayton Bissell. Chiang Kai-shek was leery of induction, since he had developed confidence in Chennault and the AVG. Chennault also opposed the scheme, feeling that it was criminal to sacrifice the spirit and experience of the group for a change in uniform. The other two generals disagreed, stating that for reasons of command and control there could not be an independent group operating in the theater. Stilwell and Bissell had the support of the War Department, so there was no choice: the AVG would be dissolved on July 4 and replaced by the Twenty-Third Fighter Group, USAAC.

It was one thing to dismember the AVG and another to find qualified men for the Twenty-third Fighter Group. At the insistence of Chiang Kai-shek, Chennault was given the command of the new group as brigadier general. His superior was Bissell, a man who in the 1930s had opposed the fighter tactics advocated by Chennault and who now was convinced that he could persuade members of the AVG to continue fighting in China. He knew little about the group, and he did not realize that many had volunteered to get out of the military and that after months of combat, pilots were war-weary and eager to return to the United States. Bissell asked Chennault if he could make a speech to the group at Kunming on May 21, and I attended. Afterwards I returned to my quarters and noted in my diary keen disappointment in the way the USAAC was handling the induction, an opinion shared by other members of the AVG.

Induction, however, was the last thing on my mind two weeks later, on June 12, for I was engaged in a combat mission over Kweilin,

[2] The *New York Times*, May 14, 1942, carried the headline: "50 Planes Wrecked in Bombing of Three Airdromes—AVG Strikes at Hanoi Field."

and after I was shot down for the second time, my friends began to call me Old Hard Luck Bond.

*   *   *

May 5, 1942

I slept soundly with Doc's pills and shots, awoke at dawn, and slowly got out of bed. The number-one boy came in and helped me put on my flying suit, bound just enough to keep from slipping down. Colonel Wong, a local Chinese support officer, fed me breakfast, and Bill Bartling packed my things. It was our intention to leave Paoshan and return to Kunming.

On the way out of the hostel I passed by the infirmary, where Doc Richards had been working on the wounded. One native was dead and another had the right half of his hip missing; he was asleep, probably on Doc's dope. On the way to the field we stopped by the Paoshan hospital to pick up Benny's body. Bartling went in to help carry the body to our car. They brought Benny out in a blanket, his eyes still open. Bartling gagged and nearly vomited.

When we got to the field, we had another air-raid warning, so we went for the ditches. Two Jap reconnaissance planes came over. They were bold, flying low over the field.

We received a message that a DC-3 was coming to pick us up, and four P-40s would be sent as escort. I liked that, for we expected the Japs anytime. Bob Little's No. 33 was still in commission, so he also planned to escort. We spotted the DC-3 coming over the mountains and left the ditches. He made it in and taxied over. The mechanics had stripped the strafed P-40s of as much salvageable equipment as they could, particularly the .50-caliber guns, and the transport was loaded. Harvey Greenlaw, Bob Neale, Bartling, and I, and a few airmen were the passengers, besides Benny's body.

Overloaded, we barely made it off the field, and I was outwardly shaken. Harvey took one look at me and started rummaging through his baggage. He brought out a bottle of Johnnie Walker Black Label scotch and handed it to me. My body was on fire, and I couldn't sit still for more than a minute. Bob Neale could tell I was having problems, and he continued offering me scotch. In between swigs he would have one every now and then. In no time we both were feeling much better.

173

Right after takeoff Bob Little flew up close on our left wing and eased in tightly. We could see him in the cockpit of his P-40. He was acting crazy, wild. He kept throwing his right arm over his shoulder with his thumb extended outward. Bob Neale went forward to the cockpit to check with the DC-3 pilot. No wonder Little was acting crazy; the pilot was heading for Dinjan, India!

When we landed in Kunming, the Old Man and everybody else met us at the aircraft. I was a sight to behold. With gentian violet salve all over my upper body and face, I staggered off the plane, naked to the waist. That moment I picked up the nickname "Deep Purple."

General Chennault greeted me warmly, and Skip Adair rushed me over to our local AVG dispensary. Our wonderful nurse Jo Stewart fixed a bunk in the same room with Bob Brouk, who was still hobbling around on a shot-up leg. I tried to take a nap but couldn't. I just sat up and told my story to the guys who came to see me. I rolled and tossed a long time before falling asleep.

May 7, 1942

The days are monotonous. The main event every morning is a visit by one of the guys to bring news of action. The news today was both good and bad. The Second Squadron had gone to Paoshan yesterday and was ready for the daily Japanese raid. They got nine, but Frank Schiel is missing. The Japs have moved up an armored outfit to the Salween River, which separates Burma from the southern part of China. After retreating across the river, the Chinese destroyed the bridge, and the Japs are stymied right there. Fighting is heavy. Reports are that we are to move north to Chungking. Surely the Japs can't get across the river in that mountainous terrain and advance on Kunming.

Got letters from the folks and Doris, and that boosted my morale. They had read about my escapade in the home-town papers. That is a big boost to my ego.

The pain seems to subside during the day, but the nights are bad. I can't sleep without drugs. I have nightmares and wake up not knowing where I am. I hope this doesn't last long.

President Roosevelt sent a special message to the AVG today expressing his wish that all of us would remain in China until he could replace us with another full USAAC fighter wing. Most of the guys think lightly of the idea. All want to return to the States as soon as possible. I am not sure how this is going to turn out.

May 8, 1942

I hear the AVG hit the Jap armored column with bombs and machine gun fire at the Salween River. Apparently the enemy never made a crossing, and now they are reputed to be in retreat.

I am sleeping better at night—three different kinds of pills.

May 9, 1942

Heard this morning that Bill Bartling got a Jap reconnaissance ship at twenty-seven thousand feet over the Kunming lake yesterday. Unbelievable! I don't see how he ever got that P-40 above twenty-five thousand feet. Apparently he was on Bob Neale's wing, and Bob's ship pooped out at a lower altitude. Bart's plane had a bit more power. Now he is even with Bob for that Jap reconnaissance plane near Paoshan.

General Chennault came in for a few minutes to see how we were doing. It boosted our morale. A great guy!

May 10, 1942

Got the scoop this morning about our outfit moving to Chungking. Doc Prevo drove me over to my room to get my things packed. I got ready to go and then in the afternoon I got word that the Old Man told Doc Gentry that maybe Bob Brouk and I should stay here in Kunming a while longer and not move up north to Chungking. Seems to think the climate here is better for our wounds. I don't like that.

I cower a bit when Doc Prevo comes in. I don't like him picking around in my scabby wounds looking for infection. It just plain damn hurts. Also I don't like that purple salve smeared on my face. I have just about got it worn off. Nurses Jo and Red keep jumping on me for picking at my scabs. It has gotten to be a habit with me, particularly that deep burn on the back of my neck. My face seems to be healing fine, no scars.

May 11, 1942

Bob and I heard the good news about the U.S. Navy beating the hell out of the Japs in the Coral Sea.

More and more talk about an official induction of the AVG on July 4. Most of the guys just want to go home.[3]

Red gave me an unusually thorough bath today, and when she found I was ticklish under my arms she got as much kick out of it as I did. And Jo, bless her heart, came in tonight with a bottle of sherry. We all just sat and talked until late. How I have learned to love those two nurses.

May 13, 1942

Heard the Vice Squadron Commander Tom Jones led a flight down to Hanoi yesterday and bombed and strafed the Japs on the airport. They got some fifteen to twenty aircraft on the ground, but they lost John Donovan, who they think got hit by antiaircraft fire and crashed right near the field. Sounds like a replay of our Chiang Mai raid.

I got Jim to bring Doris's picture over and put it on my dresser. It helps just to look and think of her.

May 14, 1942

Jo came in and talked with us for a long time this morning. She is a little irked at Doc Gentry for assuming that she would stay if the AVG were inducted. She wants to go home, too.

I haven't made a trip to the latrine in several days. Perhaps burns and dope cause that. I told Bob that I'd probably have to eat some dynamite if I keep this up.

May 15, 1942

Doc Sam Prevo says our finance people are getting ready to pay everyone fully on the Fourth of July, and the AVG will be no more.

The generalissimo must have been impressed with Jones's raid on Hanoi. Jones and Frank Schiel were made squadron leaders "in rank," which means more pay for them, since we only have three squadrons and those positions are already filled by Bob Neale, Olie Olson, and Tex Hill. Lewis Bishop and C. H. "Link" Laughlin were also upped a notch.

---

[3]The desire to return home was reported in the *New York Times* and the *Dallas Morning News*, which wrote on May 4, 1942, "The Flying Fools of the AVG feel that they have earned a rest and should be granted furloughs to visit the United States before they are transferred to another Pacific war front."

May 16, 1942

The news today is horrible. Poor Tom Jones mushed into the ground on the practice bombing range today and shattered himself. After the terrific mission just the other day. How awful.

May 17, 1942

Another mission was on today to strafe trains south of the Lao Cai area in Indochina. Again we lost another man. This time it was Lew Bishop. Antiaircraft fire got him, and he bailed out over the populated area. The Japs surely picked him up. Just the other day he was visiting me and saying how much he looked forward to going home and seeing his wife and baby.

Ed Rector joined Bob and me with a bad throat and signs of dengue fever. With three in here, more of the guys come in, and we really have some good bull sessions.

May 18, 1942

I went to the other ward to talk to some of the men; most are venereal disease cases. I talked to one who was really in the dumps. I couldn't help but feel for him. He zipped open his fly and showed me his bandaged penis. It was more of a glove than a bandage, and when he removed it to show me his problem, I was sickened. Doc had slit open his penis from the head to the root in order to lay it open for treatment. It was a mass of puss and rotten flesh.

May 20, 1942

This was a great day. Doc let me and Eddie Rector go and warned me to quit picking at my scabs and be careful. I hated to say goodbye to Jo and Red. They had been so good to me and they knew how much I meant it when I tried to tell them how much I appreciated their kindness and consideration. I was in the hospital sixteen days.

Bob Neale and I had a long talk about staying or leaving. I told him that if I could not get a regular commission, I was going home. He told me he was offered the rank of lieutenant colonel if he would stay, but he is planning on going home.

May 21, 1942

General Chennault announced a meeting for tonight to give us the straight and final poop on our future. He reviewed our CAMCO contracts with us. If I stay here and take a reserve commission, I will collect AVG pay until 4 July, including pay for accrued leave up to that date. I also will collect five hundred dollars for what he said is "travel pay," since the contract included our return trip to the States. Further, I will be paid a lump sum of money equivalent to the difference between my AVG pay as vice squadron leader and whatever the basic pay of the rank I would get when I was inducted into the AAC. If I elect to go home, I will receive the same amount except I will not get the lump-sum payment because I will not be inducted into the AAC. I think that is fair.

Gen. Clayton Bissell then gave us a talk. He is chairman of the induction board. He discussed what we could do, what the U.S. Army would like us to do, and what we ought to do under the circumstances. He spoke pessimistically about our chances of getting a job in the States that would prevent us from being drafted back into the service. He painted a dark picture for us if we did not stay here and accept induction.

All the fellows feel that Bissell is jamming the Army down our throats. We have a guarded feeling about anything he said. Of course he is just doing his job, and the Army wants us as a unit under the command of the USAAC. I think his talk hurt more than helped his cause. It would have been much better to have it explained by the Old Man.

Bus Keeton stood up and asked what our chances were to get a regular commission. Bissell said that was beyond his power, and that we could not take jobs with Pan-Am, CNAC, or any other airline in Asia. We know better, for many of the guys have already done their spadework concerning private lines.

After the meeting I approached General Chennault and asked him directly about my desire to get the regular commission. He said I have no alternative but to go into the service as a reserve officer, and that I should go in right here. Of course the Old Man is now a reserve general in the AAC and is in a peculiar position to tell us honestly how he feels about everything. He then offered me the rank of major if I stay. I was courteous, for the Old Man always has been good to me, but I must admit that I was steaming mad.

I walked into the bar, and all of the pilots gathered around me, since they knew I had been talking to Chennault. We cussed a lot and then discussed every aspect of what we had heard and what we should do. All the way back to our rooms we still were talking about what to do. I think most everyone has made up his mind to go back to the States and take the chance of being drafted.

I haven't made up my mind. I lie awake until the wee hours of the morning trying to decide. Here I am within reach of what I have come over here for. It has turned out exactly as I had thought: I would get combat experience by the time the U.S. got into the war and be in a perfect position to parlay that into a regular commission when the time came to integrate the AVG into the USAAC. In the meantime I would have saved up some money. And now my key and most important goal is going down the drain. What to do?

May 22, 1942

Got some terrible news today. Bob Little was killed. On a bombing and strafing mission on the Salween front Bob's plane lost a wing either from Japanese antiaircraft fire or a faulty bomb under his wing. We will never know. He went into a spin and was too low to bail out. I had just seen him the day before at the field, and he was in his usual cheerful and kidding manner. This is the closest friend yet; it gets to my innards. What a terrific person, and his contract was due to expire in forty days. Bob Neale took it awfully hard, for those two were very close. What an awful business.

Talked with a Pan-Am pilot who came in to Kunming in a B-24, and he brought us up to date on the situation in the States. He said an AVG man could write his own ticket with any airline. He suggested that I not give up about a regular commission, but go on home and personally see the top folks in the War Department. He just about sold me on that idea. That is what I will do.

I thought a lot about Mom today, since it is her birthday. How wonderful it would be just to sit in her kitchen and have a cup of coffee and talk the way we used to do. God bless her heart!

May 23, 1942

Jim and George came in today with their flight of P-43s, or what was left of their flight. The P-43s are for the Chinese Air Force, and we were helping them ferry the birds in from India. Chinese pilots on the flight lost six aircraft on the trip back from Karachi, India.

May 24, 1942

After days of poor weather we got ready to leave this morning for Chungking. I helped put all of Bob Little's personal stuff on the DC-3. Jim had ear trouble and got permission to go up on the DC-3 with me rather than fly a P-40. We were so overloaded it took the entire length of the field to get us off, and then we had to use some flaps.

It so happened that Edgar Snow, the writer, was on the same flight. We talked all the way to Chungking. A very impressive man.

As we neared Chungking I got a good look at the huge, muddy Yangtze River. We didn't land at the river island airport, but instead headed west and set down at Peishihyi Field, about thirty-five miles from Chungking. This will be our base of operations in this area.

We were driven to our hostel area from the grass field and found it to be much like the one at Kunming. This one had apparently just been completed. I opened a bottle of sherry, and several of us had a house warming. The food at dinner tonight was excellent, more on the American style.

May 26, 1942

Jim Cross left for the city this morning and a job that he is supposed to take immediately. He now is our liaison officer in Chungking with the Chinese Air Force.

I spent some time assigning pilots and men to hostel rooms and making up schedules for duties. At least I could try to get things prepared for the arrival of the outfit. Doc Rich, who was driving overland from Kunming, came in tonight, and he was filthy. Shortly following him came the dentist, Doc Bruce, and Charles Kenner. They said the road from Kunming to Chungking was worse than the Burma Road.

May 27, 1942

To kill time and cut boredom I decided to walk the perimeter of the airfield. Quite a distance, several miles. At one point I was passing a Chinese Army cantonment and stopped to watch them doing calisthenics. Some were jumping, others running, still others working out on bars. Some were drilling in close-order formations. Many looked as though they could not have been over twelve or thirteen years old.

May 28, 1942

With nothing else to do, some of us decided to drive into Chungking and see the place. I now understand why it takes an hour and a half to drive the sixty kilometers. The road is rough and unpaved and it winds around and through mountainous country. The mountains didn't look that high from the air. We passed through many small villages that were clogged with Chinese peasants, and we saw all means of transportation: rickshaws, sedan chairs, diesel trucks, vehicles running on coal, hundreds of bicycles, and countless two-wheeled carts drawn and pushed by a couple of Chinese. How they got those loads up the steep slopes, I'll never know.

As we entered the outskirts we came around the peak of one mountain and looked down on the Kailing River, which at the city meets the larger Yangtze River. Both rivers are dirty yellow and are filled with sampans. The airport for CNAC and serving the city is on a small island in the middle of the Yangtze River. There are countless air-raid shelters dug back into the mountainous cliffs, one right after another. In many cases they are homes where the people live. Bomb damage is evident all over. This city has been bombed more than any other city in the world, and the population is still close to a million. As in any other large city there are slums, modern buildings, and an attractive business district. We stopped in front of an old two-story residential building which is the AVG hostel.

Jim came out to meet us, and I kidded him about loafing here in the city. After some discussion he drove me and Doc Rich over to a nearby garage where AVG vehicles are being repaired. Spark plugs cost about eighteen U.S. dollars! Everything is dearly expensive in this city. We went to a tailor shop to check if they would make a uniform out of some gabardine that George Burgard brought back from India and had given me as a birthday gift. The cost? Two hundred dollars U.S. Arguing didn't have any effect, so I told the tailor okay. It will take a week. After that I tried to find a place to buy a Parker fountain pen. When I found one and the clerk said eighty-five dollars U.S., I nearly blew my top—I didn't buy it.

May 29, 1942

Jim and I drove over to the garage to pick up Doc Rich's Chevrolet so I could drive it back to the field. The weather was rainy and murky, so we didn't have to worry about Jap bombings. We said goodbye to Jim and started out on our trek back to the field. When we arrived I found out that the electricity was not hooked up yet, and we will have to continue with candles.

After lunch I decided to separate my personal belongings into two footlockers. I will take one home with me, and the other I will sell to any Chinese who will buy it. I marked the price of all the clothes and some items like pocket knives, billfolds at 17,300 Chinese National dollars or about six hundred dollars U.S.

May 30, 1942

Another drizzly, dull day. After some cribbage games I sat down and started composing a letter to Senator Tom Connally of Texas to seek his support in getting me a regular commission. I let Doc Prevo read it, and he thought it was good but suggested that maybe all of us in the AVG should draw up a petition to President Roosevelt, sign it, and attach it to a letter of recommendation signed by General Chennault.

After dinner I got my radio set up, since now we have electric power. I tuned in San Francisco, but the Japs were jamming the frequency so badly that I gave up.

May 31, 1942

When I awoke this morning I lay there thinking of the trip home. I figure I have only thirty-four more days before starting.

Our radio operator came in to tell us that he had picked up news that Yunnanyi was hit by twenty Jap bombers yesterday. The Kunming pilots got into the air, but we have no reports of contact being made. How I wish I could have been there. Suddenly I realized how long it has been since I was in the cockpit of a P-40—twenty-seven days. Hell's bells! What have I been doing? I have to get back into the action.

June 1, 1942

We got another radio report that our boys bombed Lao Cai. I guess the Old Man is going to let up on us between now and 4 July.

I prepared a petition to the president. I intend to let Bob Neale and George Burgard look at it when they arrive from Kunming, and then we will decide how to approach General Chennault.

June 2, 1942

A DC-3 came in from Kunming with another load of supplies, and the pilot briefed us on life down there. The outfit is still bombing and strafing along the Salween front and the Indochina border. Also the Japs again hit Yunnanyi. I suppose they are trying to knock out the Russian-built Chinese bombers that were deployed there last month.

June 3, 1942

I sold my topcoat, my Sam Browne belt, a medical first aid kit, and six shirts to some Chinese for about $165 U.S.

George and six others came in from Kunming with the Old Man on a DC-3. They are to meet the regular commission board tomorrow and take a written exam. George said General Chennault told him that maybe I could get a waiver on my age. I decided to go with them and take the exam in any case.

George told me of a sickening incident a few days ago in the Hump area. The USAAC in India sent six B-25s out of Dinjan on a raid against the Japs at Lashio, after which they were to recover at Kunming. Some higher-up made them load on an extra thousand pounds of bombs at the last minute before takeoff. As a result, one B-25 recovered at Kunming, and he would not have made it had it not been for George on air patrol over Kunming. George picked him up coming in about the time the Jap fighter flight intercepted him. The Japs fled, but only after the B-25 radio operator was killed during the attack. We heard that one bomber turned back to Dinjan and are fairly sure that the other B-25s ran into the mountains because of the bad weather. Someone should "burn" for that mission.

Also, to top off the bad day, a B-17E took off from Dinjan with General Brereton aboard headed for Kunming. After wandering around lost for hours, it finally landed wheels-up in a rice paddy just north of Kunming. What a SNAFU operation.

June 4, 1942

We left the field about 8:00 A.M. for Chungking to take the exams. We picked up Jim at the hostel and then drove over to the U.S. Military Mission, where we took a physical exam. I had trouble on my hearing test, but they skimmed over it and said I probably just needed my ears cleaned out.

I ran across General Chennault at the mission, and he asked me if I was over my burns and wanted to go back to Kunming. I replied, "Yes, very emphatically." He said okay. At noon we gathered back at the hostel for lunch, and again I saw the Old Man. I asked him what my chances were for a regular commission. As usual he said he couldn't give me a definite word. I decided to go ahead and take the written exam with George and the others.

The exam contained some very simple, even silly questions. Name some countries in South America. From what is aluminum made? Why is Trinidad famous? Who owns Samoa? What is the Monroe Doctrine?

After I handed my paper in, I asked General Bissell about my chances of getting a regular commission. I told him the date I graduated from flying school, and he said one word: "Impossible." Then we discussed a second lieutenant's future after the war.

He gave me no encouragement at all, and at times I might have irritated him with my persistent questions. When leaving, I said, "I hope I have said nothing that will go against me."

"You haven't," was all he said. I think that I impressed him with my honesty and sincere desire to have a military career.

Others didn't fare so well. Charlie Sawyer's ears are too bad; I doubt that he'll be offered a regular commission. One of the other pilots has syphilis.

June 5, 1942

The trip to Kunming was monotonous. I talked with Frank Schiel and Erik "Mortimer" Shilling. At other times I just stared out the window.

June 6, 1942

The outfit assembled this morning at the big hangar so the Chinese could decorate many of us. Chinese troops were lined up in formation, and a small band struck up some music. When my name was called, I arose and stepped in front of Colonel Wong, saluted smartly, and stood at attention. He took a medal from the aide and tried to pin it on my coveralls. For some reason or other he couldn't get it pinned on, so he unzipped the upper part of my coveralls with the idea of pinning it on my undershirt. I had none on. He started laughing, turned to General Chennault and said something in Chinese, and then just handed the medal to me. He got another medal of a different kind and also handed that to me. We shook hands and I returned to my seat.

The first decoration was the Fifth Order of the Cloud Banner, one of China's highest decorations. The other was the Chinese Ten Star

Wing Medal, which is a lesser honor and is in recognition of the number of enemy aircraft that I have shot down. I have not reached ten yet, but they gave it to me anyway.

I took a flight up and assembled them over the city as though we were heading north to Chungking. When we got out of sight of the city, we turned back and came toward the field just above the trees from a different direction. The idea is to let the spies in the city assume the AVG has departed Kunming and left it undefended. Maybe that will entice the Japs to lay on a big effort against Kunming. We will be waiting for them. There is no doubt that the Japanese have their informers in Kunming just as the Chinese have ours in Hanoi. General Chennault has done this before and it has worked. I welcomed getting back in the air, feeling a P-40. It has been thirty-three days since I had a throttle in my hand.

June 7, 1942

The usual alert today. Lounging around, gabbing about this or that, playing cribbage or acey-deucie, reading or strolling outside. It gets awfully boring and tedious.

Went out to lead a flight of six P-40s to an outlying dispersal field we had named Generalissimo Field. Somehow the orders were misinterpreted and Bill Bartling took off with another flight of four. He tried to land at the field downwind and touched down too fast. Seeing he was going off the end of the field, he tried to ground loop the plane and tore off the landing gear. The others in his flight followed him, and suddenly there were three P-40s piled up at the end of the field, all badly damaged. The fourth man managed to stop.

Bartling had a few scratches, but his pride was the main thing that was hurt. The other pilots were okay. He admitted that he was headed downwind in a fast glide. We got in the station wagon and drove back to the field, where I found Bob Neale to tell him about the disaster. As soon as he saw me he jumped down my throat about not having a six-ship formation. I got him to settle down and then told him of the three damaged P-40s. He called us into the adjacent office and proceeded to give Bartling pure hell. He then blamed me for the disaster, and that got me heated up! I blew up, and we had a violent argument. He finally settled down, but then turned to Bartling and called him a liar. Bart just looked at him as great big tears swelled up in his eyes. I stared at Bob, told him he should never had said that, and stalked out of the office. Later, after our tempers had cooled, Bob, Bart, and I talked it over again, and Bob, being the real guy he is, apologized for calling Bart a liar.

I have a heavy heart, wondering if I was responsible for losing three planes.

June 8, 1942

Bob and I have to figure out a way to get the three P-40s repaired and back to the main field. The weather is rainy and foggy, so we put it off till tomorrow when the airfield won't be so soggy.

June 9, 1942

The Chungking weather was good, so I called Bob and started preparations to leave. I had six P-40s in my flight, and Bob and George each led nine P-40s. Ed Rector took the Second Squadron up about an hour ahead of us.

We caught sight of the field at Chungking and changed course just enough to fly directly over the city and circle it, giving the impression of a large Flying Tiger outfit stationed at Chungking.

I taxied up and cut my engine, and Red and Jo, our two nurses, came up to greet me. It was good to see them again and to hear news of the Japanese defeat at Midway Island.

Bob Neale and I then made plans to take the First Squadron to Kweilin tomorrow. The Second Squadron will remain here. Kweilin is being hit frequently by Jap bombers, and we want to slip in undetected and be prepared to hit them the following morning.

June 10, 1942

Was up at 3:15 A.M. Everyone was in good spirits and looked forward to leaving Chungking and getting to Kweilin, but the weather soured, so we delayed departure until tomorrow. A DC-3 did get off, however, taking some of the maintenance people.

Learned tonight that the Old Man and some of his staff are also going down to Kweilin. Maybe we will have another Rangoon series there. The place was hit three times yesterday and today, and the Jap bombers were without escorts. We look forward to some real fighting.

June 11, 1942

Our plans called for a 10:30 takeoff for Kweilin. After getting in the air and up to cruising altitude, my engine started cutting out badly; I returned to the field. George had the same problem, and we sat around while the mechanics checked the troubles.

After lunch George and I took off, and the engines purred like kittens. We made it with no problems. The Kweilin field is surrounded by high mountains that look like inverted ice cream cones. The valley is lush, and the field is the biggest and best I have seen in China. It is over a mile long and has revetments that can take B-17s. The runway is a hard surface, gravel mixed with clay. Our operations office is up a slope and back a hundred yards in a huge cave at the base of one of the giant mountains. The cave is naturally cool inside and provides a beautiful view of the entire field.

We dispersed the ships about the field and boarded an old rattletrap bus to go to the hostel, about five miles away. The hostel is very nice with camphor wood construction, American furniture, and showers. In the club room we actually have a pool table. This is the best layout yet.

We told Bob Neale of our engine problems, and he said that Matt Kuykendall was missing. A few hours later old Kirk came riding in with some Chinese fellow and told us that he had to abort into an intermediate field. Upon landing, the plane nosed over and caught fire. Fortunately he got out unscathed.

Before turning in, we got together to discuss our formation and tactics for the expected action tomorrow. I hope the Japs continue to come over in separate small formations. We may even get some action like strafing Canton. The general has asked for fifty belly tanks for our planes. We shall see.

June 12, 1942

Our early-morning game of cribbage was interrupted by an alarm of a Jap observation plane coming over. We took off and circled west of the field, Neale with a flight of four at eighteen thousand feet, George with a flight of three at twenty thousand feet, and me with a flight of four at fifteen thousand feet. They came, and we started after them. On my wing Joe Rosbert moved in close and fired his guns to get my attention. He pointed to a flight of five Japanese bombers to my lower right. I had almost commited my formation to Japs at my left front, but with the altitude advantage I agreed with Joe. We attacked the lower formation. After two passes we still saw no enemy fighter escort. On the third attack I closed up fast on the tail of the bomber on the outside of the vee formation, firing short bursts. Suddenly five of my guns quit working, so I had only one left. Damn! I concentrated on the recharge hydraulic buttons in the lower cockpit, and when I looked up I caught a glimpse of six I-97 fighters high and to my right and one twin-engined bomber by itself which I figured was a cripple.

I pulled away to get my guns working again, but none would work. Then I noticed the glaring yellow coolant overheat light—the indicator went clear over to the peg! Smoke was curling out from behind my instrument panel. Obviously my cooling system had taken some return fire from the bomber. That eventually damaged the hydraulic system that worked the guns.

I cut down and away and then noticed what was on my tail: two Jap I-97s. One pulled off, but the other stuck with me to within a thousand feet of the ground. I was in a maximum dive because I was trying to save the engine long enough to make a try for the field. Pulling back on the throttle, I was staying ahead of the Jap fighter just enough to stay out of range of his guns.

I was beginning to feel that my number was up this time. My oil pressure dropped to zero. Speed about 315 MPH. I hunched behind the armor plate, listening for the pings of the Jap's guns while trying to make a decision about bailing out or belly landing. Luckily, the Jap must have thought I was a goner, for he turned his fighter away and climbed back to the battle area. A second later, my propeller stopped. I stared at one of the three blades straight up in front of the nose of my ship.

I was dropping fast toward an area of rice paddies located at the base of a mountain. I was too low to bail out, so I decided to risk a wheels-up landing. I picked out a field and glided in, rolling my canopy back. I tried the flap levers. Hell, they wouldn't work! I was going to overshoot the field. I wasn't over a hundred feet above it, and my speed was giving out fast. I risked a drastic bank and turn, trying to hit the slope of the rice paddy.

It worked. Just as I flattened out my wings, I hit the ground. I bounced out of one muddy rice paddy, sailed over a small dike, and smashed down into another water-filled paddy. What a jolt! I was thrown against my safety belt. My head flew forward, and the right side of my forehead caught the gunsight. I was momentarily dazed but brought back to my senses by the sound of the canopy slamming back shut.

I rolled the canopy open again, unsnapped my safety belt, hit my parachute release button, and jumped out of the cockpit onto the wing. The fuselage was smoking, but no fire had started. The propeller and gear housing had torn loose from the nose and had become a curled mass of junk about fifteen feet in front of the plane. The oil and coolant radiators had been torn off and were strung out behind the ship. What a mess.[4]

God, I was glad to be alive! I looked up for signs of aircraft, particularly Japanese. There weren't even any sounds of aircraft. I retrieved my helmet, oxygen mask, goggles, and earphones and moved out toward the left wingtip. My head ached. I reached up and felt a couple of deep gashes in my forehead from the gunsight. Fortunately they weren't bleeding heavily.

Several natives with hoes were chopping in the rice paddies nearby, but they wouldn't look at me. Perhaps they thought I was Japanese. There was a cluster of shacks across the way, and I sloshed off through the mud and water to look for help. I wanted a phone just as I did the other time. Approaching some Chinese with sign language, I tried to indicate I needed a phone. Finally, after holding a "phone" to my ear while jabbering, "Wah, wah, wah," which is how they sound talking on a local phone, they got the idea. One motioned to follow him, and we started out along the rice paddy dikes towards another cluster of shacks.

The shacks turned out to be something like a schoolhouse, and in them was a phone. There were several Chinese in the room, and they stared at me in blank silence, not making a move. One of the natives picked up the phone and contacted someone. He shoved the instrument towards me and backed away. I picked it up and started saying, "Hello! Hello!" I was amazed; someone on the other end replied in English. He asked who I was and what I wanted and said that he was a Catholic missionary, Reverend Herbert Elliott. I talked to him for twenty minutes, but for some reason I could not make him understand that I needed to return to my airfield. I must have been partly in shock

---

[4]The crash and the entire air war over Kweilin are described in Hotz, *With General Chennault*, chap. 17.

and not making myself clear. Eventually he said that I was to come to Yungfu, a small town where he was and where he could get help for me.

It was a good walk of three and one-half hours. I trailed behind a Chinese native, carrying my parachute over one of my shoulders. Eventually we came to a narrow river, and I sat down to bathe my feet. I saw someone across the river who did not look Chinese; it was Reverend Elliott.

A boat was brought over to ferry me across, and we shook hands. It was a relief to see an American. He gave me a drink of fresh water and looked at the cuts on my forehead, and then we walked to the little village where his mission was located. A large crowd gathered behind us, and he took me straight to the mandarin's (mayor's) office. There they washed my face thoroughly. They still were suspicious of me being a Japanese because of my dark face, still not completely healed from my previous accident. I explained carefully everything to the reverend, who then told them in Chinese. I could see the relief on their faces.

After that we went back to the mission, where I bathed, had a nice lunch, and sat down while they cleaned and treated the cut on my forehead. They put something on it and bandaged it with clean gauze.

The mandarin and some of his officials made a call on me after lunch and then they took me to the railroad station. We were joined by four Chinese soldiers, and along the way we picked up groups of curious natives. It turned out to be a parade down the main street. Many little children tugged at my hands, and the soldiers began lighting strings of firecrackers and throwing them in our path. Some crackers were still popping as we passed over them, and I got several small burns on my lower legs. The experience was almost as nerve-wracking as the belly landing, and I was relieved when we got to the station.

The reverend told me that this was the greatest moment in the life of the village. The Flying Tigers are heroes to them, and now they had seen one. I must admit that in spite of all my misery I felt very proud and honored.

The passenger train pulled into the station and we bade each other goodbye. I thanked the reverend from the bottom of my heart, and he knew it. The train master took me over and put me in a comfortable seat in his best car. The train was surprisingly modern and comfortable. As we pulled out of the station, I heard more firecrackers popping. Soon the aisle next to my seat was crowded with passengers who came to see the American Flying Tiger hero. The train master had to keep shoving them away. The trip lasted only an hour or so, and I was in Kweilin, getting into a car and being taken to the field.

All the gang met me. They had gotten word from Reverend Elliott by phone that I was okay. Not worried about me, they immediately turned the episode into a celebration and joked about "old hard luck Bond."

We critiqued the fight. George got two. Bob Neale was surprised by one of the "twin-engined bombers," which he quickly found out was a new type of twin-engined Japanese fighter.[5] The Japs surprised us with them. Bob said there must have been a total of twenty-one enemy aircraft and that we think we got nine or ten. Allen Wright's plane was shot up, and he came in with a dead stick, hitting the overrun of the field. His aircraft flipped over, and he got a wrenched back. Wright and I were the only ones who got hurt. General Chennault chided me about "bad luck" and then smiled and said he hoped it was over. I responded, "So do I." We were all excited and jubilant.

Doc Prevo checked my head wound. No stitches were necessary, so I went to dinner and turned in. Thank God—I have survived again.

[5] Kawasaki Ki-45 Toryu. See Appendix A.

8. *A Volunteer Returns Home*

Monsoons drenched southern China in May, and it rained on and off until July. As a result, we spent most of the time in air defense posture and saw little combat during the last two months before being replaced by pilots of the new Twenty-third Fighter Group. The new group had been organized and trained early in 1942, and in March the men boarded a ship for the long trip to the Orient.

AAC pilots slowly began arriving in China during late May and June, and they surprised us by bringing a squadron of B-25 bombers. With a half-dozen bombers at his disposal, Chennault had more tactical flexibility, and he again shifted the mission of the AVG. During clear days we escorted the AAC bombers on strikes aimed at disrupting the enemy supply bases and halting the Japanese advance in eastern China. Late in June, B-25s raided Hankow, an important railroad and supply center, and in July they attacked Canton.

The Japanese counterattacked over Hengyang on July 4, the last official day of the AVG. They were determined to knock us out before all replacements arrived, but what the enemy did not know was that the Old Man had asked for volunteers to stay an extra two weeks. Most men refused, but eighteen pilots and about thirty airmen agreed. In the battle over Hengyang we shot down six enemy planes while losing none, but unfortunately it was during those extra two weeks that two volunteers, John Petach and Arnold Shamblin, lost their lives in combat.

On July 9, Pete Wright shot down the last enemy aircraft credited to the AVG, and on July 18 most of us boarded an old DC-3 for the first leg of the long journey back to the United States.[1] Five other volunteers decided not to go home and instead accepted induction into the USAAC and remained with Chennault. They were Tex Hill, Ed Rector, Frank Schiel, Charles Sawyer, and Gil Bright. Schiel, unfortunately, died in

---

[1] Pete Wright diary, July 9, 1942.

December, 1942, when he flew into a mountain during bad weather. Hill and Rector continued to perform to the highest standards. Tex eventually earned twelve aerial victories, and both men left the service after the war as colonels. Sawyer eventually became a colonel, but Bright left the service a few years after returning to the States.

*   *   *

June 14, 1942

General Chennault and General Mow of the Chinese Air Force reviewed the situation with me and Ed Rector. I was in charge today, and they had to return to Chungking for a conference with General Brereton. They don't think the Japs will hit us here at Kweilin again for some time. The Old Man directed us not to take missions other than local interception. He also told me that I was almost killed after I crashed at Yungfu—the natives suspected me of being Japanese.

June 15, 1942

Nothing to do. For a diversion, Bob Neale and I decided to explore some caves in the mountains behind our operations area.

June 17, 1942

There has been much talk lately about the red-light district in Kweilin, wild tales of unbelievable sights. Bob Neale and I got our curiosity aroused after hearing some tales, and the men dared us to go see for ourselves. The weather was so bad the Japs wouldn't come over, so we decided to go.

The city is much like other Chinese cities except it seems much cleaner. We parked near a bridge that spans the wide river near the center of the city. One of the airmen led us across the bridge and into a section typically Chinese—dirty, smelly, and clogged with natives dodging the mudholes in the tiny streets. We came to an intersection with an alley, and we were at the entrance to the red-light district.

At first I got the impression that we were going to parade down a street where local Chinese females had been lined up to cheer us. Then I realized they were prostitutes. The women and girls were almost shoulder to shoulder on both sides of the narrow alley. They were all ages: some just ten or twelve and others into their forties. All were in traditional dress.

193

The airman motioned for us to follow him down the street. As we strolled through the two lines of women, they reached out and grabbed our arms, giggling and chattering in Chinese. When two or three pulled in the same direction, we had to dig our heels into the cobblestones to keep from being dragged into a brothel room. When we got loose from one, another down the line would reach for us. They continued to laugh and yell. We didn't see any men or pimps around, so we just laughed and fought them off as we continued moving from doorway to doorway. Both sleeves of Bob's shirt were torn off, and the belt of my bush jacket had vanished. Buttons were torn from the front of my blouse. One girl slapped me soundly on the burned shoulder, and I yelled loudly. That really drew response from them; they thought they were getting me into the spirit. I really had a fight on my hands to stay in the street and out of a room.

Further along Bob and I spotted a cute little girl who couldn't have been over fourteen years old. We jumped across the street towards her and acted as though we meant business. She stood there and giggled loudly into her hands clasped across her face. Although the girls close by left us alone for a minute as though a decision was being made, there was no such thing as privacy. Above, girls were hanging out the windows observing the business. We wondered what her charge would be, but no interpreters were around, and neither one of us was serious whatsoever. As we left, we handed her a few Chinese National dollars, and she grabbed them and giggled in delight.

The other guys had moved down the street. We finally caught up with Frank Schiel, who was in a conversation with two Chinese men, the first ones we had seen since starting our escapade down the alley. They were obviously pimps, and they could speak broken English. It came through loud and clear that they had a "different type of establishment" nearby that they were sure we would like. We agreed to take a look.

It was different. The establishment was around a corner and on a much wider and cleaner street. The entrance opened up into what appeared to be a small grocery store with canned goods lining both walls. The men were strictly business and proceeded to explain what they had to offer. While standing there and listening to them, young Chinese girls crowded around us and started fanning us with Chinese fans to keep us cool, for it was very hot and humid.

We were led through a doorway into another room that was much like an American living room with elegant, overstuffed chairs and coffee tables. We were offered tea. One of the men went through another doorway and came back with a Chinese girl. Without a doubt she was one of the most exquisite and exotic women I have ever seen. Our surprise was picked up immediately by the two pimps, for there was no doubt that all three of us were impressed. She reminded me of Miss Lace in the comic strip "Terry and the Pirates." She was dressed in a black, ankle-length mandarin gown that clung to every curve of her body. Her skin was like ivory, and her oriental eyes were made up perfectly. Her hair, typically black, was combed in a long page-boy style down to her shoulders. She was small and slender, and her poise and demeanor gave the impression of a fine lady rather than a sexy, imported, professional prostitute from Hong Kong. She spoke rather good English, and we engaged her in conversation.

There was no pressure on us, strictly business, and she was interested in a long-term relationship. Her price was one thousand Chinese National Dollars, or about fifty dollars American. This only was for the first night, during which she would serve a fine dinner, sing and dance, and of course sleep with her buyer all night. After that she was his woman, but only as long as he kept her in money and paid the costs of keeping her in the position she was—a beautiful, professional prostitute. In plain words, she was sold to you for a period of time.

It soon became obvious that we were not serious, but neither the Chinese men nor the girl seemed concerned or disappointed in not making a deal. I could only conclude that the word would get around at the field and the advertisement was worth their time. What a business. What a deal!

We talked about what we had seen all the way back to the field and had to admit that it was something else. Before turning in I took a good shower and threw my bush jacket into the wastebasket.

June 18, 1942

The rain is so bad that we who were scheduled for alert were dismissed.

Just fifteen days, and the outfit breaks up and we go home. Everyone is getting impatient. The more we think about it, the more time seems to drag. I am leaning right now towards going with Pan American Airways and not with the Army Air Force, particularly after the episode last night. Everyone's sleep was disturbed by the loud and rowdy ruckus in the club. Capt. Ajax Baumler, a USAAC pilot already attached to us, got pickled and was arguing with an airman and Doc Sam. He began kicking the furniture around, and after about fifteen minutes of lying awake and listening to it I went over to try to stop it and get them to bed. It wasn't easy. I had Ajax by the collar up against the wall and ordered him to bed. He ended up lying in the middle of the floor on a crying jag. The airman was more reasonable, and Doc Sam and I carried him to his room and dumped him in bed. What a night!

June 20, 1942

The Chinese brought a Japanese prisoner to our office, the only one I've ever talked to. He was a gunner in one of the aircraft George Burgard shot down and was dressed in khaki jodphurs, a collarless khaki shirt, and rope-soled sandals. He looked Chinese to us but had higher cheekbones and was cleaner cut than most Chinese. We asked him questions through interpreters. He was twenty-six years old and was a chicken farmer before entering the service. He was transferred out of the army into the air force and became a gunner in a bomber. He told us much about the new "Number 45" fighter, as he called it. He did not think it performed as well as the Japanese Zero, but it did have two 13-mm cannons in the wings and one 18-mm in the nose. Wow! Some of the guys had been thinking of head-on passes at those new fighters!

He had heard much about the Flying Tigers, especially that it was a strong organization. He answered questions quickly and courteously, and we gave him water and cigarettes. We also took him over to the P-40E and let him examine it, particularly the six .50-caliber guns. He was intensely interested. We introduced George to him as the one who had shot him down—he refused to look at George.

The city of Kweilin arranged a big banquet for the AVG tonight. The mandarin was the host, and we were wined and dined and showered with praise and even a few gifts. The hostel club was decorated by the Chinese, and it was without a doubt the most elaborate affair I had attended since being in China. They even had cigars at each place setting. We received beautiful pieces of embroidery—eagles pouncing on

196

the Japanese red sun. Bob and I sat beside the mandarin and talked with him through an interpreter. He made a short speech, and then George countered with a few remarks and introduced all of the pilots. When he introduced me, he commented that I had just been shot down the second time but was still going strong. I took two bows. By the time the party was over, everyone was having a rip-roaring time, even the Chinese. They surprised me as they drank bourbon or scotch right along with us.

June 21, 1942

The U.S. Army Induction Board came to see us in Kweilin. Colonel Haynes brought them in a DC-3, and with them was General Chennault. There also was a member of the U.S. Navy, and his talk was slanted toward the former Navy pilots. He was too abrasive and arrogant. We all listened to an Army colonel about induction and our alternatives. Later, Bob Neale and I got together and agreed that it was time to make up our minds; it wasn't easy. We decided to go home. My conscience is bothering me for not staying, but I'm going to Washington, D.C., to try personally to get a regular commission.

June 22, 1942

The induction board meetings were held in the cave adjacent to our operations room. Sitting in the area, I could overhear the discussions until it came my turn. Colonel Sanders of the USAAC did the questioning, and General Chennault sat next to him and observed. Sanders opened the interview: "What are you going to do, Charlie? I'm sure you're going to stay with us, aren't you?"

I said slowly, "Colonel Sanders, I'd stay here without a moment's delay if I were given a regular commission in the Air Corps."

Colonel Sanders was honest when he replied that he couldn't do a thing about that, and he appreciated my feelings. He continued to try to talk me into staying anyhow and said something about high chances of getting torpedoed aboard ship on the way home.

That riled me. I came right back, "Colonel, I assure you, that thought doesn't bother me after all I've been through in the last several months!" General Chennault understood, looked at me and laughed softly. Colonel Sanders then laughed about the comment. That was just about all there was to talk about.

About noon Bob Neale started getting sick and went back to the hostel to check with Doc Sam, so I took command. Then came a phone call from Ed Rector, who was at the field at Hengyang, some forty miles north. He wanted help. They had been caught with some of their planes on the field by fourteen Japanese fighters. The weather was closing in, so I delayed my takeoff until General Chennault came down and suggested that I go ahead and try to get through anyhow.

I led a flight of eight P-40Es and P-40Bs. Everyone got off, and we started north. The rain got heavier and the clouds kept getting lower. I tried to penetrate the stuff, but soon was at treetop level trying to get under the clouds. It simply was too dangerous. During one turn I saw that my wingman, Lieutenant Dumas of the USAAC, was gone. That worried me, so I decided to abort the mission and return to the field. There was Dumas. I asked him what happened, and he replied sheepishly, "I just didn't want to go through that stuff." I looked at him a few seconds, turned away, and went to the operations shack.

I felt bad about not getting help to Ed, and I wanted to let him know we tried. Ed had gotten six ships into the air and had engaged the Japs, but they didn't get a single one. I just couldn't believe it. Maybe I'll learn more tomorrow, for I'm sure we'll be going to Hengyang for a big fight with the Japs.

At the hostel I checked on Bob Neale. They think he may have a case of dengue fever. Also, he's almost a nervous wreck.

The induction board isn't having much luck. Some of the airmen have agreed to stay, but so far no pilots. Jim Cross and Pappy Paxton came in from Chungking this evening, and since Pappy is our finance officer, I figured we would get our final pay. I drew $1,500 and will get another $1,750 when I get home.

My respect for the Old Man soared higher than ever tonight. George Burgard told me that in a discussion with Chennault the general told George that he didn't blame any of us for not staying. That made me feel much better. Maybe I can sleep now.

June 23, 1942

Ed Rector got reports of several waves of Japs coming toward him at Hengyang. The weather had broken considerably by noon, so George took a flight of five planes up to be on alert with Ed. I kept my flight on the field and sat around in operations watching the plotting board. The waves of Japs never appeared, and George returned to our field.

General Chennault thought it would be better if I took my flight up to Hengyang and stayed there to help Ed Rector. It seemed that the Japs were not about to come back to Kweilin and now their target was Hengyang.

I had my flight of seven ships at the end of the runway at 5:30, just about ready to start takeoff, when ground control held me up. No wonder. Here came six B-25s from Kunming, and they started landing right past us. I was glad to see them, and when they were clear we took off for Hengyang.

I circled Kweilin widely to the south in order not to tilt our hand to possible spies in the city that Kweilin defenses were being cut by seven P-40s. The weather was still marginal, but I was determined to make it this time. It was getting dark fast, and I became more concerned about that than the weather. I spotted the field and we flew very low and angled away from the city to the southeast. The idea was to keep our boosted strength at Hengyang a secret and be prepared to really hit the Japs. We landed just before darkness, and Ed and some of his pilots met us. The tension showed on their faces. A big fight is expected tomorrow.

My pilots were picked up in station wagons and driven to the hostel about two miles from the field. On the way Ed pointed out the remains of a Jap dive bomber that had been shot down and while coming down made a last effort to try to hit one of our planes. The hostel was different from the others. It was three stories and reminded me of a huge college dormitory. I had a room with Ed, and after a fairly good dinner we talked and turned in. It reminded me of old Toungoo days: eat and then go to bed.

June 24, 1942

After just a few hours in bed we were roused by men running down the hall yelling, "The Japs are on their way!" It was a night bombing raid, for the weather wasn't too bad. The moon could be seen at times shining through a thin overcast. We evacuated the building and sat along the banks of the river nearby in anticipation of the bombing. No Japs. They apparently were targeted for Changsha just to the north. We went back to bed.

Up at 3:00 and out at the field to get our ships parked for a quick scramble. While waiting we tried to catch a little more sleep. We picked up a plot on what was probably a Jap reconnaissance plane. We had two P-40s up and circling the field just in case. Tension was high. Nothing happened. The weather was too bad. It was a long day.

June 30, 1942

Ed Rector got a message from General Chennault today: "Prepare to leave today." How good that sounded.

Later in the day General Chennault came in from Chungking in a DC-3. Mail came in with him, and it was good to hear from home and Doris. The mail cheered me up considerably, but it didn't last long, for Bob Neale came into the alert shack from a meeting with the Old Man and called in all of the First Squadron. I immediately sensed something wrong. Bob asked, "How many of you are willing to stay two more weeks beyond the fourth to permit the USAAC to arrive here and get in shape to replace us?" There it was; I knew it! Several of the pilots and mechanics said, "Hell, no!"

I was mad as hell. I knew my conscience wouldn't let me do anything about it but say yes. I blame it all on the U.S. Army. They knew we were supposed to be disbanded on the fourth. Why the hell didn't they lay their plans accordingly and get their replacements in here? How can I say no under the circumstances? The Japs have threatened to wipe out the USAAC after the AVG leaves. We picked it up on all their radio frequencies; the Old Man is using this crutch. Now he can tell the Japs: We dare you to try it. Perhaps he is right. He is the USAAC commander on the spot and he is doing what he considers his job. Sometimes I wonder if he doesn't have more emotional problems than us pilots.

I did an awful lot of soul-searching the rest of the day. I was downright mad—irate—angry as hell! I had offered to stay on and continue fighting if only they would give me a regular commission so I could realize my dream and have a military career. But hell, no, they decided I was a few months too old! Well, it's over. I volunteered to stay.

So did Bob Neale and George Burgard. They then went back to Kweilin in the DC-3 to get our stuff together and bring it down here to Hengyang. George also decided to stop off at Chungking for some dental work.

After a sorry dinner I crawled in the bunk and lay there a long time before going to sleep. This has been one of the longest days of my life.

July 1, 1942

Bob Neale came back from Kweilin. We now have seven P-40s at Hengyang and seven pilots in our squadron. That's all.

I hope to get over my resentful feeling. Instead of three days to go, I have seventeen before I can leave for the States.

The weather broke this afternoon, and we got four B-25s off to hit Hankow. The fifth one got mired down in the mud off the runway, and the sixth turned up with a broken brake line. Ed Rector sent up five P-40s to escort them. They were gone over two hours when we picked up what appeared to be a Jap reconnaissance plane. I put up a flight of three to patrol the area and look for the enemy plane. Matt Kuykendall took Dick Rossi and Bus Loane to intercept, but it turned out to be a lone B-25 returning to Hengyang.

The bombers got lost, and Ed had to take over and direct them to the target twice. They finally released their bombs on some little village on the Yangtze River. Immediately after the bomb run they passed directly over the designated target—the Jap field at Hankow. The field was covered with planes, and there was no Jap opposition in the air. Everyone was either disgusted or just downright embarrassed about the fiasco.

The citizens of Hengyang decided to have a banquet for the AVG similar to the previous one at Kweilin. It was almost exactly the same, and there were many distinguished Chinese. I went but couldn't get in the spirit.

July 3, 1942

Again we were rousted out of our bunks—this time it was 2:10 A.M. The Japs were on their way. I gathered up a few guys and drove over to the field. Bob Neale drove up in a jeep with some more of our pilots. Suddenly we decided that we had better get into the revetments off the edge of the field. We drove down to the riverbank and huddled up near a stone culvert.

Just in time. We could hear the bombers. They passed overhead, circled, and headed back. We managed to pick them up from their exhausts. Five were in a tight vee formation. Down came the bombs, but they missed the field by several hundred yards.

About noon the B-25s got off with an escort of four P-40s to hit the Jap airfield at Namchang. They did a good job—damaged the hangar and runways and knocked out a few fighters. Antiaircraft fire and Japanese I-97 fighters were encountered. Bob Raines got one Jap for sure, but Harry Bolster must have been hit, for he bailed out on the way back inside Chinese lines. He is okay. The B-25s got back with no damage.

Later we scrambled and met incoming Jap fighters. I was in the same airplane, No. 114; what a lemon. It had no fuselage tank and instead a belly tank. Upon spotting the Japanese Zeros, I dropped the belly tank. One came in on Bus Loane's tail. I turned into it and it broke off. I shot at it, but my bursts were low. It went up into a climb, a turn, and then a shallow dive. I looked back and found myself alone. I climbed back up to the fighting altitude, and Raines came up on my wing. He was in the old P-40 photo ship, which had no guns!

I scanned the skies for aircraft and finally picked up one in the distance. It was too far away to identify until it got closer. Then I picked out the outline of the radial engine—a Zero. We passed each other at about seventeen thousand feet, and both of us immediately went into a violent bank to get around behind the other. In no time he was getting the advantage, so I began a vertical dive to the lower cloud level. He followed me at first. I hit 410 MPH when my radio antenna tore off, but I lost the Zero in the clouds.

I was running low on fuel. My tachometer was out and my engine was missing badly, so I decided to head for Lingling, a small field just south, rather than risk getting strafed while landing at Hengyang. I had just sighted Lingling when my red fuel warning light started glowing. Damn! Can I make it? I made up my mind; if the engine quit before I got into my glide path toward the field, I would bail out.

I headed for the field. Fortunately I had the advantage of a little altitude, so I put my wheels down while nearing the field. I knew I would never have time to put them down if the engine quit. I waited to use the flaps. Down they went. I was coming too fast, so I pulled the flaps back violently. I made it.

I had enough fuel to taxi over to the hangar line, and to my surprise I found that several B-25s and P-40s and the DC-3 also had recovered here. I got out of the cockpit and just stood there cussing, disgusted with my fate on having a lemon plane and bad luck.

We got an all-clear message and took off to go back to Hengyang. When we arrived, we learned that no one got any Japs, but neither did we lose anybody.

Bob took Bus Loane and Dick Rossi to Lingling and told me to follow them. I gathered my personal belongings, loaded them in the P-40, took off, and landed at Lingling. After I dispersed my plane I was driven to the living area, where I found Bob and the others. Bob had a bottle of bourbon, and a swig of it helped a lot. I told him of my experience and said I ought to quit at the rate I am going. He grinned, gave me another drink, and then said the Old Man had guaranteed airlift all the way to the States for those who volunteered to stay the additional two weeks.

Tomorrow Dick Rossi, Bill Bartling, Matt Kuykendall, and Joe Rosbert will be leaving. I will miss them.

July 4, 1942

The glorious Fourth of July! The Japs really gave us some fireworks last night. They came over Lingling the same way they did the other night at Hengyang. They dropped their bombs in two salvos. I could see the bomb flashes through my window. I presume they meant to hit the field with the first drop and the second salvo was meant for our barracks. They had it figured out just about right. The second salvo hit just short of my barracks and shook me out of my bunk. My heart almost beat out of my body. That was close.

Dick Rossi and I this morning took our P-40s to Kweilin, where we stood alert. I scrambled once when the warning net indicated an unknown coming up from the south. It was the B-25s coming back from a raid on Canton and recovering at Kweilin. I covered their landing and then came in myself. No sooner had I taxied up, when we got another alert. Off I went again. This time it turned out to be Bob Neale and Bus Loane coming in from Lingling.

During the day Ed Rector's boys tangled with another raid on Hengyang and got six out of twelve. That is more like it!

Jim Cross and George Burgard already have departed China for the States. They were reported to be in Karachi. I heard that those who had decided to leave on July 4 already have started stacking up in

Kunming. Seems like all the transports are occupied with problems in North Africa. Also heard that the Old Man can only promise remaining survivors air transportation to Calcutta.

I have felt bad the last few days—mentally bad. My nerves are ragged and I'm irritable as hell.

July 5, 1942

Had an unusual diversion today. A couple of USAAC B-25 pilots who in April had hit Tokyo with Gen. Jimmy Doolittle dropped in on us for an overnight stay. The Chinese got them out of the Jap-occupied area and were shuttling them into our area to get them back home. Their story was fascinating. Further, it gave us a big boost in morale.

Nine of the gang came in from Kunming today, meaning nine more P-40s for us at Kweilin. Boy, do we need them. Tex Hill led them in. He is now a major in the Army Air Corps. Tex decided to stay in China.

July 6, 1942

The B-25s hit the docks in Canton today, escorted by four P-40Es. John Petach got one I-97, and Tex Hill claimed a probable.

General Chennault came in and with Bob Neale and Lt. Colonel Cecil E. Combs, USAAC, planned several more bombing missions.

July 9, 1942

Another DC-3 came in today bringing some Sixteenth Squadron airmen of the USAAC from Kunming to Lingling. Looks like the Army is finally moving in.

July 10, 1942

The Japs moved 150 aircraft into Canton. Guess they have decided to try to stop our B-25 raids. Another report revealed that Japanese Navy Zeros are replacing their older Army Zeros in Hankow. They are determined to wipe us out.

On a flight down towards Namchang to bomb a Japanese Army headquarters John Petach was killed. Also Arnold "Red" Shamblin is missing. Only two of four returned from that flight. The word is that Petach's plane exploded in midair on his bombing dive. Poor devil. He is one of us who volunteered to stay another two weeks. The news will really kill Red, our nurse. They were married just a few months ago.

Johnny Alison came in today with a flight of nine P-40s from Kunming. I haven't seen Johnny in at least two years, since our days at Langley Field. It was like a reunion. After they had refueled and rested a little, I led them up to Lingling, where they will be based. We got an air raid and I started their indoctrination right then. I told Johnny we had to get all the planes in the air. We did. No Japs showed up.

July 11, 1942

While on alert I discussed Japanese tactics in the air and our tactics in fighting them. Johnny and his pilots are very interested and enthusiastic. He sent his pilots for local flights during the day to familiarize them with the area.

When we returned to the barracks, we learned that some men suddenly had become ill and were seized with violent vomiting spells. Every few minutes we noticed that someone would leave the dinner table and run for the door. I looked out and saw ten airmen in convulsive fits, vomiting. Those of us who came in and ate later began sweating it out. It soon hit us. My stomach started griping badly. I walked off to the side of the terrace and vomited everything. Then it hit me from the other end. We were the sickest bunch of human beings I had ever seen. Out of twenty-five men, only seven were lucky.

The Chinese authorities were concerned, and it didn't take long to track down the problem. The Chinese cook had sent one of his men into town to buy some cooking oil for the fish, and the enterprising young man had too much cumshaw (profit) in mind and bought cheaper oil. He returned with tung oil, used in production of paints and lacquer, and pocketed the savings. The dinner fish had been fried in paint oil.

I am unhappy, disgusted, feeling ill, and just about at the end of my rope. These are awful conditions. The barracks are overcrowded, and when I get in my bunk I have a fight with the bedbugs. Lingling is the worst base we have occupied in China.

July 12, 1942

We got in touch with Bob Neale and told him of our situation here. He came up and was loaded with castor oil, epsom salts, aspirin, and several big cans of Flit for the bedbugs. He listened to the tale, took one look at me, and ordered Jim Howard to come up from Kweilin. I took off, and after I arrived in Kweilin, Doc Sam Prevo told me I was to take a big dose of castor oil. I could have slugged him.

July 13, 1942

Lolled around, read some magazines, and talked with some of the new AAC pilots. General Chennault and Colonel Haynes came in and talked. All of the remnants of the AVG are here in Kweilin.

The USAAC personnel are here in strength, and they laid on a party for the AVG, but I skipped it because I didn't want to get in bad shape again.

July 14, 1942

Bob Neale said the Old Man told him that we could leave in two days.

July 16, 1942

The weather was too bad to leave today.

Had a long bull session with Col. Meriam Cooper, a rather famous old character who had been in the war between Poland and Russia. He was here in some capacity in intelligence with the AAC. It is unusual to meet a person like that, and it was well worth the time. Seems like a fine old man.

The bombers went up to Hengyang. They refueled there and then took off for Hankow. Six P-40s escorted them. The bombing was excellent, and they met no opposition. There was a fiasco on the return to Hengyang, however, for the warning net apparently picked up some penetrating Japs. Fighters at the base scrambled, and everything got fouled up. Freeman Ricketts mistook one of the returning B-25s as an enemy bomber and shot it down. Five of the crew bailed out, but the pilot stayed aboard to try to belly it in some place. No report on them yet.

I told Johnny Alison goodbye tonight. He said he wished he were going with me. I wish the war was over and everyone could go home. I am very tired.

July 17, 1942

The AAC pilots were scheduled for alert this morning, but Bob, Bart, and I got up and went down to the line also. Heard that the B-25 crew and pilot that were shot down yesterday are okay.

Talked with Colonel Cooper. He gave me a letter to his brother, a vice president with Pan American Airlines, who might help me get a job. Sounds great. I am also taking some messages home for Colonel

Haynes, who wrote a letter of recommendation for me to Generals Bob Olds and Hal George. He is pulling for me to get that regular commission. What a grand old man.

July 18, 1942

Was up at 4:30 ready to start on a flight halfway around the world. Since we were going the western route, I will complete an around-the-world trip when I get home.

Van Shapard was still asleep on his "agony bench," as he called his bamboo bunk. I jostled him and told him to get up, this was going-home day. That was all I needed to say. We ate a good breakfast and then rode to the field for the last time in our old ambulance. The weather was good, and I completed all the goodbyes. Twenty-one of us got aboard the old gooney bird and left Kweilin on the first leg of our journey.

Skip Adair met us at the field in Chungking. He called Bob Neale and me off to the side and persuaded us to take Red Petach with us and to take care of her all the way. He told us that she is pregnant. She has borne up very well after hearing of her husband's death. Skip is staying in China.

I spent most of the day selling my personal belongings. I kept just enough clothes to get home. I ended up collecting about $325.

I went with Bob and one of our finest line chiefs, Harry Fox, to see the Old Man for the last time. General Chennault told Bob and me that he had submitted our names to the RAF for their Distinguished Flying Cross. He asked us to do all we could to arouse public support for the American air effort in China. I got a frog in the middle of my throat when I shook hands with him and said goodbye. Fox almost broke into sobbing. Afterwards, Skip, Bob, and I got into a bull session with a bottle of bourbon. Skip hates to see us go as much as we hate to tell him goodbye.

July 19, 1942

We bade everyone goodbye, especially Skip, and climbed aboard the gooney bird to fly to Kunming. Upon landing we found that one of our main tires had gone flat. Fortunately it didn't blow on the touchdown.

Got hold of Frank Schiel and sold him my rifle for one hundred dollars. He decided to stay and is now a major. He seems quite satisfied. Seven of the AVG pilots have joined the Chinese National Aviation Corporation. They want five more pilots. I'll check with Chuck Sharpe in Calcutta.

After we landed in Dinjan, India, a truck transported us to the officer's club, where we sat down to the first real American-style dinner in almost a year. The coffee was out of this world.

July 20, 1942

Up at 3:30 to file for priority for Bob, Red, and me on the lone DC-3 heading for Calcutta. Many of the AVG men are going to Allahabad and Karachi, the most direct route. By 8:30 we were booked on the DC-3 and soon on our way. Upon landing we went straight to see Chuck Sharpe. We talked about working for him. I told him I wanted to go home first. He balked, saying the transportation was tight from here to the States. In any event, he is giving us a letter of intent to hire us, which he said might come in handy if the draft board meets us at the field in Miami. We laughed, but we did think of it for a while afterwards.

We went into town and got rooms at the Great Eastern Hotel. Later we joined some of the other returning AVG men in the lobby over some drinks and discussed our intentions. Some are staying and going on immediately with CNAC. Others are going home first, then coming back and becoming copilots with CNAC at $450 a month. After checking out as pilots, they will draw $800 a month.

July 21, 1942

Off to the Calcutta Police Department and the American consul to register and get passports and visas. While at the consulate I put in a call to Tenth Air Force Headquarters in New Delhi to ask Col. Don Olds about air transportation for us three. He painted a very dismal picture and suggested that we give thought of catching a ship out of Bombay. I thought of General Chennault's promise about air transportation home if I stayed another two weeks in China.

We had a hard time getting our passport visas, going to three different places to get a transit visa across India. To make matters worse, I was billed twenty-seven dollars for the phone call to New Delhi. Bob paid half of it.

Red is down in the dumps, and I can understand it. She doesn't relish the idea of going home by boat. She is pregnant but doesn't know that Skip told us.

July 22, 1942

We ran into one of the crew chiefs of the AVG who had come in from Karachi. The boat situation there is not good.

I made up my mind to go to New Delhi and at least try to get Red air transportation home. I learned that a USAAC gooney bird at Dumdum Airport was leaving tomorrow for New Delhi, so I started checking on the crew. Luckily the pilot was an old buddy of mine from Mac-Dill Air Base. I called him and told him my story, and he said he would be glad to talk to Colonel Olds and even Brig. Gen. Earl Naiden, Tenth Air Force Commander. That boosted our spirits considerably.

July 23, 1942

Had breakfast with Red and Bob and told them about hearing from a friend of mine who was a pilot with Pan American assigned to the Army Air Corps. He said the Army would not allow him to take any passengers going west out of Karachi. If we travel west, we will have to get Army authorization and also pay for the tickets. There is no doubt that the Army induction board in China really "fixed up" the AVGers who wanted to go home. What a shame.

We went to New Delhi with my buddy on his DC-3. As soon as we landed, we went to a hotel and I ran into Col. Charlie Caldwell. I did a little groundwork on our problem with him, and as usual he was a wonderful guy. Said he would see what he could do.

As soon as I got in my room I put on my full-dress AVG uniform with all the ribbons. Red had sewed them on. Off I went to corner Colonel Caldwell. I pleaded for Red, at least, and he buzzed General Naiden and got a quick interview for me. Naiden remembered me from Langley days, and we talked about them for awhile. He said he would look into my problem.

July 24, 1942

I took Bob and Red with me to call on Colonel Caldwell. We spent all morning with him. He was wonderful to Red—made her feel like a heroine! At luncheon all four of us worked up a cable for General Naiden to send to Gen. Hal George, who is running Air Transport Command in Washington. We proposed it to General Naiden, he thought a moment, and then he decided to readdress it to Gen. Hap Arnold! I thought Red and Bob would faint right there.

Bob begged off a dinner date with Colonel Caldwell, so Red and I went without him. It turned out to be a good-sized dinner dance party at the Maiden Hotel. We had a wonderful time and didn't get in until about 2:00 A.M. The colonel's secretary was a little doll, and she and I danced up a storm. My AVG uniform was rather conspicuous, since it was the only one of its kind in the ballroom. I could hear comments often: "That's an AVG pilot." I'll have to admit that I felt proud.

July 28, 1942

We had to get something settled soon, so Bob and I went to the railroad station and firmed up reservations to Bombay. Then we struck out to check in with Colonel Caldwell—still no news.

Nothing to do, so we talked the colonel's secretary into going to a nice lounge with us. We got comfortable, ordered a drink, and then in came Colonel Caldwell, beaming from ear to ear! He had a cable in his hand, signed by General Arnold: "Request approved. Grant all three highest priority!"

How wonderful! And how much I loved Colonel Caldwell. He doesn't think we will have to pay for tickets and already has us booked on a flight tomorrow leaving New Delhi and going to Karachi.

Back at our hotel, we could hardly wait to tell Red. She had returned from a side trip to Agra, where she toured the Taj Mahal. I thought she would break down and cry when we told her of the good news and that we had to leave tomorrow morning. Her reaction was expected: "If I can be ready by then," she said! She could be ready in ten minutes.

July 29, 1942

Up early and went over to tell Colonel Caldwell and the others goodbye and swear my undying gratitude to Charlie Caldwell. We boarded a gooney bird at the field and were soon winging our way on another leg of the long trek home. About thirty minutes out of Karachi our left engine started throwing oil badly and started sputtering. It worried me a little, and I wondered about my luck lately. The problem cleared up, however, and we landed at Karachi with no problems.

Upon landing we learned that we will have to pay a fare of $252 from Khartoum, Egypt, to Accra, Gold Coast. The Army will fly us to

AVG pilots lined up after an awards ceremony in Kunming in which they received Winged Star and Fifth Order of the Cloud Banner medals from Chinese Air Force officials, June 6, 1942. *Left to right*: Snuffy Smith, Bill Bartling, myself, George Burgard, J. Gilpin Bright, Dick Rossi, Bob Neale, John Petach, John Dean, Joe Rosbert, Fritz Wolf, Bob Prescott, Bill Reed, and Ken Jernstedt. (*Courtesy, J. J. Harrington*)

Captured Japanese gunner shot down by George Burgard in June, 1942, at Kweilin. *Left to right*: Lewis Bishop, Snuffy Smith, Joe Rosbert, Bill Bartling, Dick Rossi, Burgard, and Bob Neale. (*Courtesy, Jim Cross*)

Among the first USAAC aircraft sent to China in June, 1942, to assist and replace the AVG were B-25 bombers. (*Courtesy, U.S. Air Force*)

With Doris in front of our quarters at Orlando, Florida, at Christmastime, 1942. Doris was pregnant with our first child, and I was a major in the USAAC. Notice the Chinese Air Force wings over my right blouse pocket.

Me, Tex Hill, and Eddie Rector back together to receive the British Distinguished Flying Cross in Washington, D.C., in August, 1943. British Ambassador Lord Halifax presented the medals, along with one awarded posthumously to Jack Newkirk.

A C-87 (B-24 conversion) of the type I flew for Ambassador Averell Harriman later during World War II. (*Courtesy, U.S. Air Force*)

Briefing USAF Chief of Staff Gen. Curtis LeMay during "Desertstrike," a joint Army–Air Force exercise in 1965 at Luke Air Force Base, Phoenix, Arizona.

With President Lyndon Johnson and Lt. Gen. Albert ("Bub") Clark in 1968 at Bergstrom Air Force Base, Austin, Texas. As commander of the Twelfth Air Force, I was accepting the "E" award for my officers and men, who had exceeded goals for purchasing war bonds.

Khartoum from here. At Accra we will have to make further arrangements or pay for a Pan American flight. The technicalities were of such a nature that they were still abiding by General Arnold's wire.

August 1, 1942

Was up at 4:30, had coffee by lantern light, rode to the field in an RAF "dune buggy," and was in the air by 6:30 on our way to Salala, Arabia. The haze was as usual—practically instrument weather. We were on a Pan American DC-3 chartered by the USAAC. We were in the air almost seven hours on this leg, reading and playing cribbage.

We landed on what was supposed to be a strip but looked like part of a sandy beach next to the Indian Ocean. Had some good American coffee and then took off for the leg to Aden. The countryside was the same until we approached the huge RAF base at Aden, where the desert became green with vegetation.

Many ships were in the harbor, and there were countless oil tanks inland near the hillsides. Barrage balloons were tethered over the area. The field had paved runways and taxiways and large hangars.

Taxiing in, I saw several U.S. Lockheed Hudson bombers. Apparently these were the A-29s we thought we would get at one time in the AVG.

August 2, 1942

We were up before daylight and in the air by 5:50 on our way across north central Africa. We were cruising at eleven thousand feet to get over the mountains, and it was cold. We crossed the Red Sea and then headed almost due west over Eritrean territory to Sudan. The country now took on the appearance of a vast wasteland, and we soon gained sight of the Nile River and Khartoum. The field was El Fasher at Khartoum, and it was covered with P-40s, Hudson bombers, B-25s, and some B-24s. All, I was told, are headed for Egypt. The U.S. is really pouring the aircraft into the area.

The control officer met us at the plane and greeted us warmly. He talked about the history of the area while the plane was being refueled. He also told us that we should proceed right on through on the same DC-3. Our spirits soared. He said he was sending us through to the west coast of Africa, where we could catch the Pan American Clipper to Miami. He said it is all set up. I thought Red was going to kiss him.

August 3, 1942

Left Khartoum about 6:00 A.M., and again it was a routine flight, dozing, talking, and playing cribbage with Bob and Red.

All three of us are getting along great. All of us like to kid each other. Red is wonderful. She is a tall redhead with lots of freckles. She has a big frame but is not buxom or heavy—an attractive gal. We all are at ease around each other, and when someone wins at cribbage or tells a joke, often we shove, push, or hit each other. Red laughs and hits us right back. She is a wonderful sport and is not showing any signs of her pregnancy or revealing her condition.

We landed at Kano, Nigeria, and the field had all types of aircraft in every corner. I saw some Spitfires and B-26s. After refueling, we were again on our way—this time for Accra, Gold Coast. Soon we picked up the Atlantic Ocean shore and flew out over the water before cutting back west again in order to skirt wide of the Vichy French territory. After over four hours we set down on the busy Accra air base. I haven't seen this many airplanes in a long time.

We got word almost immediately that we had been booked on the TWA Stratoliner leaving at midnight. That meant all the way to Miami with a few stops in between. We were delighted.

We took off in the darkness of the African night at 1:00 A.M. The plane was loaded with Pan American ferry pilots going back to pick up more planes to fly to Egypt. About dawn we hit a little island in the middle of the ocean: Ascension Island. The U.S. Army was busy cutting off a side of a mountain to widen and lengthen the runway.

August 4, 1942

Off we went for Natal, Brazil. Eight hours later we got our first glimpse of the northeast tip of the country. Soon we were on the field and unloading. I recalled the time back in November, 1939, when I was a brand new second lieutenant and came in here from Rio de Janeiro with a flight of six B-17s on a good-will flight.

August 5, 1942

I'm too excited to sleep now that I'm getting close to the States. Got up about 5:30 and went over for breakfast. I joined our pilot, Captain Churchill, and we discussed my chances of going to work for TWA. He gave me a story similar to the one I had heard in Karachi: looks like

Air Transport Command of the U.S. military is going to take over all the private airlines.

Red and Bob showed up, and soon we were airborne again and on our way to Belem, Brazil.

August 6, 1942

Waited until about 5:30, at which time we left Brazil en route for Puerto Rico. Almost!

August 7, 1942

Up at 4:30 and in high spirits. Today is the day!

We got off at 6:15 and watched Puerto Rico fade behind us. Played cribbage: won a dime from Red and lost a quarter to Bob.

Soon we caught our first glimpse of the Florida coastline, and there was Miami. I just sat silently. After all those experiences in far-away places, how good it was to see America. As we flew over the city, Red, Bob, and I acted like little kids.

We glided in and sat down on the runway at 11:30 A.M. I had just completed my first trip around the world. I was back home.

Epilogue: Mission Accomplished

The Flying Tigers made aviation history in 1941 and 1942. Without a doubt they were one of the most effective military forces in history. The group never had more than seventy trained pilots or more than forty-nine planes ready for combat. When it was replaced by the Twenty-third Fighter Group, Chennault had only twenty-nine planes operational. His force faced an enemy usually equipped with ten times as many planes. During the battle of Rangoon, for example, two squadrons of the AVG opposed 464 bombers and 371 fighters of the Japanese Air Force.

Considering such odds, the Flying Tigers' record was impressive. In the air they were credited with the certain destruction of 299 enemy planes and the possible destruction of an additional 153. On the ground, the AVG estimated that it destroyed another 200, bringing the total number of enemy aircraft destroyed to approximately 650. In contrast, the Japanese destroyed just a dozen P-40s in the air and caught sixty-one on the ground (twenty-two of which the AVG burned when evacuating Loiwing), for a total of only seventy-three. While the AVG killed as many as fifteen hundred Japanese personnel, the group only lost ten pilots in combat and the same number in aircraft accidents. Three others were killed during air raids, and three were taken prisoner.[1]

This incredible record resulted in the AVG being glamorized and in some volunteers becoming heroes. "Claire Chennault: American Hero" was the headline in one magazine, and *Newsweek* labeled the

---

[1] The combat record appears in Chennault, *Way of a Fighter*, pp. 173–74, and in Greenlaw, *Lady and the Tigers*, p. 139. For a monthly breakdown, see a report by Harrison Forman, *New York Times*, July 3, 1942, p. 6. The Japanese told their people that their air force had destroyed 554 enemy planes over Burma and China during the first five months of 1942, completely annihilating the British and AVG forces. *Japan Times and Advertiser*, May 16, 1942.

pilots "aerial Sergeant Yorks."[2] Twenty-nine of the pilots became aces, destroying five or more enemy planes in aerial combat, and thirty-three pilots and three crew chiefs received decorations from the Chinese government. Eight pilots also earned medals from the British for valor over Rangoon. By 1943 at least five books had been published adulating the Flying Tigers, and the shark's teeth were being painted on other fighter planes as the symbol of air superiority.

The price tag for the group was only about eight million dollars: three million in salaries and five million for planes and equipment. Chennault was upset that the cost exceeded his original estimate and apologized to Dr. T. V. Soong, who replied: "The AVG was the soundest investment China ever made. I am ashamed that you should ever consider the cost."

Another sincere statement was written by the government that benefited from the work of the volunteers. The Chinese wrote: "General Chennault and his company of air knights will always be remembered by the Chinese people as comrades in arms and the friendly representatives of a friendly people."[3]

The five pilots and thirty-four ground personnel who accepted induction in China and remained with Chennault became the cadre for the Twenty-third Fighter Group and eventually the Fourteenth Air Force. The rest were eager to return home, but some never got farther than India, where about twenty went to work for the Chinese National Aviation Corporation. Dick Rossi, for example, stayed with CNAC throughout the war and during that time set a record with more than 750 flights over the Hump; after the war he returned to the United States and in 1950 joined the Flying Tiger Airlines. Many others reached home in 1942 and rejoined their old units in the Army Air Corps, Navy, or Marines. Pappy Boyington returned to the Marines and became an ace in the Southwest Pacific. After shooting down twenty-eight enemy aircraft, he too was shot down and taken prisoner. Later he received the Medal of Honor, an award also bestowed upon Jim Howard for an outstanding aerial engagement with thirty enemy fighters over Germany. Walt Dolan, my crew chief who kept my P-40

[2] *New Republic*, March 3, 1942, pp. 288–90, and *Newsweek*, April 6, 1942, pp. 20–21.

[3] Chennault, *Way of a Fighter*, p. 174; *New York Times*, July 1, 1942, p. 12.

No. 5 purring in spite of bullet holes and a lack of spare parts, re-enlisted in the Air Corps. Within a year he was back in China, repairing aircraft for the Fourteenth Air Force. Another airman, Donald "Rode" Rodewald, entered Army flight school, became a fighter pilot, and after an exemplary career retired as a colonel.

Others signed with airline companies. Bob Neale, George Burgard, Jim Cross, Bus Keeton, and several more became pilots for Pan American Grace Airlines, New York. Neale subsequently retired from flying and bought a fishing marina in his home state of Washington. Bob Prescott made a name for himself as a pioneer in large-scale air freight business and established and directed the Flying Tiger Airlines. Doc Richards established a thriving medical practice in California. Jo Stewart became a high school teacher in Dallas, and Red Petach, after delivering a baby girl and naming it Joan Claire after the Old Man, went back to her nursing profession at Yale University. Charlie Older went to law school and later became a judge in Los Angeles, and Ken Jernstedt was elected to the senate of Oregon.

Chennault, of course, continued in China. His remaining years in war and peace were marked with controversy, as had been his earlier life. In March, 1943, he was promoted to major general and given command of the Fourteenth Air Force. For the next year and a half he was in conflict with his superior, Lieutenant General Stilwell. It was the classic case of attempting to fight a war with too few supplies, personal animosities, and different objectives. President Roosevelt grew to favor Chennault's views, and Stilwell eventually lost his command. Before the defeat of Japan in the summer of 1945, Chennault was recalled to Washington.

After the war he again returned to China, organizing air transport operations aimed at rebuilding that war-torn nation while supporting the Nationalist government of Chiang Kai-shek. His last battle came in 1958, this one with cancer. While dying in Walter Reed Hospital, Washington, he received word from President Eisenhower of his promotion to lieutenant general in recognition of his outstanding service to his country.

As for me, I had accomplished some of my objectives in the AVG, returning to fighters and recording a fine combat record—almost a double ace. I had also saved several thousand dollars which could be used to buy my parents a comfortable home. Yet I still did not have a regular commission in the Army Air Corps, a secure career, and that is why I proceeded directly to Washington, D.C., after landing in Miami. I intended to take my case to the top—the chief of staff, USAAC, General H. H. "Hap" Arnold.

It was mid-August, 1942, when I entered the chief of staff's office, introduced myself to Brig. Gen. Laurence S. Kuter, one of his top aides, and asked for an audience with General Arnold. Fortunately, but unknown to me, the news media had been questioning General Arnold about the "superiority" of the Japanese Zero over the P-40, and General Kuter quickly seized on the opportunity to gain some intelligence from a P-40 ace just returning from combat with Zeros.

General Arnold was sitting with his blouse unbuttoned and with one foot in the lower drawer of his desk. He welcomed me with a warm grin, shook my hand, and invited me to a chair nearby. A group of ranking staff members crowded into the room, eager to hear my comments. Wasting no time, I bluntly presented my case. I wanted a regular commission in the Army, and if offered one I was prepared to return to China or go to any other assignment. He listened patiently and then told me it was beyond his power; it would require an act of Congress.

Abruptly he changed from listener to questioner. "Bond, what do you think of the P-40 versus the Zero? How did you men do it?" Caught off guard, I tried to return the conversation to my interests. It was no use; he was in charge. He repeated the question, and for the next half hour I told him and his staff about the P-40, the AVG tactics, and how to beat the Zeros. They listened intently, and the chief thanked me.

I left the office extremely disappointed and rode across the city to the TWA office at National Airport. There I inquired about a job and accepted a position as one of their air transport pilots.

I did not have to report for work for a couple of weeks, so I left for Dallas. I was greeted as a returning hero. My family, friends, and even strangers wanted to hear my tales. The Dallas Junior Chamber of Commerce selected me as the most outstanding young Texan of 1942.

It took little time to fulfill two other objectives. I bought a nice little home for my parents, and on September 14, Doris and I were married in her home by her father, a minister in the Church of Christ. We left on our honeymoon for Washington, D.C.

My employment with TWA lasted just sixteen days. Deep inside I remained a military man, and with the nation at war I was eager to get back into uniform. Doris agreed. I reentered the Army at the Pentagon on October 14, 1942, as a second lieutenant. As agreed upon before the induction, I was promoted to first lieutenant the next week, captain the next, and major the third week. I was confident that someway, someday, I would get that regular commission.

My Flying Tiger experience was a primary factor in my initial Air Corps assignments. First I was ordered to Orlando, Florida, to command the Eighty-first Fighter Squadron, a unit in the Air Force School of Applied Tactics, where realistic combat tactics and techniques were taught to the members of newly activated fighter groups of the rapidly expanding USAAC. While on that tour I was promoted to reserve lieutenant colonel.

In September, 1943, I was selected by General Arnold to accompany Ambassador Averell Harriman to Moscow, where for the next year I was his Army Air Corps aide, personal pilot of his C-87 transport aircraft, and chief of the Air Division of the U.S. Military Mission to the USSR.

That year of duty in Russia is a story in itself that must be told elsewhere, but the manner in which I was selected for the assignment is interesting. My commander called to tell me that I had been recommended to the chief of staff, USAAC, for a top-secret job. He said nothing more except that the chief "wanted to interview a field-grade officer of at least lieutenant colonel rank who had combat experience, had flown many different types of aircraft, and who knows how to use his head." Upon arriving at the Pentagon I met three other lieutenant colonels. All of us were called in and lined up in front of General Arnold. He started down the line asking only one question of each of us: "Are you ready to go back overseas?" The first three answered in a positive manner but with some reservations. One wanted more time with his baby daughter, another would leave immediately if given command of a P-51 Mustang fighter group, and the third wanted a longer rest before leaving the United States.

The chief looked at me and asked, "Bond, are you ready to go back overseas?" We were eyeball to eyeball, about a foot apart.

"Yes, sir!" I replied, "But I think I should remind you that you promised General Chennault that I could return to his command in China if and when I returned to combat."

He stared at me without changing his expression, then turned and walked over to his office window overlooking the city. He stood there for a moment with his hands in his pockets. Slowly he turned around, looked at me, folded his arms across his chest, and with that characteristic grin declared, "I rank Chennault!"

Later I learned from President Roosevelt's aide, Harry Hopkins, that within twenty-four hours that story got halfway around the world to Chennault.

About the middle of my Russian tour I was promoted to full colonel; in two years I had risen in rank from second lieutenant to colonel, USAAC Reserves. I was still a reserve officer, but fortunately, a few years after my return from Russia, while on assignment with the Air Corps Air Staff at the Pentagon, the opportunity for a regular commission arose. Congress passed the Armed Forces Reorganization Act of 1947, which was the culmination of lessons learned from the war and an attempt to improve the effectiveness of the new Department of Defense. One of the key provisions was the establishment of the U.S. Air Force as a separate and independent department of the armed forces. Included was authority to increase the number of regularly commissioned officers in the USAF. As a result, I was selected on July 1, 1948, as a regular colonel. I had achieved my ultimate objective, a secure military career.

By this time Doris had presented me with two beautiful little daughters, Rebecca Ruth in August, 1943, during the Orlando, Florida, assignment and Cynthia Sue on Christmas Day, 1945, while I was on duty in the Pentagon. Indeed, it appeared that I now had realized the dreams I had while flying AVG P-40s over the skies of China.

The next step in my career was to get the single star of a brigadier general. It also was obvious that my chances for such a promotion were slim, for I did not have a college degree. Again I was fortunate, for the Department of Defense implemented a policy to improve the educational level of commissioned officers. Certain officers would be permitted to apply for colleges and remain for two years to obtain a degree or establish a good basis for subsequent schooling which would ultimately lead to a degree. I applied immediately and was accepted in the program.

In January, 1947, I was on my way to the school of my choice, Texas A&M College. It was a unique situation for the college as well as for me. I was a thirty-two-year-old Air Force colonel sitting in classes with teen-aged members of the cadet corps. My primary duty was to cram as much education into two years as possible. I obtained special concessions from the registrar's office to pursue an ambitious curriculum—twenty-eight credit hours per semester and eight during each of the two summer sessions. In the first year I completed the equivalent of two years of college. With that as leverage I obtained an extra semester from the Air Force to allow me to obtain my degree. In June, 1949, I received my B.S. in management engineering. It had been not only a grueling grind for me but also a hard, stressful time for Doris. She lost a little boy in labor in 1947, and in June, 1949, she gave birth to our third daughter, Mary "Jeannie" Jean.

After earning my degree, I was eager to get back into the mainstream of the Air Force. I was assigned to Continental Air Command headquarters, Mitchell Air Base, New York, which was the beginning of my involvement in air defense over the next eleven years. I was on duty in many locations throughout the United States, Canada, Greenland, and Iceland in the pioneering days of what is now known as NORAD (North American Air Defense Command), planning, supervising, operating, and commanding elements of air defense units.

The most memorable and meaningful tour of duty was in 1954 through 1957 at NORAD headquarters in Colorado Springs. There Doris presented me with our fourth child, a little boy, Charles R. Bond III, born in December, 1954. I also received my first star, being promoted to brigadier general in August, 1957. Gen. Earl Partridge, commander-in-chief, North American Air Defense Command, was one of the first to congratulate me, adding, "Now that you're a general you're not going to have any more fun!"

Subsequent tours in Europe as deputy commander, Fifth Allied Tactical Air Force, Vicenza, Italy, followed by a tour as vice commander, Ninth Air Force, Tactical Air Command, Shaw Air Force Base, South Carolina, reoriented my specialty from air defense to tactical air operations. I had also been promoted to major general before leaving Italy.

With my broad background and tactical experience, it was certain that during the mid-1960s I would be assigned to Southeast Asia. The Air Force chief of staff, Gen. John P. McConnell, briefed me for the position, stating that it was necessary to activate a small, streamlined

Air Force headquarters in Thailand in order to maintain closer control over the growing number of units scattered throughout that country, particularly since those planes were the main strike forces used against North Vietnam. He continued that the current command structure was unorthodox and unacceptable—all USAF personnel based in Thailand were erroneously considered, by many high-level civilian and military leaders alike, to be under a joint command led by a U.S. Army major general. Thus, General McConnell activated a small headquarters at Udorn, Thailand, and appointed me deputy commander of the Seventh and Thirteenth Air Force headquarters.

The chief stated that he chose me to represent the Air Force in Thailand because of my background and experience with American diplomats and foreign military officials, noting that I had been in the Orient with Chennault. Leaving his office, I wondered if after twenty-five years my days with the Flying Tigers were still influencing my career.

I served eighteen months in that war-torn area from January, 1966, through the middle of 1967. It is another experience in my career that deserves special treatment elsewhere and represents the peculiar nature and outcome of that strange war. Oftentimes while flying near Chiang Mai on some of my field visits, I would look down at that airfield and relive that attack by the Flying Tigers.

I returned to the States in June, 1967, departing the combat zone of Southeast Asia in a pessimistic mood. My arrival at home was considerably different from that in the summer of 1942 when I returned from the same part of the world as a hero. The antimilitary, antiwar attitude was surprising; while in Asia I had no idea of the intense feeling of the American public.

Upon returning, I was awarded the Air Force Distinguished Service Medal and given command of the Twelfth Air Force, headquartered at James Connally Air Base, Waco, Texas. My pessimism disappeared in the excitement of such good fortune. I now had an assignment that general officers dream about, and I considered myself at the peak of my career. I felt proud, and apparently my old Flying Tiger buddies felt the same way, for they selected me to receive our 1967 Flying Tiger AVG Trophy for Outstanding Aviation Achievement at our July 4, 1967, reunion at Ojai, California.

Then suddenly in the spring of 1968 my fortune changed abruptly.

Doris suddenly became gravely ill. After surgery at the local hospital, complications arose, and she again was placed on the operating table. For several hours her life hung in the balance. It gave me enough time to agonize over the many years she had faithfully supported me in my career. She had been a wonderful wife and mother and had weathered some difficult times with a man married to his profession. I had realized my dreams; perhaps it was her time now. She recovered miraculously, and we agreed that it was time for me to retire.

Arrangements were made for a traditional Air Force flyby retirement. Gen. Gabe Disosway, my Tactical Air Command commander, honored me with his presence, and I retired on July 31, 1968, at James Connally Air Base. Those moments on the reviewing stand were filled with pride and satisfaction. For a fleeting second my thoughts wandered back to China. I felt that the Old Man, wherever he was, would be happy to know that one of his men had followed closely in his footsteps. I returned to the U.S. Air Force as he did and ultimately commanded a tactical air force as a major general just as he did. I feel I owe him thanks as much as I do my other air force contemporaries.

Aircraft Mentioned

United States

FIGHTERS

CW-21   This Curtiss Wright single-engined, low-wing, all-metal mono-plane, powered by a radial engine, was a fighter built for export in 1939. It was highly maneuverable, with a top speed of 375 MPH.

P-12   This Boeing fabric-and-metal biplane was first flown in 1928 and later was used as an advanced pursuit trainer. Small and extremely maneuverable, with a 450-HP radial engine and a top speed of about 170 MPH, it was a great acrobatic aircraft.

P-26   Boeing developed this low-wing, cantilever monoplane in the early 1930's. Powered with a 600-HP radial engine, and with a top speed of 225 MPH, it became the mainstay of Air Corps pursuit squadrons until 1939. Some P-26s were exported to China in the early phases of the Sino-Japanese War.

P-35   A Seversky fighter, developed in 1935, this plane was one of the first to have the World War II look: an all-metal, low-wing monoplane with an enclosed cockpit and retractable landing gear. It also could carry 300 pounds of bombs.

P-36   Curtiss designed and built this low-wing, cantilevered, radial-engined monoplane, which was used in the late 1930s and early 1940s by Army Air Corps pursuit wings. It was powered by a 1,200-HP Wright Cyclone engine for a top speed of 323 MPH. The export version was known as the Hawk 75, and Chennault used one in his first duties with the Chinese Air Force. China eventually had over one hundred of these fighters. With an in-line engine installed, this design was later developed into the P-40.

P-40   Described on pp. 38–39.

P-43   Republic Aviation's Lancer was a metal, low-wing monoplane powered by a 1,100-HP turbosupercharged radial engine. It was extremely capable at high altitudes and had a top speed of over 375 MPH. Produced in 1941, it was exported to China through Lend-Lease. This plane was a forerunner of the famous P-47 Thunderbolt, which proved to be a formidable fighter over Germany later in the war.

P-51   The North American Mustang fighter, first flown in 1941, was powered by a liquid-cooled, in-line engine, usually either an Allison V-1710 or a Merlin V-1650. A low-wing, monoplane design, it had the "look" of a modern fighter and a top speed of 400 MPH. The aircraft proved to be a highly effective weapon system and was a favorite of many pilots in World War II.

BOMBERS

A-28   The Lockheed Hudson light to medium bomber had an all-metal monoplane wing. It was powered by two Pratt & Whitney R-1830 radial engines or two similar Wright Cyclone engines. It was first conceived and developed as a transport in 1938 and was redesigned the next year as a bomber. With a top speed of only 275 MPH and a service ceiling of only 24,500 feet, it became obsolete in the early part of World War II.

B-17   The Boeing Flying Fortress was a heavy bomber powered by four 1,200-HP Wright R-1820 turbosupercharged engines. Top speed was 325 MPH at 24,600 feet, and it could climb to 37,000 feet. The bomb load was at least 4,000 pounds, depending on the range, and the B-17F had a maximum range of 4,400 miles. A total of 12,731 were built from 1935 to the end of the war, and the plane became the mainstay of the Army Air Corps, validating the concept of daylight strategic bombing.

B-24   In this Consolidated Vultee heavy bomber, called the Liberator, the high, cantilevered wings had four turbosupercharged, 1,200-HP Pratt & Whitney R-1830 radial engines. The plane held a crew of from seven to ten, depending on armaments, and had a speed of 320 MPH with a service ceiling of 26,000 feet. Its range was 3,200 miles, and its maximum bomb load was 8,000 pounds. The Liberator was first produced in 1940 and was used extensively in World War II.

B-25   The North American Mitchell medium bomber was powered by two Wright Cyclone GR-2600 radial engines. It had a tricycle landing gear, a high monoplane wing, and a plexiglass nose for the bombardier. Developed in 1939, it was designed to carry a bomb load of 3,000 pounds.

PBY   The Consolidated PBY-5 Catalina was a flying boat powered by two Pratt & Whitney Twin Wasp radial engines, of 900 to 1,200 HP each, mounted on a high parasol wing over the fuselage. Its top speed was less than 200 MPH, but the plane could loiter at 130 MPH, giving it a range of over three thousand miles. As a long-distance reconnaissance, patrol bombing, and air-sea rescue aircraft, the PBY had a long and distinguished career with the U.S. Navy.

TRAINERS

BC-1   See BT-9

BT-8   A trainer version of the P-35, this plane was greatly underpowered compared to the fighter, but it proved to be a little too advanced as a trainer for cadets. It was extremely tricky to handle on landings, and many instructors ground-looped it again and again.

BT-9   This North American basic trainer had a 450-HP Pratt & Whitney radial engine. Of all-metal construction with a low cantilevered monoplane wing, it had a two-seat, canopied cockpit. It was used during the late 1930s and early 1940s. The BC-1 and the BT-14 trainers were variations of the same design, and all resembled the famous AT-6 Texan.

BT-14   See BT-9.

PT-13   A Boeing (formerly Stearman) primary trainer, this plane was usually powered by a 220-HP Lycoming R-60 radial engine. It was a two-seat open-cockpit biplane of fabric and metal construction, and it, too, was used during the 1930s and early 1940s.

Ryan ST   These planes were developed in the 1930s as all-metal, low-wing cantilever monoplane trainers. The first in the series were designated PT-16, 20, 21, or 22 by the USAAC. They were powered by a six-cylinder, air-cooled engine for a top speed of 149 MPH. Many countries bought them, including the Netherlands East Indies.

TRANSPORTS

Beechcraft   Designed and developed in the 1930s, the Beechcraft series of light transports and trainers proved to be a popular and useful line in the USAAC and U.S. Navy in World War II. Several versions were produced, all basically the same: twin-engined, low-winged, cantilever monoplanes with twin-rudder tails and retractable landing gear. Most types were powered by two 450-HP Pratt and Whitney radial engines for a cruising speed of 220 MPH.

C-87   This plane was Consolidated Aircraft's transport version of the B-24 Liberator. The bomb bay was redesigned as a passenger compartment, and the C-87 performed slightly better than the B-24.

DC-3

Designed by Douglas as a commercial airliner in the 1930s, the C-47, as the Air Corps designated it, was used as a medium troop and cargo transport. Called the Dakota, Skytrain, sometimes Skytrooper, and always affectionately "gooney bird," it seated twenty-eight passengers as an airliner. A low-wing monoplane powered by two 1,000-HP Wright Cyclone radial engines, it produced a top speed of 230 MPH at 8,500 feet. It was a workhorse for the armed forces in World War II and afterwards. A similar earlier version was the DC-2.

Great Britain

FIGHTERS

Brewster Buffalo

Originally built as a U.S. naval aircraft (the F2A-2), the low-wing monoplane Buffalo was also exported to Great Britain and other nations before the United States entered the war. As used by the British in the Far East, it was equipped with a 1,000-HP Wright Cyclone radial engine which gave it a top speed of 337 MPH. Two .50-caliber machine guns were set into the engine cowling, and one .30-caliber machine gun was mounted in each wing outside the propeller arc. Though it was highly maneuverable, its rate of climb was greatly outmatched by that of the Japanese Zero.

Hurricane

First built in 1934 by Hawker Aircraft, the Hurricane was a single-place, low-wing monoplane similar to the P-40. It was powered by a liquid-cooled, 1,185-HP Merlin V-type in-line engine. Armament varied, but most Hurricanes in Burma had four to eight .30-caliber machine guns mounted in the wings. Top speed was about 340 MPH at 18,500 feet. The plane is best remembered for its role in the Battle of Britain, during which it shot down more enemy aircraft than any other fighter.

BOMBERS

Blenheim

Developed by Bristol in 1936 as a light day bomber, and powered by two 840-HP Mercury XX radial engines, the Blenheim was a midwing monoplane with a bomb load capacity of 1,000 pounds and a top speed of 295 MPH at 15,000 feet.

OBSERVATION AIRCRAFT

Lysander

Built by Westland originally as a two-seat target-towing trainer, and used early in the war as an attack aircraft, this high-wing monoplane was powered by a Bristol Mercury XX 825-HP radial engine. Its top speed was 206 MPH. In Southeast Asia it was used primarily for visual reconnaissance roles, although it did perform some bombing missions.

Japan

FIGHTERS

I-96   The Mitsubishi Type 96, code-named "Claude" by the Allies, was a single-seat, open-cockpit fighter and light dive bomber with fixed landing gear. Designed as a carrier-borne fighter, it was Japan's first naval monoplane. A 730-HP Mitsubishi radial engine gave it a top speed of 250 MPH at 9,000 feet. It mounted two 7.7-mm machine guns in the fuselage.

I-97   The Nakajima Type 97, code-named "Nate," was an extremely maneuverable single-seat fighter developed in the mid-1930s. With its fixed landing gear it was similar to the Mitsubishi Type 96 in appearance except for its enclosed cockpit. A low-wing monoplane powered by a Nakajima or Hikari radial engine of 750 to 850 HP, it had a top speed of 270 MPH at 15,000 feet. Armament varied from two to four 7.7-mm machine guns.

Ki-45   The Kawasaki Toryu ("Dragon-slayer"), code-named "Nick" by the Allies, was a two-seat, long-range escort fighter. Used by the Japanese Army, it was their first twin-engine fighter, entering service in September, 1941. It had 13-mm guns in the wings and one 18-mm gun in the nose.

Zero   Described on pp. 38–39.

BOMBERS

Sally   The Mitsubishi Type 97 medium bomber (called "Sally" by the Allies) was a mid-wing monoplane powered by two Kinsei IV 870-HP radial engines. Early armament was six to eight 7.7-mm machine guns. Top speed was 224 MPH, maximum gross weight was 22,000 pounds, and cruising range was reported variously to be 1,800 miles to nearly 2,500 miles.

Roster of the AVG

1. Adair, C. B. "Skip"	Staff, Operations and Supply	1—Major
2. Adkins, Frank W.	Flight Leader	
3. Allard, James L.	Auto Mechanic	
4. Alsop, Joseph W., Jr.	Staff Historian	5
5. Anderson, Frank A.	Crew Chief	
6. Armstrong, John Dean	Wingman	2
7. Atkinson, Peter W.	Wingman	2
8. Bacon, Noel R.	Flight Leader	4
9. Bailey, George R.	Crew Chief	1—M/Sgt.
10. Baisden, Charles N.	Armorer	
11. Bartelt, Percy R.	Flight Leader	4
12. Bartling, William E.	Flight Leader	3
13. Baugh, Marion F.	Wingman	2
14. Baughman, Edmund C.	Communications	
15. Beaupre, Leo A.	Clerk, Transportation	
16. Bell, Donald	Clerk, Transportation	1—1st Lt.
17. Bent, Morton W.	Clerk, Operations	3
18. Bernsdorf, Donald R.	Wingman	4
19. Bishop, Lewis S.	Vice Squadron Leader	5
20. Blackburn, John Ed., III	Wingman	2
21. Blackburn, William J.	Crew Chief	3
22. Blackwell, Harold	Crew Chief	3
23. Blaylock, Glen O.	Crew Chief	4
24. Bohman, Morris P.	Wingman	4
25. Bolster, Harry R.	Wingman	3
26. Bond, Charles R., Jr.	Vice Squadron Leader	3

CODE: 1—Entered service in China at rank shown
2—Died in the Far East
3—Volunteered to remain fourteen extra days
4—Left AVG before its disbandment
5—Was captured and repatriated
6—Either was captured and escaped, or evaded
7—Missing in the Far East

27. Bonham, Ernest O.	Communications	1—1st Lt.
28. Boyington, Gregory	Flight Leader	4
29. Brady, James E.	Clerk, Transportation	
30. Breeden, Kenneth V.	Clerk, Administration	
31. Brice, George	Crew Chief	
32. Bright, John G.	Flight Leader	1—Major
33. Brouk, Robert R.	Flight Leader	
34. Brown, Carl K.	Flight Leader	3
35. Bruce, Everett W., D.D.S.	Dental Surgeon	
36. Bryant, Alfred W.	Clerk	4
37. Bugler, Carl F.	Chief, Administration	
38. Burgard, George T.	Flight Leader	
39. Buxton, Richard H.	Clerk, Medical Orderly	4
40. Callan, Michael R.	Crew Chief	
41. Carney, Boatner R.	Staff	
42. Carter, John B.	Line Chief	3
43. Cavanah, Herbert R.	Flight Leader	
44. Ceder, Melvin E.	Staff, Police	
45. Chaney, Charles	Crew Chief	
46. Chennault, Claire L.	Group Commander	1—General
47. Christensen, Keith J.	Armorer	
48. Christman, Allen Bert	Staff, Intelligence; Flight Leader	2
49. Clouthier, Leo P.	Clerk, Operations	
50. Cole, Thomas J., Jr.	Wingman	2
51. Colquette, Leon P.	Crew Chief	
52. Conant, Edwin S.	Staff, Transportation; Flight Leader	
53. Cook, Elmer J.	Wingman	4
54. Cornelius, Jack	Crew Chief	
55. Cribbs, Charles D.	Clerk, Medical Orderly	
56. Criz, Albert	Wingman	4
57. Croft, John S.	Flight Leader	
58. Crookshanks, Jesse R.	Crew Chief	
59. Cross, Harvey G.	Communications	
60. Cross, James D.	Flight Leader	

CODE: 1—Entered service in China at rank shown
2—Died in the Far East
3—Volunteered to remain fourteen extra days
4—Left AVG before its disbandment
5—Was captured and repatriated
6—Either was captured and escaped, or evaded
7—Missing in the Far East

61. Crotty, John D.	Clerk, Operations	4
62. Curran, George F.	Crew Chief	
63. Cushing, Albert D.	Clerk, Operations	
64. Daube, Otto W.	Crew Chief	3
65. Davis, Doreen	Steno-Typist	
66. Davis, William H. S.	Staff, Asst. Operations	1—1st Lt.
67. Dean, John J.	Flight Leader	
68. Dolan, Walter J.	Crew Chief	
69. Donovan, John Tyler	Wingman	2
70. Doran, Francis R.	Clerk, Administration	
71. Dorris, Carl E.	Chief, Administration	
72. Dudzik, Francis P.	Clerk, Administration	4
73. DuPouy, Parker S.	Vice Squadron Leader	
74. Durbin, Estill E.		4
75. Durall, Eugene C., Jr.	Clerk, Intelligence	
76. Dyson, James P.		4
77. Engle, Charles R.	Crew Chief	
78. Engler, John R.	Communications	1—1st Lt.
79. Ernst, Richard J.	Communications	1—CPO
80. Farrell, John W.	Staff, Transportation; Flight Leader	
81. Fauth, John Edward	Crew Chief	2
82. Fish, William H., Jr.	Wingman	
83. Fobes, Edwin L.	Clerk Administration	
84. Foshee, Ben Crum	Wingman	2
85. Foster, Emma Jane	Nurse (married John E. Petach, Jr.)	3
86. Fox, Henry E.	Line Chief	3
87. Francisco, Charles H.	Communications	
88. Frillmann, Paul W.	Chaplain	
89. Fritzke, Allen W.	Armorer	3
90. Fuller, Henry W.	Instructor	4
91. Gallagher, Edward F.	Crew Chief	
92. Gallagher, Robert	Nurse	1—M/Sgt.
93. Gasdick, Joseph	Crew Chief; Sheet Metal Worker	

CODE: 1—Entered service in China at rank shown
2—Died in the Far East
3—Volunteered to remain fourteen extra days
4—Left AVG before its disbandment
5—Was captured and repatriated
6—Either was captured and escaped, or evaded
7—Missing in the Far East

230

94.	Gee, Chun Yuen	Engineering Helper	
95.	Gentry, Thomas C., M.D.	Chief Surgeon	1—Major
96.	Geselbracht, Henry M., Jr.	Flight Leader	3
97.	Gilbert, Henry G.	Wingman	2
98.	Gorham, Lloyd L.	Crew Chief	
99.	Gove, Irving P.	Crew Chief	
100.	Goyette, Edgar T.	Flight Leader	
101.	Graham, Richard E.	Crew Chief	4
102.	Greene, Paul J.	Flight Leader	
103.	Greenlaw, Harvey K.	Staff, Operations	
104.	Greenlaw, Olga S.	Clerk, Administration	
105.	Groh, Clifford G.	Flight Leader	
106.	Gunvordahl, Ralph N.	Wingman	4
107.	Hall, Lester J.	Wingman	3
108.	Hammer, Maax C.	Wingman	2
109.	Hanley, Lee D.	Armorer	4
110.	Hardesty, Martin L.	Crew Chief	4
111.	Harpold, Clayton M.	Mess	4
112.	Harrington, Jasper J.	Line Chief	1—1st Lt.
113.	Harris, David H.	Staff	
114.	Harris, Edward J.	Chief, Administration	1—1st Lt.
115.	Hastey, Raymond L.	Wingman	4
116.	Hauser, John B.	Crew Chief	4
117.	Haywood, Thomas C., Jr.	Flight Leader	
118.	Hedman, Robert P.	Flight Leader	
119.	Heller, John E.	Clerk, Transportation	4
120.	Henderson, George G.	Clerk	4
121.	Hennessy, John J.	Flight Leader	
122.	Henson, Thomas M.	Clerk, Medical Orderly	
123.	Hill, David Lee	Squadron Two Leader	1—Major
124.	Hodges, Fred S.	Flight Leader	
125.	Hoffman, Louis	Flight Leader	2
126.	Hoffman, Roy G.	Staff, Armorer	1—Capt.
127.	Hooker, Burton L.	Parachute Rigger	3
128.	Houle, Leo J.	Wingman	4
129.	Howard, James H.	Vice Squadron Leader	3

CODE: 1 —Entered service in China at rank shown
2—Died in the Far East
3—Volunteered to remain fourteen extra days
4—Left AVG before its disbandment
5—Was captured and repatriated
6—Either was captured and escaped, or evaded
7—Missing in the Far East

130. Hoyle, Daniel J.	Chief, Administration	
131. Hubler, Marlin R.	Clerk, Operations	1—2nd Lt.
132. Hurst, Lynn A.	Wingman	
133. Jacobson, Frank A.	Crew Chief	
134. Jaeger, George B.	Auto Mechanic	4
135. Janski, Edwin A.	Propeller Specialist	
136. Jernstedt, Kenneth O.	Flight Leader	
137. Johnston, Leon H.	Clerk, Operations	4
138. Jones, Jack D.	Armorer	4
139. Jones, Thomas A.	Staff, Transportation; Vice Squadron Leader	2
140. Jordan, Joe T.	Clerk, Finance	
141. Jourdan, Walter C., Jr.	Clerk, Meteorology	
142. Kaelin, Albert V.	Clerk, Administration	3
143. Keeton, Robert B.	Flight Leader	
144. Kelleher, John P.	Wingman	4
145. Keller, Daniel W.	Crew Chief	
146. Kelly, Thomas D.	Telephone Lineman	
147. Kemph, Merlin D.	Crew Chief	3
148. Kenner, Charles D.	Crew Chief	
149. Kepka, George B.	Crew Chief	
150. Kiner, Melvin W.	Telephone Lineman	
151. King, Robert J.	Communications	
152. Knapp, Donald R.	Wingman	4
153. Kustay, Stephen	Armorer	
154. Kuykendall, Matthew W.	Flight Leader	
155. Kwong, Lawrence C.	Staff	
156. Lancaster, George R.	Clerk	4
157. Laughlin, C. H., Jr.	Flight Leader	
158. Lawlor, Frank L.	Flight Leader	
159. Layher, Robert F.	Flight Leader	3
160. Leaghty, Charles C.	Parachute Rigger	
161. Lee, Joseph S., M.D.	Flight Surgeon	
162. Lee, Pak On	Engineering Helper	1—PFC
163. Leibolt, Edward J.	Flight Leader	7
164. Lindstedt, Robert K.	Communications	

CODE: 1—Entered service in China at rank shown
      2—Died in the Far East
      3—Volunteered to remain fourteen extra days
      4—Left AVG before its disbandment
      5—Was captured and repatriated
      6—Either was captured and escaped, or evaded
      7—Missing in the Far East

165.	Linton, Jack R.	Armorer	3
166.	Little, Robert L.	Staff, Engineering; Flight Leader	2
167.	Loane, Ernest W.	Wingman	3
168.	Locke, Robert P.	Propeller Specialist	
169.	Loomis, Elton V.	Communications	1—2nd Lt.
170.	Losonsky, Frank S.	Crew Chief	
171.	Lum, George L.	Engineering Helper	
172.	Lussier, Joseph E.	Communications	1—2nd Lt.
173.	McAllister, Gale E.	Crew Chief	
174.	McClure, Edgar B.	Crew Chief	1—CPO
175.	McDowell, Mark H.	Crew Chief	4
176.	McGarry, William D.	Wingman	6
177.	McGuire, Maurice G.	Wingman	4
178.	McHenry, Sharon L.	Clerk, Engineering	
179.	McKinney, Eugene R.	Armorer	1—M/Sgt.
180.	McMillan, George B.	Vice Squadron Leader	
181.	Mangleburg, Lacy F.	Wingman	2
182.	Martin, Neil G.	Flight Leader	2
183.	Merritt, Kenneth T.	Wingman	2
184.	Metasavage, Frank G.	Crew Chief	4
185.	Mickelson, Einar I.	Wingman	
186.	Milhalko, Alex	Communications	1—CPO
187.	Miller, Arvold A.	Communications	1—2nd Lt.
188.	Misenheimer, Charles V.	Crew Chief	
189.	Moore, Lawrence C.	Clerk	4
190.	Moss, Kenneth R.	Clerk, Meteorology	3
191.	Moss, Robert C.	Flight Leader	
192.	Mott, Charles D.	Flight Leader	5
193.	Mundelein, Charles D.	Crew Chief	4
194.	Musgrove, Willard L.	Crew Chief	
195.	Musick, James H.	Armorer	1—T/Sgt.
196.	Neal, Robert J.	Armorer	3
197.	Neale, Robert H.	Squadron One Leader	3
198.	Neumann, Gerhard	Propeller Specialist	1—S/Sgt.
199.	Newell, Ferris E.	Clerk, Administration	4
200.	Newkirk, John Van Kuren	Squadron Two Leader	2

CODE: 1—Entered service in China at rank shown
2—Died in the Far East
3—Volunteered to remain fourteen extra days
4—Left AVG before its disbandment
5—Was captured and repatriated
6—Either was captured and escaped, or evaded
7—Missing in the Far East

201. Older, Charles H.	Flight Leader	
202. Olson, Arvid E., Jr.	Squadron Three Leader	
203. Olson, Henry L.	Crew Chief	
204. Osborne, Harold L.	Crew Chief	
205. Overend, Edmund F.	Flight Leader	
206. Overley, John L.	Crew Chief	3
207. Paull, Preston B.	Crew Chief	
208. Paxton, George L.	Staff, Finance; Flight Leader	3
209. Peeden, Joseph N.	Crew Chief	
210. Peret, Richard C.	Staff, Engineering; Line Chief	
211. Perry, Paul J.	Armorer	
212. Petach, John E., Jr.	Flight Leader	2
213. Pietsker, Joseph H.	Photographer	
214. Pistole, Herbert	Armorer	
215. Pon, Kee Jeung	Engineering Helper	1—PFC
216. Poshefko, Joseph A.	Armorer	3
217. Power, John D.	Crew Chief	4
218. Power, Robert H.	Wingman	4
219. Prescott, Robert W.	Flight Leader	
220. Prevo, Samuel B., M.D.	Flight Surgeon	1—Major
221. Probst, Albert E.	Flight Leader	3
222. Quick, Carl	Crew Chief	3
223. Raines, Robert J.	Flight Leader	3
224. Rasbury, James D.	Mess	4
225. Rasmussen, Robert P.	Crew Chief	1—M/Sgt.
226. Rector, Edward F.	Vice Squadron Leader	1—Major
227. Reed, William N.	Flight Leader	
228. Regis, James E.	Photographer	
229. Regis, Stanley J.	Crew Chief	
230. Reynolds, George B.	Crew Chief	4
231. Richards, Lewis J., M.D.	Flight Surgeon	
232. Richardson, Charles A.	Crew Chief	4
233. Richardson, Randall S.	Clerk	4
234. Richardson, Roland L.	Communications	1—1st Lt.
235. Ricketts, Freeman I.	Flight Leader	3

CODE: 1—Entered service in China at rank shown
2—Died in the Far East
3—Volunteered to remain fourteen extra days
4—Left AVG before its disbandment
5—Was captured and repatriated
6—Either was captured and escaped, or evaded
7—Missing in the Far East

236. Ricks, Wayne W.	Propeller Specialist	
237. Riffer, Clarence W.	Armorer	
238. Ringey, Joseph E.	Auto Mechanic	4
239. Roberts, Carson M.	Communications	1—2nd Lt.
240. Rodewald, Donald L.	Armorer	1—1st Lt.
241. Rogers, Robert W.	Crew Chief	
242. Rosbert, Camille J.	Flight Leader	3
243. Rossi, John R.	Flight Leader	
244. Rumen, John N.	Armorer	3
245. Rushton, Edwin H.	Wingman	4
246. Sandell, Robert J.	Squadron One Leader	2
247. Sanger, Kenneth C.	Communications	4
248. Sasser, Ralph W.	Communications	1—CPO
249. Sawyer, Charles W.	Flight Leader	1—Capt.
250. Schaper, Wilfred E.	Crew Chief	3
251. Schiel, Frank, Jr.	Staff, Intelligence; Vice Squadron Leader	2, 1—Major
252. Schiller, Ralph F.	Armorer	
253. Schramm, Leo J.	Crew Chief	
254. Schur, Carl E.	Crew Chief	4
255. Seamster, Loy F.	Communications	
256. Seavey, Edward H.	Clerk, Operations	
257. Seiple, Wilfred R.	Crew Chief	
258. Shamblin, Arnold W.	Wingman	3, 7
259. Shapard, Van, Jr.	Wingman	3
260. Shapiro, William D.	Clerk	4
261. Shaw, John E.	Clerk, Medical Orderly	
262. Shee, George Leo Wing	Engineering Helper	
263. Shields, Milan R.	Propeller Specialist	
264. Shilling, Eriksen E.	Flight Leader	
265. Shreffler, Roger	Communications	
266. Smith, Corbett J.	Mess	4
267. Smith, Curtis E.	Staff, Group Adjutant; Flight Leader	
268. Smith, George	Administration	4
269. Smith, Robert A.	Crew Chief	
270. Smith, Robert H.	Flight Leader	

CODE: 1—Entered service in China at rank shown
     2—Died in the Far East
     3—Volunteered to remain fourteen extra days
     4—Left AVG before its disbandment
     5—Was captured and repatriated
     6—Either was captured and escaped, or evaded
     7—Missing in the Far East

271. Smith, Robert M.	Communications	
272. Smith, Robert T.	Flight Leader	
273. Sommers, John T.	Clerk, Operations	4
274. Stewart, Jo B.	Nurse	
275. Stiles, Edward L.	Crew Chief	
276. Stolet, Irving J.	Crew Chief	
277. Stubbs, Gail L.	Instructor	4
278. Sutherland, William L.	Auto Mechanic	
279. Swartz, Frank W.	Wingman	2
280. Sweeney, Joseph H.	Communications	
281. Swindle, Estes T., Jr.	Wingman	4
282. Sykes, William A.	Communications	1—1st Lt.
283. Terry, Julian E.	Clerk, Administration	
284. Towery, William H.	Mess Supervisor	1—2nd Lt.
285. Trumble, Thomas C.	Staff, Secretary to Group Commander	3
286. Tuley, Chester A.	Crew Chief	
287. Tyrrell, George	Crew Chief	
288. Uebele, John J.	Crew Chief	
289. Unger, William H.	Armorer	4
290. Van Timmeran, Frank E.	Line Chief	
291. Vaux, Morgan H.	Communications	
292. Viverette, Hugh J.	Clerk, Medical Orderly	
293. Wagner, Earl F.	Armor	3
294. Wakefield, Manning, Jr.	Crew Chief	3
295. Walker, Harold H.	Crew Chief	4
296. Wallace, Stanley H.	Wingman	4
297. Walroth, Robert H.	Wingman	4
298. Walsh, Andrew A.	Clerk	4
299. Walters, George F.	Clerk, Administration	
300. Watson, Eugene A.	Wingman	4
301. Whelpley, Donald A.	Clerk, Meteorology	
302. White, John E.	Crew Chief	4
303. Whitehead, R. G.	Staff, Asst. Operations	4
304. Whitwer, Eloise	Steno-Typist	
305. Wiggin, Edwin D.	Chief, Administration	4
306. Williams, John M.	Staff, Communications	1—Capt.

CODE: 1—Entered service in China at rank shown
    2—Died in the Far East
    3—Volunteered to remain fourteen extra days
    4—Left AVG before its disbandment
    5—Was captured and repatriated
    6—Either was captured and escaped, or evaded
    7—Missing in the Far East

307.	Wilson, Clifford H.	Auto Mechanic	
308.	Wirta, Harvey C.	Armorer	
309.	Wolf, Fritz E.	Flight Leader	
310.	Woodward, Melvin	Crew Chief	
311.	Wright, Allen M.	Wingman	3
312,	Wright, Peter	Flight Leader	3
313.	Wu, Lem Fong	Engineering Helper	
314.	Wyatt, Louis G.	Communications	3
315.	Wyke, William R.	Asst. Group Adjutant	4
316.	Wylie, Harold G.	Clerk, Finance	
317.	Yarbery, Glen L.	Crew Chief	4
318.	Yee, Francis T. F.	Engineering Helper	1—S/Sgt.
319.	Young, John P.	Clerk, Engineering	

SOURCE: Larry M. Pistole, *A Pictorial History of the Flying Tigers*, App. C. Reprinted by permission.

CODE: 1—Entered service in China at rank shown
2—Died in the Far East
3—Volunteered to remain fourteen extra days
4—Left AVG before its disbandment
5—Was captured and repatriated
6—Either was captured and escaped, or evaded
7—Missing in the Far East

Notes on Sources

So much has been written on the China-Burma-India theater that a complete bibliography would itself make a small book, so the following discussion will note only sources concerning the American Volunteer Group.

Since the AVG was not part of the U.S. armed forces, official documents were not maintained by the Army Air Corps and therefore are not housed at the modern military branch of the National Archives. In fact, an investigation of the archives resulted in finding just one document concerning the group—an order for .50-caliber machinegun bullets.

A more rewarding collection is at Albert F. Simpson Historical Research Center, Maxwell Air Force Base, Montgomery, Alabama. The material on Chennault and the AVG is scattered but includes news clippings, some correspondence and intelligence reports, and oral history interviews with Thomas Corcoran, Jerry Costello, Tex Hill, Joe T. Jordan, Gale McAllister, Bob Neale, Robert Prescott, Donald Rodewald, Robert M. Smith, Thomas G. Trumble, and John Vivian. In general, most of the collection concerns the period after the AVG was replaced by the Fourteenth Air Force.

The largest personal collection of materials is that of Larry M. Pistole, a nephew of an AVG armorer. He will open it to researchers by appointment and can be contacted by writing P.O. Box 400, Kennesaw, Georgia 30144. His collection includes combat reports, interviews, logbooks, scrapbooks, memorabilia, and about ten thousand photographs. More important are letters, notebooks, and the diaries of Skip Adair, George Burgard, Carl E. Dorris, Charles D. Mott, Arvid E. Olson, Robert M. Smith, and Peter Wright. A complete list of Pistole's holdings is in his fine book *A Pictorial History of the Flying Tigers* (Orange, Va.: Moss Publications, 1981). Another pictorial study of less value is Malcolm Rosholt's *Days of the Ching Pao: A Photographic Record of the Flying Tigers—14th Air Force in China in World War II* (Amherst, Wis.: Palmer Publishers, 1978).

The University Archives of Texas A&M hold the oral biography of General Bond and copies of diaries of George Burgard, John Donovan, Olga Greenlaw, Robert B. Keeton, Arvid Olson, Robert M. Smith, and Peter Wright.

Finally, one should consult the personal papers of Claire Chennault. They are found in fourteen boxes of papers housed at the Hoover Institution, Stanford University, and they also are on microfilm at the Library of Congress; the first nine reels of microfilm concern the AVG. The papers contain correspondence, memoranda, personnel sheets, orders, and messages to Chiang Kaishek and Madame Chiang. The most informative part of the papers is the group war diary, which includes operation and combat reports and intelligence summaries. Unfortunately, the papers do not include a diary by Chennault or any comments revealing his attitudes toward his men and associates.

Memoirs are the best source of information on the AVG. Chennault's *Way of a Fighter: The Memoirs of Claire Lee Chennault* (ed. Robert Hotz. New York: Putnam's, 1949) remains the standard reference. Unfortunately, Anna Chennault's *A Thousand Springs* (New York: Paul S. Eriksson, 1962) is only the "biography of a marriage," and *Chennault and the Flying Tigers* (New York: Paul S. Eriksson, 1963) is based on her husband's memoirs. A few volunteers have written about their experiences. Although entertaining, these books are personal stories and usually do not examine historical issues. Gregory Boyington's *Baa, Baa, Black Sheep* (New York: Putnam's, 1958) is the rambunctious story of a two-fisted pilot and is concerned mostly with later combat in the Pacific. Olga S. Greenlaw's *The Lady and the Tigers* (New York: Dutton, 1943) discusses being a woman with the group and reproduces a few documents from Chennault's office, where she worked. The chaplain for the AVG, Paul Frillmann, collaborated with Graham Peck to tell his story in *China: The Remembered Life* (Boston: Houghton Mifflin, 1968). This account includes interesting passages about the black market, morale problems, and relations between the average Chinese people and the American pilots and presents a more human side of Claire Chennault. Finally, a man who never was an official member of the group and who later commanded the Twenty-third Fighter Group, Robert L. Scott, Jr., has written *God is My Co-pilot* (New York: Scribner, 1943), *Flying Tiger: Chennault of China* (New York: Doubleday, 1959), and *Boring a Hole in the Sky* (New York: Random House, 1961), all of which tell his adventures and add little to our knowledge of the AVG.

Many books concerning the group were published during the Second World War. The best is Robert B. Hotz's *With General Chennault: The Story of the Flying Tigers* (New York: Coward-McCann, 1943). The author was a journalist who visited China in 1942 and by the next year was serving under Chennault as a captain in the USAAC. Hotz was assisted by many members of the AVG, especially George Paxton, Bob Neale, and Parker DuPouy, and the book includes an excellent list of men who joined, quit, received honorable and dishonorable discharges, and became aces.

Other wartime books tend to glorify the group and its leader. Keith Ayling's *Old Leatherface of the Flying Tigers: The Story of General Chennault* (Indianapolis: Bobbs-Merrill, 1945) and Joe Archibald's *Commander of the Flying Tigers: Claire Lee Chennault* (New York: Julian Messner, 1966) are aimed at children, as is Sam Mims's *Chennault of the Flying Tigers* (Philadelphia: Macrae-Smith, 1943). Russell Whelan's *The Flying Tigers: The Story of the American Volunteer Group* (New York: Viking, 1942) is a war story which was written hastily for the popular market. Finally, a volume edited by Maude Owens Walters, *Combat in the Air* (New York: Appleton-Century, 1944), contains one chapter on AVG member Gil Bright.

Unfortunately, no professional historian has written a scholarly monograph about the group or a biography of Chennault, so books published after the war have relied on *Way of a Fighter* and have been aimed at capturing the market. Ron Heifermann's *Flying Tigers: Chennault of China* (New York: Ballantine, 1971) is weaker than Bernard C. Nalty's *Tigers over Asia* (New York: Elsevier-Dutton, 1978). John Toland's *The Flying Tigers* (New York: Random House, 1963) is superficial, and just one chapter concerns the group in Dick Wilson's *When Tigers Fight: The Story of the Sino-Japanese War, 1937–1945* (New York: Viking, 1982) and in Martin Caidin's *The Ragged, Rugged Warriors* (New York: Dutton, 1966).

Some "official histories" of the war in Asia briefly mention the AVG. These have been commissioned by governments and rely on government sources. Wesley Frank Craven and James Lea Cate have written the multivolume *The Army Air Force in World War II* (Chicago: University of Chicago Press, 1948–1958); volume one, *Plans and Early Operations*, mentions the group, and volume seven, *Services Around the World*, discusses the problems of flying supplies over the Hump. Charles F. Romanus and Riley Sunderland published three volumes of *The China-Burma-India Theater* for the Office of the Chief of Military History, Department of the Army, and the most relevant book in that series is *Stilwell's Mission to China* (Washington, D.C.: Government Printing Office, 1953). The official British history is S. Woodburn Kirby's *The War Against Japan* (London: Her Majesty's Stationery Office, 1957–1969), which rarely mentions the AVG, even when discussing the battle of Rangoon.

Two other books about the war are useful. F. F. Liu's *A Military History of Modern China, 1924–1949* (Princeton: Princeton University Press, 1956) is a detailed account, and Wanda Cornelius and Thayne Short's *Ding Hao: America's Air War in China, 1937–1945* (Gretna, La.: Pelican, 1980) is an obscure book which has a chapter on the AVG.

Some scholarly histories are relevant to the Flying Tigers. Herbert Feis's *The China Tangle: The American Effort in China from Pearl Harbor to the Marshall Mission* (Princeton: Princeton University Press, 1953) is a fine survey, as is Paul A. Varg's *The Closing of the Door: Sino-American Relations, 1936–1946* (East Lansing: Michigan State University Press, 1973). Two books by Michael Schaller discuss Chennault's attempts in Washington, D.C., to assemble planes and pilots for the AVG; they are *The U.S. Crusade in China, 1938–1945* (New York: Columbia University Press, 1979) and *The United States and China in the Twentieth Century* (New York: Oxford University Press, 1979). The best book concerning economic relations is by a former advisor to China, Arthur N. Young: *China and the Helping Hand, 1937–1945* (Cambridge, Harvard University Press, 1963), in which chapter seven details supply problems during 1941–42. Tang Tsou's *America's Failure in China,*

1941–1950 (Chicago: University of Chicago Press, 1963) summarizes the feud between Chennault and Stilwell.

Finally, most books concerned with Stilwell do not tell much about the AVG but do discuss his debate with Chennault. The standard survey is Barbara W. Tuchman's *Stilwell and the American Experience in China, 1911–1945* (New York: Macmillan, 1970), which is favorable toward its subject. Theodore White edited *The Stilwell Papers* (New York: Schocken, 1948), and they are more valuable than the five volumes edited by Riley Sunderland and Charles F. Romanus, *Stilwell's Personal File: China, Burma, India, 1942–44* (Wilmington, Del.: Scholarly Resources, 1976).

Index

Dr. Cyclops (film), 72
Dumas, Lieutenant, 198

Eddy, Bill, 25
Eddy, Nat, 25
Elliott, Rev. Herbert, 189–91

Farrell, John, 75, 99, 104
Fauth, John, 118, 130, 131, 137
Fish, Willie, 149
Flying Tigers: and Army Air Corps, 74; books about, xiii; and Chinese Air Force, 46; insignia of, 44, 127; record of, 214–15; and *Time* and *Collier's*, 115
Foshee, Benny, 168, 173
Foster, Emma Jane "Red," 19; in Chungking, 186; in Kunming, 72–73, 175, 176, 177; later career of, 216; and Petach's death, 204; in Toungoo, 42, 47; and trip home, 207–13
For Whom the Bell Tolls, 147
Fox, F. E., 131
Fox, Harry, 207
Frillmann, Paul, 19, 70, 128

Gandhi, 51
Gentry, Thomas C., 45, 148, 175, 176
George, Colonel, 128
George, Gen. Hal, 207, 209, 210, 211
Geselbracht, Henry, 18, 93, 133, 136
Ghost Breakers (film), 45
Gilbert, Henry, 18, 66, 79, 166
Goyette, Edgar, 43, 107, 156, 157
Green, Colonel, 20
Greenlaw, Harvey, 19, 35; and Calcutta, 152–53; in Kunming, 68, 70, 127, 143–46, 149; in Paoshan, 173
Greenlaw, Olga, 19, 127, 149
Groh, Cliff, 161
Gunvordahl, Luke, 24

Hall, Miss, 129
Hammer, Maax, 39
Hansens, the, 90
Harriman, Averell, 218
Hastey, Raymond, 159–60
Hawaii, 22–23
Haynes, Caleb, 15, 160, 161, 197, 206, 207

Haywood, Tom, 18
Hedman, Robert "Duke," 19, 125, 126
Hengyang, 192, 198–202
Hennessy, John J., 49, 54, 148, 150
Here is My Heart (film), 67
Hill, Tex, 176; and dive-bombing, 171; at Kunming, 146–47, 160; at Lashio, 152; at Loiwing, 139; and morale, 141–42; stays in China, 192, 193, 204; in Toungoo, 53
Hodges, Fred, 131, 143
Hodges, Roy, 137
Hoffman, Louis, 18, 82–83, 84–85
Holbrook, Roy, 7, 8
Hopkins, Harry, 219
Howard, Jim, 205, 215
Huang, General, 68
Hunter, Chuck, 137
Hurricane (aircraft), 82, 84, 89, 90, 92, 93, 94, 95, 96, 97, 99, 100, 107, 110, 112, 118, 121, 124, 131, 153
Hurst, L. A., 24, 92

Idzumo (ship), 9
I-96 (aircraft), 86–87, 88, 161
I-97 (aircraft), 94, 104, 111, 161, 188, 202, 204
insignia, 43–44, 51
Intercontinental Aviation Corp, 12
Irvine, Rutledge, 18

Japan: U.S. relations with, 3–5
Java, 25–26, 31–33
Jensen, Mr., 83, 84, 89, 90, 91, 101
Jernstedt, Ken, 18, 118, 128, 216
Joe (barracks boy), 51
John Haig airstrip, 109, 114
Johnnie Walker airstrip, 86, 89, 93, 96, 98, 115
Johnson, Mr., 43
Johore, 34
Jones, Tom, 171, 176, 177
Jouett, Col. Jack, 8

Karachi, 152–58
Keeton, Robert "Buster," 18; at Chiang Mai, 133, 137; in Kunming, 178; later career of, 216; in Toungoo, 96
Kenner, Charles, 69, 180